Martin Christopher is Professor of Marketing and Logistics Systems at Cranfield School of Management, where he is Head of the Marketing Faculty, one of Europe's largest centres for marketing teaching. He has acted as consultant in this field for major international companies in North America, Europe, the Far East and Australasia and is a non-executive director of a number of companies. He has written numerous books and articles and is on the editorial advisory boards of several professional journals in the marketing and logistics areas.

Malcolm H. B. McDonald is Professor of Marketing Planning and Director of the International Marketing Planning Centre at the Cranfield School of Management. He has extensive industrial experience, including a number of years as Marketing Director of Canada Dry, and runs seminars and workshops on Marketing Planning in the UK, Europe, India, the Far East, Australasia and the USA. He has written fifteen books, and is editor of *International Marketing Review*.

Martin Christopher and Malcolm McDonald

MARKETING:
An Introduction

PAN BOOKS
London, Sydney and Auckland

First published 1991 by Pan Books Ltd,
Cavaye Place, London SW10 9PG
9 8 7 6 5 4 3
© Martin Christopher and Malcolm McDonald 1991
ISBN 0 330 32046 7

Photoset by Parker Typesetting Service, Leicester
Printed and bound in Great Britain by
Cox & Wyman Ltd, Reading, Berkshire

Contents

List of Figures

Preface

There has probably never been a time when effective marketing has been more crucial than at the present. The search for competitive advantage has taken on the equivalence of the search for the Holy Grail in the turbulent business environment of the nineties. The role that marketing plays in guiding corporate strategy is crucial and yet it is still the weak link for so many companies in the process that binds the customer to the organization.

Marketing in the past has often been misinterpreted and oversimplified. It has been confused with selling – itself a crucial activity – or with a naïve concept of 'giving the customers what they want'.

Through our work as teachers and consultants we have come to the strongly held view that marketing's role in the business is to find opportunities which allow the organization to reap a greater return on its assets, in particular its marketing assets. The marketing assets of a business include such things as corporate image, brand names, sales and distribution networks, supplier and customer relations and, of course, its people. Incorporated as part of total corporate strategy, marketing becomes a powerful machine for building and developing these crucial assets.

This book is designed to explore these ideas in a simple-to-read format. Whether you are an experienced marketing professional or entering marketing for the first time, or if your work is in a non-marketing function but you need to know more about marketing, we believe you will find this book helpful.

Whilst we have sought to put our own interpretation on the marketing concept and techniques described in this book we owe a large debt to many marketing professionals and teachers, including our past and present colleagues at Cranfield, for their pioneering work in developing the large body of knowledge that now exists in the area. An equal debt is owed to Dorothy Martin and Lee Smith who struggled with the manuscript, and to John Leppard who helped in the development of much of the material.

Martin Christopher
Malcolm McDonald

Cranfield, 1991

CHAPTER 1

Introduction:
Marketing's Role
in the Organization

AFTER DOMINATING the world motor-bike market for the best part of fifty years, with famous names like Norton, Triumph and BSA, the British volume motor-bike industry is dead. Similarly, the British ship-building industry is a shadow of its former self, with yards that were known around the world now closed and derelict. On the other hand Jaguar Cars, Rolls-Royce Engines and ICL Computers, having at one time all been close to collapse, have strengthened their positions and survived, albeit under new management and ownership.

What are the factors that lead to success or failure in the market place? Why is it that companies in the same industry have widely differing success in achieving sales?

This books seeks to explain the roots of success to show quite simply that the difference between success and failure in the market place is due to something that can be termed 'competitive advantage' and that marketing is ultimately about how that advantage is achieved.

WHAT IS MARKETING?

Marketing is often misunderstood. To many it is just a fancy word for 'selling'; to others it is about advertising and promotion. Still other people think of marketing as market research

– finding out what customers want. In a sense, marketing is about all of these and yet it is much more. Marketing is not selling, yet the culmination of successful marketing is a sale. Likewise advertising and promotion may be a highly effective means of communicating with potential customers to inform them about our product or service and to convince them of its merits. Similarly, without an understanding of real customer needs, provided perhaps by market research, we are unlikely to be successful in the market place.

Clearly marketing is concerned with customer satisfaction and with the identification of marketing opportunities; it is also concerned with the harnessing of the firm's resources and the focussing of those resources upon the most appropriate opportunities.

The simplest definition of marketing is that it is the process of matching the resources of the business with identified customer needs. In other words, marketing is concerned with customer satisfaction and with the focussing of the organization's resources to ensure that the customer is satisfied – at a profit to the business. The idea of customer satisfaction is a basic article of faith in marketing. The marketing-oriented company is one which 'puts the customer at the centre of the business' and seeks to focus all its activities towards creating satisfied customers.

Philosophically there is little to argue with in this notion. However, it must be recognized that in any business the ability of the organization to produce offerings that meet real needs will generally be limited to some very specific areas. More particularly, what we find is that an organization's skills and resources are the limiting factor determining its ability to meet market place needs. For example, a slide rule manufacturer would find it difficult to compete in the age of electronics with pocket calculators. The strengths and skills of that company, whatever they may be, are quite definitely not in the manufacture of electronic calculators, whereas they may well have a strength in marketing and distribution in specialized markets – this possibly providing an opportunity to distribute other manufacturers' products aimed at those markets.

What we are in effect saying is that marketing should really be seen as the process of achieving *the most effective deployment of the firms' assets* to achieve overall corporate objectives. By assets in this context we refer specifically to those assets which might best be described as 'marketing assets'.

THE COMPANY'S MARKETING ASSETS

What are marketing assets? Typically when we talk about assets we think first of financial assets, or more precisely those assets that are recognized in the balance sheet of the business. So fixed assets, such as plant and machinery, and current assets, such as inventory or cash, would be typical of this view of assets.

In fact the marketing assets of the business are of far greater importance to the long-run health of the business and yet paradoxically would not appear in the balance sheet. Ultimately the only assets that have value are those which contribute directly or indirectly to profitable sales, now or in the future. Included in our categorization of marketing assets would be such things as:

▶ **Brand name:** What is the strength of the image or the 'values' that are created in the market place by the brand name (e.g. Schweppes or IBM)?

▶ **Market 'franchise':** Are there certain parts of the market that we can call our own? (The loyalty of customers and distributors will be a factor here.)

▶ **Distribution network:** Do we have established channels of distribution which enable us to bring products or services to the market in a cost-effective way?

▶ **Market share:** The 'experience effect' and economies of scale mean that for many companies there are substantial advantages to being big. For example, costs will be lower and visibility in the market place will be higher.

▶ **Supplier relationships:** The ability to have access to raw materials and low-cost components, for example, can be of substantial advantage. Additionally, close cooperation with suppliers can frequently lead to innovative product developments.

▶ **Customer relations:** *'Close to the customer'* has become the motto of the 1990s and many organizations can testify to the advantage of strong bonds between the company and its customers.

▶ **Technology base:** Does the company have any unique skills, processes or 'know-how' strengths that can provide a basis for product/market exploitation?

It is only through the effective use of these and any other marketing assets that the company can build successful marketing strategies.

Asset-based marketing should not be confused with that hallmark of the past – the 'production orientation'. A production orientation typifies those businesses which are so wrapped up in their own processes and technology that they ignore the customers' real needs. Many companies which were once customer-focussed have gradually lost that focus because they have failed to recognize changes in the market place and have continued to look inwards rather than outwards. On the other hand, asset-based marketing seeks constantly to identify opportunities for exploiting skills and resources rather than products. Products are simply the vehicle whereby the needs of the customer are met. Indeed, in the growing service sector of the economy there is no physical product in any case, but rather an 'encounter'. To encompass this idea of the product or the encounter as a vehicle for achieving both customer satisfaction and corporate goals (e.g. profitability) we will be using the concept of 'the offer' throughout the book. The offer represents the totality of elements that the company provides and that the customer perceives himself to be receiving. As Figure 1.1 suggests, there has to be a match between the offer and the need if corporate goals and objectives are to be met.

Essentially the offer is a 'promise of benefits'. In other words, the customer is induced to buy the product or service in the expectation of acquiring desired benefits. It is an old saying in

Figure 1.1   Matching Customer Needs with Corporate Resources

marketing that, 'people don't buy products, they buy benefits.'
So people might buy a TV set to be entertained, to be informed or
even to *keep up with the Jones*; but not because they want to buy a
cathode ray tube and all the electronics that go with it.

Many companies still fail to recognize this basic fact and
continue to focus upon features rather than on benefits. This is
particularly true in industrial marketing. Pick up any trade magazine in, say, the engineering field and examine the advertisements. Mostly these advertisements will highlight the technical
aspects of the product rather than what the product will do for the
customer. Thus a manufacturer of roller bearings might stress the
'track and roller profile' whereas the customer benefit is actually
less friction and greater efficiency. This is not to say that technical
information is unimportant, but rather that successful marketing
is based upon selling solutions to perceived problems.

The same principle applies if we are marketing to another
company rather than to the end customer – what is sometimes
called 'business-to-business' or 'industrial' marketing. Buyers in
such organizations are also seeking benefits or, put another way,
they seek solutions to problems. To succeed in the market place
therefore our offer has to provide desired benefits or solutions. If
it does not, or is not perceived to do so, no amount of high-
pressure selling will persuade people to buy it.

Thus the offer should be viewed as a bundle of benefits and/or
solutions and not merely as a set of product features. One way of
expressing this idea is as a 'halo' or 'surround' that encircles the
core product or service (See Figure 1.2). In effect, this 'surround'
reflects the added values for the customer and thus will provide a
means of differentiating the core product or service from competitive offers.

Figure 1.2   Added Values Enhance Basic Features

The surround comprises such sources of added value as the corporate image, the customer service that is provided, any financial 'packages' that assist the purchase, technical support, after sales service and, of course, brand or corporate image.

The larger the surround in relation to the core, the more likely it is that the offer will be strongly differentiated from the competition. If, on the other hand, we only emphasize the core product in our promotion, then we are encouraging the customer to see it purely as a 'commodity'. It is relatively easy for competitors to imitate the core product – even if we think we have a patent protection. In so many markets there has been a convergence of technology; for example in hi-fi, in personal computers, in compact disc players and in digital watches. The way in which companies like Bang & Olufsen, Apple, Sony and Seiko differentiate themselves is not through technology – good though it may be – but through the wider dimensions of design, user-friendliness, quality reputation and breadth of range.

THE SEARCH FOR DIFFERENTIAL ADVANTAGE

What is the reason that Coca-Cola outsells Pepsi, even though in many cases 'blind' tests have shown that people prefer the taste of Pepsi? Why do large numbers of people pay more for a sports shirt with a designer label than one of equal quality from Marks and Spencer? Indeed why, in most markets, is there a 'brand leader'?

The answer is simple: successful companies are those which have worked to produce strongly differentiated offers. Their products or services are not *me too*'s. Customers recognize the added value that, in their minds, enhances the product. Sometimes that added value may be psychological or emotional, as in the case of Coca-Cola; other times it will be because there are specific benefits that are perceived to attach to one offer as compared to that of its competitors.

The strength of Coca-Cola's emotional appeal was well illustrated in 1985 when, after ninety-nine years, the Coca-Cola Company decided to counter the competitive threat in the USA from Pepsi-Cola by introducing an improved formula with a taste which tests had shown was judged superior to that of Pepsi. The new formula was thoroughly researched – about $4million was spent on taste tests and research with nearly 200,000 consumers. Some of the tests were 'blind tests', i.e. the consumer did not know the name of the product. Other research asked the question 'What if this were a new Coke taste?' but none of the questions addressed the issue: 'What if the old familiar Coca-Cola you have known and loved for years were to be removed from the market and replaced by something called "New Coke"?'

When the product was launched in the USA as a replacement for the traditional Coca-Cola there was a national outcry. Sales fell away, pressure groups were formed, primetime TV news programmes reported the issue in great detail. Within months Coca-Cola were forced to bring back the old formulation, now called Coca-Cola 'Classic', complete with the traditional script and logo.

What Coca-Cola had failed to realize was that customers were not primarily buying a taste but an *experience*. Coca-Cola's strength – its source of differential advantage – was its image and the customer values that were delivered by the traditional name and logo.

The concept of *differential advantage* lies at the heart of strategic marketing. Indeed it could be argued that the ultimate role of marketing management is to achieve and maintain maximum positive differentiation over and above the competition in the eyes of customers.

In seeking to differentiate its products the company needs to recognize that the potential customer is concerned with **benefits** rather than **features** *per se*. Theodore Levitt, one of marketing's most original thinkers, once wrote 'people don't buy ¼" drills, they buy ¼" holes.' The essence of that statement is that the drill is purely a vehicle for the provision of the benefit – a means of solving a 'buying problem'. What this means is that the successful offer is one which promises to deliver *solutions* to customers' buying problems in a superior way to competitive offers.

A useful concept here is the idea of the 'benefit proposition'. That is: 'What does our offer promise to deliver by way of benefits and solutions that makes it different from competitive offers?'

It is important to recognize that different people will react in different ways to benefit propositions. Take, for instance, non-drip paint. The covering power of non-drip paint is less than regular paint. However, to the do-it-yourself painter the promise of 'non-drip' is a key benefit proposition. On the other hand the primary benefit sought by the professional painter is cost per square metre and thus this part of the market is unlikely to respond to that particular benefit proposition.

In 'high-tech' marketing there is a similar need to focus on customer benefits rather than upon the technology. For example, computer-integrated manufacturing (CIM) is making slow progress in terms of widespread adoption in manufacturing industry. One of the reasons for this is the apparently high costs involved. Using traditional investment appraisal techniques such as payback period or discounted cash flow (DCF) it often appears to be uneconomic in terms of the cost reduction that it promises. However, the major benefits of CIM, as the Japanese are demonstrating, exist primarily not in terms of reduced costs but rather in the greater manufacturing flexibility that it provides, the shorter through-put times and the reduction in working capital. This translates into direct marketing benefits to the manufacturing company. For example, companies using this technology can respond more rapidly to customer needs; they can produce greater variety with little or no cost penalty; they can reduce inventories and thus boost return on investment (ROI).

Thus to convince the potential customer of the advantages of this type of investment requires a focus upon that customer's market place and its characteristics. Rather than selling cost reduction *per se* the CIM equipment manufacturer must sell enhanced market share, even survival.

Careful research of the market and an understanding of the 'problems' that customers seek to solve will assist in the process of achieving differential advantage by selling benefits rather than features.

MARKETING AND THE BOTTOM LINE

A frequent criticism of western management is that it is too short-term in its thinking and its focus. There is still a tendency, it is argued, to seek to maximize this year's profit – even at the expense of longer term development of the business. Part of the blame must be placed on the general financial orientation of many senior managers. This is reflected in the accounting mentality whereby costs in general, and product costs in particular, are paid greater attention than the means of revenue improvement. This is not to say that costs are unimportant, but rather to assert a basic truth: products don't make profits, but

customers do. The search for long-term profitability must therefore focus as much upon the customer as it does upon the
product.

Whilst profitability can be increased in the short term by
productivity improvements – i.e. by producing the same sales
volume at less cost – long-term growth in profitability can only
be achieved by increasing volume. **Volume growth together
with productivity improvement holds the key to profitability.**

Figure 1.3 summarizes the options that are available to the
business in its search for sustainable profit improvement.

Figure 1.3   The Sources of Profit Improvement

Saunders, J. Attitudes, structure and behaviour in a successful company. In
Journal of Marketing Management vol. 3, no 2, winter 1987 (modified)

Let us explore some of these ideas in more detail.

Opportunities for productivity improvement tend to be self-
limiting, in the sense that costs can only be cut so far and price
and product mix adjustments can only be made with limited
frequency. On the other hand the opportunities for innovation

and improved competitiveness are limited only by imagination and creativity. A primary concern of the marketing task within the business is to seek to innovate through product and market development and to strive to enhance competitive performance.

In both cases it is only by placing the customer at the centre of the business that success can be achieved. Innovation that is not based upon the satisfaction of a customer need, either existing or latent, will not succeed – the world is littered with 'better mousetraps'. Similarly the search for competitive advantage will only be successful if based upon a strategy of meeting customer needs more effectively than competitors.

Ultimately, therefore, the role of marketing in the organization is firstly to ensure that the orientation of the business is towards the customer, and secondly to seek to marshall the resources of the business in such a way as to be perceived by the market as providing superior benefits than are available elsewhere.

There are thus two aspects to marketing. The first is about corporate values and culture and the second is about strategy and execution. It is important to recognize that to have a marketing orientation and to achieve competitive advantage it is not necessary to have a marketing department or even a single marketing executive. What is essential is that every move the organization makes is guided by the principles of marketing and that a customer orientation pervades the organization.

Recently, many books and studies have appeared which have sought to explain the factors that determine business success. Books like *In Search of Excellence*, *The Winning Streak* and *The IBM Way* have all drawn the same conclusion: put very simply it is that those companies where customer satisfaction is an article of faith rather than a convenient slogan will tend to succeed. The surprising thing is that it has taken so long for such a simple concept to gain widespread acceptance!

INDUSTRIAL, CONSUMER AND SERVICE MARKETING

There are still some managers who believe that 'marketing' only applies to toothpaste or other so-called 'fast moving consumer goods' – FMCG for short. This attitude belies the reality of the marketing concept, i.e. the achievement of corporate goals through customer satisfaction. The relevance of the marketing concept is equally strong in the case of marketing special steels to industry as it is to marketing designer jeans to the fashion-conscious young – or, for that matter, to the marketing of an appeal for famine relief.

The key point to stress is that the principles of marketing have universal application; what does differ is the way in which the implementation is achieved.

Typically, in *industrial markets* there will be fewer buyers making purchases less frequently, and at higher prices, than will be found in consumer markets. Often the buyer will be a professional purchasing manager, sometimes with specific training in negotiation skills and with detailed product know-ledge. However, it can be argued that these differences are only a matter of degree. What, ultimately, is the difference between a housewife shopping on behalf of a family and a purchasing officer buying on behalf of a corporation?

Where there *is* a difference between consumer and industrial marketing is in the emphasis placed upon the different elements of the marketing mix. Thus in the case of marketing special steels the role of TV advertising may be limited in contrast to that of marketing designer jeans. On the other hand there will be a greater emphasis placed upon personal, technical selling in the former case compared to the latter.

The distinctions between **services marketing** and **consumer marketing** are equally blurred. What makes marketing a service different is that the product on offer is 'intangible'. It is based upon a relationship, an experience, an encounter. It quite clearly is focussed upon people rather than on things. However, in reality there are few industrial or consumer products that do not have a personal or 'relationship' dimension involved somewhere along the line. Indeed, a point that was made earlier in the context of the discussion of the 'product surround' was that service is a powerful means of differentiating the product.

Again it is sometimes suggested that services are different because they are perishable and cannot be stored. In other words, a hotel bed, if not sold today, cannot be sold tomorrow; a professional accountant cannot hold his time in 'inventory' whilst he goes on holiday. Once more though, if we reflect on this issue, we will recognize that the distinction is again one of degree. A newspaper, a popular record or this season's fashion have very short lives and the service offer in a sense is just an extreme case of a 'time sensitive' product.

SUMMARY

For many years marketing was thought by many to be just another word for 'selling' or, at best, an activity that was appropriate for fast-moving consumer goods but not for the world of industrial products. Recently, however, this attitude has changed and there is now a greater recognition of the fundamental importance of marketing as the keystone for business success. Marketing, as we have seen, is more than simply 'giving the customer what he or she wants'. It requires a clear understanding of the asset base of the business and the means whereby it can differentiate itself from its competitors.

The remainder of this book focuses upon the frameworks and techniques through which the marketing concept can be made a reality in your business.

CHAPTER 2

Managing Marketing

THERE are two major facets to marketing: firstly there is marketing as an orientation and a philosophy and secondly there is marketing as a set of tasks and actions. The difference is between creating a marketing *culture* within the organization on the one hand, and managing the marketing *function* on the other. The responsibility for creating and maintaining the marketing culture is essentially that of the chief executive, for it is he or she who sets the style within the organization. However, the responsibility for managing and controlling the marketing function will normally require the attention of designated executives with specific skills.

This chapter is concerned with the marketing management process and with the issues and challenges facing the marketing executive. How does a marketing-oriented company take the concept of marketing and turn it into a reality?

THE MARKETING MIX

Perhaps the most fundamental task of the marketing executive is the management of the *marketing mix*. The marketing mix is the name given to the main *demand-influencing variables* that are available to the company. The classic description of the marketing mix, although something of a simplification, is as the 'four P's'. What are the four P's?

Product   What decisions relate to the product or service range?

Price   What price should we set for each product or service?

Promotion   How do we communicate with our target market and persuade them to buy our offer?

Place   What channels of distribution, what levels of service, are appropriate?

Each of these elements is capable of influencing demand either separately or together with the other marketing mix elements. Later chapters in this book will explore each marketing mix element in more detail, but at this stage it is appropriate to look at some of the general principles underlying decisions on the actual marketing mix that a company might choose to implement.

PRODUCT/SERVICE

Although customers and their needs are the focal point of the marketing process, few companies started with this in mind. Invariably somebody had a good idea for a product or service and this became the germ of the business idea.

Not surprisingly, then, many businesses see the product or service to be at the heart of the firm's marketing efforts. There may be nothing intrinsically wrong with this attitude as long as business people can see that their product or service does not have to remain as a fixed, unchanging entity – a sort of organizational straitjacket.

Instead, the company must learn to see its output as flexible, being subject to development and adaptation, just like any other component of the market mix. Because the business world is never static the company should keep asking itself the question: 'Does each product/service we offer provide relevant and desired benefits for today's customers' needs?'

Furthermore, it should not mislead itself into thinking that customers buy the product or service as an end in itself. They don't; they buy a whole package of things when they make a purchase. Here are just some of the factors that go to make the 'product package':

Technical features
Packaging
Design
Image
Functional performance
Quality
Availability
Reputation
Before-sales service
After-sales service
Range of sizes, colours, etc.
Running costs
Ease of maintenance
Ease of use
Training provided/simple instructions
Compatibility with existing equipment/services
Safety
Pollution hazard reduction

Clearly there is more to a product or service than meets the eye. You cannot force customers to buy your product or service, they must *want* the benefits which the purchase will bring them. For companies, this means finding out what particular benefits are wanted by different customer segments. Then the company should choose its customers rather than wait for customers to choose them. It is this knowledge which enables a company to offer a more attractive 'package' than its competitors. This might or might not mean modifying the actual product or service itself.

PRICE

Pricing is an area of marketing with a tremendous potential for increasing short-term profits, but unfortunately if it is done badly it can equally quickly bring a business to its knees.

Is pricing an art or a science? The short answer is that it is probably a bit of both, as we shall see when we come to examine pricing in more detail later. For now, let us just consider what options are open to us for using pricing as a flexible 'connector' which helps to match our efforts to the needs of the customers.

There is a fear amongst many business people that unless they offer the lowest possible price they will not win the order. Whilst this can be true for some businesses, it is rarely the case with market leaders. Take the case of the really successful builder who has built his reputation on quality workmanship. His business continues to thrive and prosper, whilst many other builders without the same quality reputation have gone bankrupt through quoting low prices to get a job and then doing poor quality work to make it pay.

Also, take the example of the housewife who prefers to buy goods from a local shop rather than a supermarket where she can get them at a cheaper price. Why? Quite apart from the convenience factor, she knows that she can get personal service from her local shop.

As we suggested earlier, the customer buys a 'package' of benefits and the price ought to reflect the value of the *total package*.

Clearly, price is an important element of the business transaction and, appropriately chosen, it can have not only a big impact on a company's marketing strategy in the long term but can also help to differentiate the product or service from those of competitors.

PROMOTION

The promotion element of the marketing mix is concerned with how to communicate with customers and potential customers. In practice the promotion element of the marketing mix falls into two broad categories:

1   Personal promotion (face-to-face dealing with customers)
2   Impersonal promotion (e.g. advertising, sales promotion)

1.   Personal Promotion

This is the role of selling, which might be accomplished through a sales force. Face-to-face selling has a number of advantages over impersonal methods:

1   it is a two-way process which gives the prospective pur-chaser the opportunity to ask questions about the product or service;
2   the sales message can be tailored to the needs of individual customers;
3   the salesperson can use his in-depth knowledge about pro-duct or service to identify new customer needs and over-come objections;
4   the salesperson can ask for an order;
5   the salesperson can negotiate on price, delivery or special requirements;
6   the salesperson can build a relationship with customers and thereby lay the foundations for longer-term business.

However, selling also involves a lot of 'dead' time such as preparing sales aids, phoning for appointments, travelling, failing to win an order, administration and research. Therefore it is a costly business, and needs to be regularly monitored to ensure that it provides a good return for the cost and effort that goes into it.

2.   Impersonal Promotion

Typically, this area of promotion takes the form of advertising and sales promotion.

Advertising
Many companies believe that this is the province of only the very large companies and that it is something best left to the 'experts'. It doesn't have to be like this. Rather than looking at

advertising as a *cost*, look upon it as an *investment*; like any other investment it is only going to be any good if it makes money for you.

Spots on television or billboards throughout the country; local radio; leaflets, brochures, stories in the papers and trade journals; cards on newspaper display boards; advertisements in the local paper, yellow pages, local buses and gifts such as calendars and pens are all examples of advertising. Even a company's letterheads and the appearance of its vans or trucks convey something about itself.

All advertising needs to address itself to these questions:

1 At whom is it aimed? (target customers)
2 What should it say? (message)
3 How should the message be communicated? (medium)
4 How will the result be measured?

These questions can only be answered if a company has a good understanding of its customers and potential customers – what interests them, what would motivate them to buy and what they are likely to read.

Although the various advertising media mentioned above vary in terms of their costs and potential for reaching customers, we can see that combinations of message and media will provide a company with a very flexible advertising repertoire – one that can be tailored to fit your budget.

Sales Promotions
Sales promotions are essentially short-term campaigns to influence customers (perhaps a competitor's customers, or even intermediaries) to buy more of your product or to use it faster. Some companies use promotions to encourage their own salesforce to sell more.

Generally, promotions take the form of offering a **money** incentive, such as a price reduction or coupon against next purchase, **goods** such as two for the price of one, or **services** such as free estimates and holidays.

PLACE

As we have indicated, the essential task of marketing is to match a firm's resources to customer needs in a way that gives satisfaction to both parties. However, it also means that companies have to search continuously for something which will give them a competitive advantage. We have looked briefly at how this might be achieved in the other parts of the marketing mix, but how might it be done in the frequently overlooked area of making goods or services available in the right place and at the right time?

A market gardener started a business of farming organically-grown vegetables. Immediately he was faced with several different ways of getting them to the consumer, some direct, some through intermediaries.

a)	Producer	▷	'Pick Your Own'	▷	Consumer
b)	Producer	▷	Farm Shop	▷	Consumer
c)	Producer	▷	Mail Order	▷	Consumer
d)	Producer	▷	Specialist Shops	▷	Consumer
e)	Producer	▷	Wholesaler – Retailers	▷	Consumer
f)	Producer	▷	Restaurants	▷	Consumer
g)	Producer	▷	Health Farms	▷	Consumer

This example also gives a good illustration of the 'place' element of the marketing mix and how that needs to be integrated with delivery and consignment 'packaging'.

Clearly, the cheapest channel is option (a), where getting the consumer to come along to bear the harvesting costs will save the farmer money. But suppose that doesn't appeal to people in his catchment area, or suppose he is in a sparsely populated area? A farm shop (b) would have the advantage of appealing to passing trade as well as to regular customers, but distribution costs are already escalating.

On analysis each option offers commercial possibilities; equally, each one involves costs. Also within any particular channel there are areas for cost management. For example, with option (f), should the farmer deliver to the restaurants or should they collect from him?

The essential decision for the company is to decide on distribution channels which give it a sizeable element of control at a reasonable cost. It might also want to safeguard its interests by using more than one channel to reach different customer segments. The choice of channel can also help the company to differentiate its product. A classic example of this was when Avon Cosmetics took their products into the home of the consumer, while the competition continued to trade in departmental stores and chemists shops.

Many firms make the mistake of sticking to the traditional distribution channels they know best, even though new channels are opening up all around them.

The message is clear. The company must keep an open mind about distribution channels. It should evaluate its existing channels on a regular basis, and not be afraid of investigating or experimenting with new ones.

PROGRAMMING THE MARKETING MIX

At the outset of this chapter we identified marketing's role as ensuring that the four P's – product, price, promotion and place – were successfully managed. Success means that the customer is satisfied and that the organization's resources are effectively deployed to that end.

Marketing's job is to generate the right mix of sales with customers at the right price, with the right promotion, and at the right time and place. This means that the marketing department must be organized in such a way that they are appropriately mixed together and that they are properly and effectively coordinated in a marketing plan. Later chapters of the book will explore the components of the marketing mix in detail.

Not only must each of the four P's be managed separately, but also as they interact with each other in the marketing mix. Furthermore, an adequate answer in terms of a specific mix for this year's marketing problems is unlikely to be adequate for next year's. Products will be improved or made obsolete, new ones launched; prices will need to change; promotion can be upstaged or drowned out; the place of sale can become less satisfactory as alternative opportunities and challenges develop. For example, to what extent might a higher price with more effective promotion improve the overall profit contribution and what effect will this have on market share? To what extent can increased stock availability more than recoup the extra costs in terms of sales and profits? These are marketing mix problems.

To wrestle with such mix problems and to plan for and implement such solutions most medium- and large-sized organizations establish a marketing department and appoint someone to coordinate all such activities at director or boardroom level. This is the role of the marketing function.

To compound the problem of identifying the appropriate marketing mix there are a series of fundamental changes that have taken place in the competitive environment. These changes present significant challenges to the way in which marketing strategies are formulated.

THE CHALLENGES TO THE CORPORATION

The market place has never been static, and the need to anticipate and respond to change has been a basic prerequisite for survival since business first began. However, it can fairly be said that marketing management today faces a greater number of challenges of a more complex nature and from a wider number of sources. Let us examine some of these challenges.

(i) THE IMPACT OF TECHNOLOGY

Whilst it has become something of a cliché to refer to the quickening pace of technological change, there is no denying its impact on marketing. The introduction of new technology will tend to render obsolete that which it succeeds. Products based upon yesterday's technology will normally die. Thus the impact of a faster rate of technological change is to reduce dramatically the viable life of a product. In other words, technological change affects the product life cycle.

An example of this is provided by the typewriter. The mechanical typewriter had a life cycle of thirty years; in other words a model introduced in 1920 would still be available, little-changed, in 1950. Electromechanical typewriters had a life cycle of ten years, electronic typewriters five years and now word processors one or two years.

Technology development tends to follow the classic 'S-shaped' curve, with especially rapid change taking place after a period of relatively little development. Similarly this period of rapid change is followed by a period of little change before the next quantum step onto the next S-curve. Figure 2.1 illustrates such a progression in the development of lighting technology.

Figure 2.1   S-Curves and Technology Change

The electronics industry provides many examples of shortening life cycles where technology changes follow each other rapidly. For example from 1964 to 1976 IBM only introduced two families of mainframe computers. As technology changed so did the rate of new product introduction – there were four in the period 1976 to 1980. In the electronic calculator market Hewlett-Packard did not begin selling calculators until 1972 but the technology evolved so quickly (232 models in eight years) that calculators had entered their mature phase by 1980.

It is not only in electronics and advanced engineering that the effect of technology is felt. Video games which took companies like Atari to dizzy levels of profitability dropped rapidly in popularity as 'new generation' electronic games were introduced by companies like Nintendo.

Clearly marketing in a period of rapid technology change needs to be far more responsive, far quicker to spot trends and to take decisions than in those markets where change is relatively slow.

(ii)   THE FRAGMENTATION OF MARKETS

In the past we used to talk of the 'mass market'. In other words there was a large volume demand for a standard product. The Model T Ford is perhaps the classic example of a product aimed at such a market. Now though, through wider choice, greater disposable income and customers seeking greater individuality, we have seen the replacement of the mass market with a highly-fragmented market based upon distinct segments and niches. Later in the book we will discuss market segmentation in greater detail, but in essence the idea is that the majority of markets comprise a number of 'sub-markets' which are characterized by customers that share common characteristics. Some of these segments might be distinguished by the age or sex of their customers; in industrial markets it might be by the size of company or the end use of their products. Often it will be the case that a market segment is best described by more than a single dimension.

The basic principle of segmentation, however, is that the

greatest chance of market success will occur through the careful matching of the precise needs of that customer group with a 'tailored' marketing mix of product, price, promotion and place.

In consumer markets it has been suggested that there has been a fundamental change in the 'shape' of the market. Figure 2.2(a) depicts the market as it was in the immediate post-war years when customers were first confronted with consumer marketing as we then knew it. This was the era of 'keeping up with the Jones' and the almost universal desire to acquire a TV, a family car and, perhaps, the first package holiday. In the thirty years or so that have followed that era we have seen a greater concern on the part of consumers to express their own individual aspirations through purchases that reflect that individuality. Figure 2.2(b) suggests that the mass market has been 'squeezed' to produce a diversity of fragmented niche markets. There still remains a sizeable market for 'value for money' at one end of the spectrum, but at the other end we see a multitude of customer requirements, each different from the other. Nowhere is this better typified than in the retail fashion market with stores that cater specifically for particular age groups, life styles and income groups.

(a) The mass market   (b) The polarized market

Figure 2.2(a) and (b)   The Change in Consumer Markets

This phenomenon is not limited to consumer markets. In industrial and service markets we see a similar pattern. There is no mass market for industrial lubricants or for robotics but instead very precisely expressed requirements for specification, for service and for price.

The challenge in today's market place is therefore quite different from that of the fifties, the sixties and even the seventies. The name of the game today is <u>variety</u>.

(iii) THE GLOBALIZATION OF MARKETS

One of the major characteristics of the late twentieth century is the trend towards the globalization of markets. Whilst the global brand is commonplace, for example Coca-Cola, Marlboro cigarettes and IBM computers, the phenomenon of the global company is more a reflection of the drive for the economies of scale and scope than it is from a growing convergence of customer requirements.

A global company is more than a multinational company. In the global business materials and components are sourced world-wide, manufactured offshore and sold in many different countries, perhaps with local customization.

Such is the trend towards globalization that it is probably safe to forecast that by the year 2000 most markets will be dominated by global corporations. The only role left for national companies will be to cater for specific and unique local demands, for example in the food industry.

The global corporation seeks to achieve competitive advantage by identifying world markets for its products and then developing a manufacturing and distribution strategy to support its marketing strategy. So a company like Caterpillar Tractor, for example, has dispersed assembly facilities to key overseas markets. It uses global logistics channels to supply parts to offshore assembly plants and aftermarkets. Where appropriate Caterpillar will use 'third party' companies to manage distribution and even final finishing. So, for example, in the US a third party company, Leaseway Transportation, in addition to providing parts inspection and warehousing, actually attaches options to fork-lift trucks. Wheels, counterweights, forks and masts are installed as specified by Caterpillar. Thus local market needs can be catered for from a standardized production process.

Even in a geographically compact area like the EEC we find

that there is still a significant need for local customization. A frequently cited example is the difference in preference for washing machines. The French prefer top-loading machines; the British go for front-loaders; the West Germans prefer high-speed spins but the Italians prefer a lower speed! In addition there are differences in electrical standards and differences in distribution channels. In the UK most washing machines are sold through national chains specializing in white goods. In Italy white goods are sold through a profusion of small retailers and customers bargain over price.

The challenge to a global company like Electrolux therefore is how to achieve the cost advantage of standardization whilst still catering for the local demand for variety. Electrolux is responding to that challenge by seeking to standardize parts, components and modules and then through flexible manufacture and local assembly to provide the specific products demanded by end markets.

(iv) TIME-BASED COMPETITION

Perhaps the greatest change to have an impact upon the business environment in recent years has been the growing demand by the customer for service. This is a phenomenon which is explored in detail in a later chapter but one particular facet justifies a mention now.

Put very simply, today's customer has become time-sensitive. Because the level of competition in most markets is greater than it was, and because substitutes are almost always available, the customer is not prepared to wait. If the shop is out of stock of Heinz Baked Beans only the most brand-loyal customer would look in other stores or would agree to come back in a week's time! Research shows that most customers in situations like this simply reach out for a competitive brand or even an own label. In service markets, like hotels, car-hire firms or hairdressers, almost by definition the customer wants immediate gratification with minimal waiting time. In industrial markets the picture is the same – a car manufacturer operating 'Just-in-Time' assembly lines will only carry a few hours of stock of components and will therefore insist that its suppliers provide on-time delivery.

Recognizing the importance of time and convenience, companies like Federal Express, Domino's Pizzas and Tie Rack have developed strong competitive positions. Another example is provided by Benetton, the Italian-based global fashion manufacturer and retailer.

Benetton's order system is 'Just-in-Time' as production runs are not started until orders have been received. A key aspect of its system is the dyeing of knitted goods after production, rather than dyeing yarn prior to knitting. This allows Benetton outlets to delay commitment to particular colours until later in the production cycle. Since each selling season typically begins with about ten alternative colours, with only about three usually resulting in high demand, the delay in colour choice affords Benetton an opportunity to respond directly to market demand. A retail information system provides valuable information to Benetton for production planning via daily feedback on sales. This updates production on current demand, upon which replenishment schedules for designs and colours may be used. The timeliness of this order data is crucial since popular colours will often sell out in the first ten days of a new season. This rapid response system gives Benetton a competitive edge over the less responsive competitors. Further, Benetton uses CAD/CAM (Computer-Aided Design/Computer-Aided Manufacturing) for design and cutting in order to respond to dynamic demand as rapidly as possible. Finally, the company's marketing strategy promotes simple colour fashion with heavy advertising support, which in turn maximizes the benefits from the flexible production process.

MEETING THE CHALLENGE

We have indicated just a few of the challenges that face marketing in the closing years of the twentieth century. What should be the response?

The common element in each of the challenges we have discussed has been **change** and in particular the speed of that change. This change has been influenced by technology, by market fragmentation, by globalization and by customer demands for service. The marketing response therefore has to be appropriate; specifically the marketing organization of the nineties must be tuned in to the market and be highly sensitive to trends. It must be capable of fast reaction to those trends and it must be global in its reach.

How might the organization acquire these characteristics?

(i) MONITORING AND RESEARCHING THE MARKET

Later in this book we will explore the marketing environment in detail. However, a prerequisite for monitoring environmental change is an effective marketing information system. The use of market research on an ongoing basis is vital to an understanding of the changing requirements of the customer.

The nature of business necessitates that the future is under constant review and is taken into account in forward planning. Markets are perhaps one of the most difficult business areas to forecast because there can be so many variables affecting them. They can be influenced by government legislation, competition, new technology, the economy at large and changing fashions. However, the fact that movements in markets can be more volatile and unpredictable than movements in other areas is not a justification for avoiding methodical analytical techniques. Equally, we might have to recognize when situations defy strict analysis, or the cost of in-depth research would be prohibitive. Then we must fall back to using our best judgement but still, hopefully, in a focussed and methodical manner.

Herman Khan, the American 'futurologist', is quoted as saying: 'The only good thing about the future is that it comes one day at a time.' In order that – even at this speed – it doesn't arrive before the company is ready for it, the marketer must develop forecasting procedures which generate a high level of confidence in the prognosis.

Instinctively we know many of the questions to which we seek answers:

Who are the customers?
What are they buying?
Where are they buying?
When are they buying?
Why do they buy from us?
If they didn't buy from us from whom would they buy?
Are our customers growing or shrinking as a 'group'?
What are the general growth trends in the total market?
How do our customers perceive us?
What threats might change the market situation?
What new opportunities are beginning to emerge?

Most of these questions can only be answered properly if we have knowledge about our customers, their behaviour, their beliefs and their reaction to our marketing effort. As we have stressed, the whole basis of the marketing concept is grounded in the notion that the profitable development of the company can be ensured only through a constant attempt to match the capabilities of the company to the needs of the customers. So that these needs may be identified, and the suitability of the company's market offering assessed, it is necessary that some type of information flow should be instituted between the customer and the company.

The key task facing the researcher is to understand what sort of decisions require what sort of information. At its simplest, we can identify three levels of marketing decisions which could require an investment in terms of market research:

▶ Information for strategic, long-term decisions
▶ Information for tactical, short-term decisions
▶ Information for specific, one-off marketing problems

The first two situations require a continuous *ongoing* input of market information, whereas the last needs a speedy, *ad hoc* response from the market researcher.

Today the more sophisticated companies have set up systems which provide their executives with market intelligence on a weekly, and sometimes even daily, basis. They will be provided with information about the level of sales, by product or by market area; levels of inventory throughout the distribution channels; work in progress; trend data and market share estimates. Very often all of this information existed previously within the organization, but in a fragmented and uncoordinated form. By constructing a *market intelligence system* (MIS) it is possible to provide management with a *data bank* which is designed to meet clearly specified information needs.

Companies which take this route need not limit their MIS to the analysis of current and historical data. Now it is becoming possible to incorporate data about customer attitudes and competitor activity, for example, alongside the more conventional information. Using on-line search facilities it is possible for even the smallest company to access commercial data bases covering every aspect of market information.

The benefits arising from an integration of marketing information through a formal MIS lie chiefly in the 'direction' that is given to otherwise uncoordinated data. The requirements for such a system do not necessarily imply the use of a computer, although of course the power and flexibility of any MIS can be greatly enhanced by such means.

However, for the system to work well, management must be clear about the decisions that they have to make and define their information needs, both those that are ongoing as well as *ad hoc*. Without this step being taken much valuable time and effort will be wasted.

(ii) 'FAST TRACK' MARKETING

It will be apparent that with the rate of technology change and the reduction in the length of the product life cycle companies can no longer proceed at a leisurely pace from product development through to product launch.

Figure 2.3 below reflects the penalty of lost profit and obsolete stock that has to be carried by the company that is slow to market.

In this case the product was launched too late into a short life

Shorter life cycles make timing crucial

- Less time to make profit
- Higher risk of obsolescence

Figure 2.3   Shorter Life Cycles Make Timing Crucial

cycle market and was only getting established as the market for
that technology or product variant was turning down. For
example, in a market like the personal computer, where the
market cycle for a particular technology may only be eighteen
months, to get to the market six months late means a one-third
reduction in profit opportunity.

To respond to this challenge many organizations have
focussed on reducing the time taken from the drawing board to
the market place. Some of the best examples come from Japan
where companies like Honda, Canon, NEC and Fuji Xerox have
been able to reduce dramatically the new product development
process. In the West there are other good examples of fast
response. IBM, although late into the personal computer market
initially, made up for lost time by halving the usual industry
product development time. Compaq, also in the personal computer market, even beats IBM by creating new machines in less
than a year. In Europe companies like Philips, Volvo and Rolls-
Royce have also successfully driven down the time to market.

What are the differences in approach that 'fast track' marketing requires?

There seem to be a number of basic lessons to be learned from
the companies who have mastered this new style marketing.

► **Manage in parallel, not sequentially**
Instead of product design, engineering, market testing and manufacturing following one after the other, they work together – thus eliminating delays and identifying problems at an early stage.

► **Use multidisciplinary venture teams**
Clearly related to the previous lesson is the idea of the venture team. IBM developed its personal computer by putting a multidisciplinary team together and gave them complete autonomy to bring the product to market.

► **Be prepared to overspend**
Strange as it may seem, the careful control of development costs can be counterproductive. In order to speed up the process of innovation it may often be necessary to invest heavily at the front end to guarantee profit over the cycle.

► **Involve suppliers at an early stage**
More and more innovation is supplier-originated, particularly in processes but also in products. By involving suppliers in the planning and development stage leadtimes can be reduced and potential production problems eliminated. Furthermore, innovative product features are more likely to emerge.

► **Spend time on planning, not on implementation**
Many western companies spend too little time on planning and consequently find that implementation of marketing strategies is more difficult, revisions are required and failures are higher. Typically the successful Japanese company spends longer at the planning stage, but once the decision is taken there is immediate action – no committees, no steering groups, no bureaucracy.

(iii) MAKE STRATEGIC ALLIANCES

The challenge posed by globalization presents a major problem, particularly to companies who are not established on the international scene. It may not always be feasible or appropriate for such companies to contemplate overseas expansion – and yet that will be the price of survival in the years ahead. Acquisition or merger may also be neither possible nor desirable.

Many companies in recent years have instead sought out global partners with whom they can form *strategic alliances*. The purpose of these alliances is to create complementary portfolios of marketing skills. This is a development on the old idea of 'synergy', or the '2+2=5' effect. Sometimes the alliance may be more concerned to share technology as in the case of the Rover Group and Honda, or ICL and Fujitsu. However, strategic alliances can also be effective in extending global market coverage. So, for example, British Airways was able to have an enhanced market presence in the United States through its strategic alliance with United Airlines.

This alliance offered an alternative to take-over or merger which in any case was not permitted under US law. British Airways Chief Executive, Sir Colin Marshall, was quoted (*The Times*, March 29, 1988) as saying: 'This really does offer a good solution – commercial extension and facilitation without the huge problems of culture and concern which attend any large merger.'

The marketing merger between British Airways and United allowed each airline greater presence in parts of the world where the other was a leader. Under the arrangement passengers travelling with British Airways and United shared terminals as well as coordinated schedules and joint pricing. A similar strategic alliance was also announced between the Scandinavian airline SAS and Continental Airlines in the USA.

Recently Philips and Whirlpool have joined forces to market domestic appliances making them a formidable force on the world scene, and General Electric of the US have established a similar arrangement with GEC in the UK.

Whilst these examples are all of companies of substantial size they provide guidelines for others. The general principle of the strategic alliance is to seek out opportunities to enhance and extend marketing skills on a global scale.

SUMMARY

In this chapter we have explained the concept of the *marketing mix* and looked in brief detail at the component elements of that mix. We also highlighted the particular challenges that the company must confront emanating from technology, market fragmentation, globalization and the 'time-sensitivity' of markets.

The ultimate task of marketing management is to construct a strategy for the marketing mix such that it is capable of overcoming these challenges to achieve competitive advantage.

CHAPTER 3

Scanning the Environment

SO FAR in this book we have looked at marketing, both as a concept and as a process. We defined marketing as matching the abilities of the supplying company with the needs of the customer so that they both get what they want. The limitations which militate against this matching process working well are likely to be weaknesses within the company and external factors, which can be seen as threats. However, on the positive side, companies also possess strengths and the business environment is rarely completely hostile. As one commercial opportunity dies, so another one will appear. The successful company plays to its strengths, which it tries to build, and tries to reduce its weaknesses. At the same time it identifies and concentrates on the available opportunities, while consciously negotiating a way through the threats.

THE MARKETING ENVIRONMENT

There are likely to be several important factors which can affect the extent to which it is possible for an organization to balance its resources and efforts with customer needs. This milieu in which the organization is operating is referred to as the **marketing environment** and consists of the following components:

- ▶ customers
- ▶ competitors
- ▶ social and cultural trends
- ▶ political, fiscal, economic and legal policies
- ▶ technology
- ▶ institutional patterns

It is our intention to examine in much more depth elsewhere in this book the two most obvious components of the marketing environment – customers and competitors. The ability to know who our actual and potential customers are and to understand in what ways different groups of customers have different needs is obviously central to any organization's success. Equally, since what competitors do will always affect a business, it is necessary to find ways of monitoring their activities and of building that information into decision-making.

This is why these two crucial components of the marketing environment are treated in more depth elsewhere in this book. This, however, is not to imply that the other elements listed are not important. Indeed, it is the purpose of this chapter to examine their impact on the organization and to look at ways of monitoring them, starting with social and cultural trends.

CULTURAL TRENDS

Different countries – and, in domestic markets, different regions – have different preference patterns that spring from culture and tradition. For example, preference shown by customers for one product over another may be based purely on cultural traditions or trends. Consider European breakfast habits for a moment. The Dutch prefer cheese, the British like toast and the Danes enjoy crispbread. If there are problems when marketing domestically, the problems are that much greater when it comes to differentiating between cultures. Intuitive skills in domestic markets can make a great contribution to marketing programmes, but behaviour according to the same cultural criteria in foreign markets can lead to the most elementary and expensive marketing mistakes.

Material Culture is often responsive to increased national wealth and its consequent rewards, as well as the current state of discretionary income and its impact on purchasing inclinations and abilities. Language is another aspect of culture which requires the most careful attention in the choice, for example, of brand names and in the communication of ideas. Different cultures respond differently to the acquisition of conspicuous wealth, towards changes in life styles and towards taking social risks.

Education determines whether or not written communication is possible. High levels of illiteracy make instructions on packaging pointless; training programmes for distributors and agents must take careful cognizance of the problems which result. The conduct of marketing research will also pose its own problems which can be severely restricting because such a high premium must, of necessity, be placed on objectively collated data in the face of an uncertain cultural situation.

Religion, like language, is a readily identifiable aspect of cultural differences which we find both within and across national boundaries. Its taboos and predilections must be ascertained and their impact on economic behaviour studied with care. For instance, anything to do with liquor in some Muslim countries must be handled with great sensitivity. Attitudes and values, most especially towards marketing, advertising and sales, will need to be ascertained and understood.

Even **business practices** vary between cultures and nations, as do acceptable modes of dress. For example, the conventions for making business appointments in South America and the Middle East not only vary but are alien to most European businessmen. Punctuality, or at least respect for this convention, is interpreted differently across national boundaries. Whilst a safari suit and long socks might be acceptable business dress for men in many hot climates, exposed knees and lower arms would be considered as a mark of disrespect by many native businessmen of the Arabian Gulf states. Contract negotiation, itself an art, must be adapted accordingly. What may be common negotiating practice 'at home' may be wholly unacceptable to businessmen in the country in which you are trying to develop a commercial presence.

Social organization can be seen most clearly at work in the family or in the company's purchasing department. Certain cultures respect age and status, whilst others have developed a more meritocratic stance. Some have a greater respect for womenfolk than others. Some operate through a greatly extended concept of family, whereas in other cultures the family has almost broken down as an effective social institution, even for bringing up children.

Ultimately, successful inter-cultural marketing activity is built upon an understanding of how local culture interacts with the four P's.

POLITICAL, FISCAL, ECONOMIC AND LEGAL POLICIES

The political, fiscal, economic and legal policies of the governments of the countries in which we sell our goods also determine what we can do. For example, inflation reduces the discretionary spending power of consumers, and this can result in market decline. Legislation concerning such things as labelling, packaging, advertising and environmentalism all affect the way in which we run our businesses, and all these things have to be taken into account when we make our plans.

One of the most obvious and visible examples of government policies has been the impact in certain countries of heavy taxation on tobacco and the banning of advertising. This has forced tobacco companies to seek less hostile markets in other parts of the world, but most have also diversified into other products and services in order to continue their historical growth in turnover and profits. Also, publicity about, and in many cases legislation against, unhealthy ingredients in food has caused significant changes in purchasing behaviour. In America and in the United Kingdom, for example, per capita consumption of chicken now exceeds that of beef. This is a prime example of an industry not being sufficiently aware of changing environmental trends and allowing a competitive industry to overtake them.

Turning for a moment specifically to the internal environment, **tariffs** are taxes on imports levied in order to earn revenue and to protect home industries. They affect the price of imported goods, making them less competitive than locally produced goods. Companies affected by tariffs often react by using marginal cost pricing policies, by modifying the product, by repositioning the product in a high-priced market segment or by CKD shipping (Completely Knocked Down) for local assembly, thus attracting a lower rate of duty.

Quotas are direct barriers to imports. They are much more serious because the firm has less flexibility in responding to them. Apart from attempting to obtain a fair share of quotas, virtually the only response is to set up local production if the market size warrants it.

Exchange control means that foreign exchange is in short supply and the government is rationing it. If a company is manufacturing in a country with exchange controls, it has to make sure it is able to obtain exchange for imported supplies of raw materials or component parts; or else develop local supplies irrespective of possible higher costs and indifferent quality. Also, such a country is unlikely to give high priority to profit remittance, whilst currency fluctuations can either wipe out a company's profit or create a windfall virtually overnight.

Non-tariff barriers in the form of customs documentation, marks of origin, product formulation, packaging and labelling laws can similarly have a dramatic effect on a company's freedom over the management of its marketing effort.

Political instability, boycotts, customs, unions and other environmental factors can also have a drastic effect on a company's marketing policy. For instance, one German company selling consumer products in Latin America lost most of its market share when the tariff was raised from twenty to fifty per cent. The options discussed by the local management at an emergency meeting were: to continue paying the high duty and change the product positioning to a high price segment; to import the primary ingredients and assemble locally; to ask for a lower price from the home factory; or to give up the market completely. Eventually, the company realized that it had to take a longer-term view which took account of the potential in the total Latin American Free Trade Area (LAFTA), and that this should have been done at the market entry stage rather than after a heavy investment had been made in only one market. Eventually the company set up manufacturing facilities in one of the LAFTA countries and South America is now a profitable market for the company. But, above all, the company learned the hard way that it just did not enjoy the same degree of control over its international marketing as it did over its home market.

TECHNOLOGY

Technology is constantly changing. We can no longer assume that our current range of products will continue to be demanded by our customers. For example, the introduction of non-drip paint had a profound effect on what had traditionally been a stable market. People discovered that they could use paint without causing a mess, and eventually the product was demanded in new kinds of outlets such as supermarkets. Those paint manufacturers who continued to make only their traditional kind of paint and to distribute it through traditional outlets went into decline very quickly.

More recently, companies such as Gestetner have been badly affected by the encroachment into their traditional areas of business by more effective small photocopying machines, whilst the printing industry is being affected by the development of desktop publishing. The advent of the computer, of course, has revolutionized just about every facet of business life, whilst the merging of telecommunications and computer technology is causing a fundamental reappraisal of a whole host of industries, with new ones springing up to replace those that do not keep abreast of changing technology.

Technological change is now such an accepted facet of business life that no organization can afford to ignore it. British Cellophane Limited, part of the Courtaulds group, dominated the European cellophane packaging market for many years until the invention of oriented polypropylene, based on oil. Since BCL had such a hold on the market they chose to ignore this technological development, until before long major oil companies entered traditional cellophane markets with a lower-priced product. It was only then that the company decided to embrace the new technology, via an acquisition. The result was that the company lost its dominant position in the market, and, whilst it has recovered well there is no doubt that many years of difficulties could have been avoided given a more perspicacious approach to technological change.

INSTITUTIONAL PATTERNS

Institutional patterns are another aspect of the marketing environment which contemporary marketers have inherited from previous years of trading activity. Since we have been talking about food and technology, this point can be illustrated by two well-known examples.

Until the late 1960s, the major pattern of food distribution throughout Europe was for relatively small grocers or multiple stores to operate through highly local retail outlets. The advent of mass car ownership has transformed this pattern in two decades to one of large-scale supermarkets in almost every developed country. In so doing, several other traditional retail institutions have been undermined – the pharmacist, the butcher, the greengrocer, the fishmonger, the dairy, the hardware merchant, and even the baker.

But even today changes are taking place. Supermarkets that present themselves only as discount retailers are losing out to those who are making more specialized offers to a more discerning public. The result is that in the UK, for example, Boots, St. Michael and Sainsburys have become brand names in their own right, whilst a whole new generation of specialist retailers are beginning to emerge.

The Giro method of banking, invented in Austria and widely practised throughout Europe for half a century, only reached the UK in the 1960s. It is only now that the Giro system is beginning to make any real impact on the pattern of banking behaviour amongst the two-thirds of the population who made no use at all of the clearing banks at the time of Giro's introduction, and to whom the convenience of banking services had hitherto not been effectively available.

The essential point is that the environment in which we operate is not controlled by us. It is dynamic, and hence must be monitored constantly. Let us turn briefly to the methods that are available to us to help monitor the environment.

MEANS OF SCANNING THE ENVIRONMENT

In looking at formal approaches to scanning the environment we should look first at **marketing research.**

It is sometimes said that a prime management concern in marketing is the **conversion of uncertainty into risk.** Uncertainty implies an inability to state the likelihood of any possible outcome occurring. By implication all outcomes must be treated as equally likely. Under **uncertainty** the manager must consider, say, the chance of failure in a new product launch to equal the chance of success. **Risk,** on the other hand, suggests that the likelihood of outcomes might be assessed more precisely. The marketing manager might feel that a particular new service launch has only a 5% chance of failure. Our ability to make successful decisions is enhanced if we are operating under conditions of known risk rather than uncertainty. If this conversion of uncertainty into risk is the prime marketing management task, the second is surely the reduction or at least the minimization of that risk.

To achieve either of these goals the manager requires information. Good information is a facilitator of successful marketing action. Seen in this way, marketing management becomes essentially an information-processing activity. Marketing research is therefore concerned with much more than simply telling us something about the market place. Rather, it is a systematic and objective search for, and an analysis of, information relevant to the identification and solution of marketing problems. Marketing research can be classified as being either *ad hoc* or ongoing.

Ad hoc marketing research refers to situations where the identification of a research problem leads to a specific information requirement. So when a French manufacturer of proprietary pharmaceuticals found that sales of its long-established cough remedy were falling, it decided to conduct a study of consumer attitudes and beliefs about cough remedies and used the information gained to relaunch the brand.

Ongoing marketing research, as the name implies, provides more of a monitoring function, resulting in a flow of information about the market place and our performance in it. The Confederation of British Industry (CBI) maintains a regular monitor, based upon surveys, of business confidence and investment intentions in the United Kingdom, for example.

Sometimes there is a dichotomy between two other forms of marketing research, **external** and **internal**. Much valuable intelligence can be gained from internal marketing analysis, and external information gathering should be seen always as a complement to such internal information and not an alternative.

External marketing research is conducted within the market and the competitive environment in which the company exists.

Internal marketing research is based upon an analysis of company data gained from information such as sales trends,

Figure 3.1   A Framework for Marketing Research

changes in the elements of marketing – price, for example – and advertising levels.

There are a number of headings under which the methods of marketing research might usefully be examined. Figure 3.1 provides a summary and useful framework for discussing the forms of marketing research activity that are encountered most frequently.

REACTIVE MARKETING RESEARCH

As the phrase implies, **reactive** marketing research is information about the market place and the customers who inhabit it. It can involve us in asking questions, such as in a survey or during an interview. Equally it can involve experiments. Figure 3.2 summarizes the principal options.

Figure 3.2 Forms of Reactive Marketing Research

Questionnaires are the favoured means of data gathering. They are a flexible instrument and can be administered by an interviewer or by the interviewee. As we know only too well from the experience of being stopped in the street, or receiving questionnaires in the mail such as reader survey questionnaires in subscription periodicals, this process can take place in various situations. It may even be conducted as a telephone conversation or discussion. However, before embarking on this method of marketing research, it is well to be aware of the pitfalls that can result from the use of a questionnaire if it has not been carefully pre-planned and checked.

Loaded questions can have a distorting effect, as can ambiguous phrases. Even the order of the questions may upset the final result. The errors in the final population estimates from a questionnaire administered to a sample are called *bias* or *systematic error* of the estimates. In other words, the true characteristics of the population – for example relative preferences between several types of industrial compressor – may be different from the estimate produced by the sample survey. This bias may result from the way in which the sample was chosen or from the means by which the survey data were collected.

Such pitfalls can be reduced by carefully designing the questionnaire and then by *pilot testing* it. In other words, give the survey a trial run on a subgroup of the intended sample to isolate any problems, ambiguities or omissions that may arise in the responses.

Group discussions may be a more appropriate way to gather market information as they attempt to draw insights for marketing action from smaller-scale, more detailed studies. Such studies are intended to provide qualitative cues, rather than quantitative conclusions.

In such circumstances a group discussion is a loosely structured format where the leader – often a trained psychologist – attempts to draw from the group their feelings about the subject under discussion. The group is chosen to be representative of the population in which the researcher is interested, although naturally any conclusions emerging from the discussions can only form the basis of qualitative generalizations about that population. Such interviews need not be conducted in groups. They can be equally effective in pairs or alone with the interviewer.

Single interviews are an alternative way of deriving information. Sometimes they are extended or in-depth interviews and do have the advantage that both the interviewer and inter-viewee can explore certain lines of discussion more rigorously if this is perceived as being of mutual benefit, whereas a group discussion must always maintain a degree of structure if it is to be meaningful. Such a form of single in-depth interview will be used more often when information regarding specialized markets is required in industrial marketing research.

Experiments are another type of reactive marketing research. Earlier in this book we assessed the benefits of test-marketing new products. Marketing experiments can also help us to gain a better understanding of how marketing processes work.

For example, a manufacturer of confectionery wanted to know if the effect on sales of a 'money-off' offer was greater than spending a similar sum on in-store merchandising improvements. The information he needed to answer the question could only be obtained from the experiment, whereby a number of stores were selected in different areas of the country and used as the testing ground for these alternative promotional approaches. The stores chosen for the experiment were as near alike as possible in terms of turnover on the brand in question and served similar types of customers.

One-third of the stores ran the 'money-off' promotion, one-third used the improved in-store merchandising, and the remaining third carried on selling the product without any changes. After a period of two months the manufacturer felt able to draw conclusions about the relative effectiveness of the two promotional methods by comparing store results with those stores where no changes were made.

Market experimentation need not necessarily involve the setting up of large-scale experimental designs such as the one just discussed. Sometimes laboratory-type situations can be used to test marketing stimuli. Often advertisements will be pre-tested in such laboratory conditions. Samples of the target audience for an advertisement will be exposed to the advertisement and their reactions to the sample will be sought. Eye cameras, polygraphs and tachistoscopes are just some of the devices that have been used successfully to record physical reactions to marketing stimuli.

Whilst the theory of experimentation in the marketing context is sound enough, there are a number of drawbacks to its operation in practice. It is very often difficult to set up experimental situations that are microcosms of the total market. There is always the problem of controlling all the variables in the experiment, for example the actions of competitors, and of course the cost of setting up and maintaining market experiments can be prohibitive.

NON-REACTIVE MARKETING RESEARCH

These methods are based upon interpretation of *observed phenomena* or extant data. By definition, they do not rely upon data derived directly from respondents. Figure 3.3 summarizes the main forms of **non-reactive** marketing research.

Figure 3.3   Forms of Non-Reactive Marketing Research

Desk research should in fact be the *starting point* of any marketing research programme. Desk research involves the use of existing information for determining the extent of prior knowledge about the subject being studied. There is often a wealth of material to be obtained from published and unpublished sources, which can reduce the need to 'rediscover the wheel'.

Official statistics such as those published by governments, OECD, the EEC and the United Nations, can provide detailed data on markets and patterns within those markets. Other sources such as newspapers, technical journals, trade association publications and published market studies will provide a 'fill-in' to any later field work that might be needed. **Internal data** derived from sales figures and salesmen's reports can also be a guide to the direction that later studies might need to take.

Observation can be a very effective marketing research technique. How people behave in the real world and how they react to stimuli can often be discovered best of all through watching and interpreting their reactions. Some observational methods, such as a camera in a supermarket, do not involve the direct participation of the researcher and this can be a limiting factor. Often the areas of activity in which we are most interested may only occur infrequently and the observation must be sustained over a period in order to capture a single activity.

'**Participant' observation**, a phrase borrowed from anthropology, involves the observer in attempting to become a part of the activity that is under observation. This form of marketing research is very limited in its scope, although one British research organization, Mass Observation, did some early pioneering work in this area in a number of studies, a famous example being a major study of consumer behaviour in public houses.

Retail audit is widely used as a secondary source of observation data. This has been developed and perfected as a technique over a period of time and, properly controlled, it can be a very accurate source of marketing information on brand shares, market size, distribution coverage and sales trends.

The audits conducted by A. C. Neilsen Ltd are perhaps the most widely known, and work on a simple basis. Within a particular product field a representative sample of stockists is chosen and their cooperation obtained. At regular periods the investigator visits the stockists and notes two things; the current levels of stock of the product group being audited, and the invoices or delivery notes for any goods in that group delivered since the last visit. With the information on stock levels obtained on the *last* visit, it is a simple matter to determine sales of each item being audited during the period between visits – i.e. opening stock plus deliveries between visits less closing stock = sales during period.

The **Consumer Panel** is another similar source of data; this is a sample group of consumers in a particular product field who record their purchases and consumption over a period of time in a diary. This technique has been used in industrial as well as consumer markets and can provide continuous data on patterns of usage as well as other data such as media habits.

INTEGRATING MARKETING RESEARCH WITH MARKETING ACTION

How should managers approach this issue? In the first place it is necessary to view marketing information as a resource. This means that we must be concerned with the problems of producing it, storing and distributing it. Marketing information has a limited *shelf life* – it is perishable. Like other resources, information has a value in use. The less the manager knows about a marketing problem, and the greater the risk attached to a wrong decision, the more valuable the information becomes. This latter point is an important consideration in assessing marketing research budgets. It implies the need for a cost/benefit appraisal of all sources of marketing information. There is no point in investing more in such information than the return on it would justify. Naturally, it is easier to determine the cost than the benefits. The managerial benefits of marketing research are difficult to pin down. They can be expressed in terms of additional sales or profits that might be achieved through the avoidance of marketing failures that could otherwise result if there is a lack of information.

One company involved in the development of an industrial application of heat exchangers in West Germany believed that there was a 20% chance that the product might not succeed, leaving them with a development and marketing bill of DM 2 million. From this they inferred that the maximum *loss expectation* was DM 400,000 (i.e. DM 2,000,000 × 20%) and that it was worth paying up to this sum to acquire information that would help them avoid such a loss. Such a cost/benefit calculation implies that the information they could acquire would in itself be totally reliable. Because such *perfect information* is rare, and in this case it could not be obtained, they budgeted a smaller sum for marketing research which effectively discounted the likely inaccuracy of the information. Such an approach can be a valuable means of quantifying the value of marketing research in managerial context.

The use of marketing research by European companies has grown considerably in the last decade or so. Its use is not confined to manufacturers selling into consumer markets; some of the most interesting work to have been conducted in recent years has been on behalf of industrial marketing organizations, service companies such as banks, and social organizations such as voluntary and government agencies.

With this growth of marketing research has come an increasing sophistication in the use of the techniques available to the researcher, now a professional whose advice is looked for more and more in marketing decision-making. Likewise, the growth of companies which provide specialist marketing research services has multiplied so that it is now a major industry in its own right. This means that the manager has the facility available to him or her to monitor the effectiveness of their marketing performance and also to gain a better feel for what opportunities exist in the market place.

Finally, let us have a brief look at the difficulties of marketing research in the international context.

INTERNATIONAL MARKETING INTELLIGENCE

International marketing intelligence is simply the systematic gathering, recording and analysis of data about problems relating to the marketing of goods and services internationally. It is concerned with the following:

► where to go
► how to enter
► how to market the 4 P's
► traditional marketing research questions within each market

International marketing intelligence involves marketing research covering additional factors not usually present in domestic marketing; and studies of many foreign markets individually.

This form of marketing research is often referred to as **comparative analysis**. It is a way of organizing information on international markets and involves comparing and grouping countries in ways useful to decision-making, thus maximizing the use of a company's international experience. For example, grouping countries according to their geographic proximity, which some companies do for the purpose of marketing control, can be a mistake if they are not homogeneous in characteristics important to the company's marketing. Grouping countries according to stage of economic development, for example, can be a useful way of filling data gaps, for the missing values can be assumed to be similar to those available in the small group. Also, the expense of researching in many small markets can often be avoided by carrying out research in a sample of countries and extrapolating the results to other countries in the same group.

A large electronics company carried out a comparative analysis of its markets worldwide by first identifying the characteristics that were important to its international marketing decisions, then grouping different countries according to their similarity in these dimensions. They found three distinct groupings and began to develop marketing strategies for these three groups, rather than developing separate marketing strategies for each individual country as previously. The result was reflected in great savings for the company and also an improvement in the company's control.

There are a great number of problems in international market research not normally present in domestic research. These centre around cultural problems and economic problems. In some parts of the world only oral communication is possible, with several languages being spoken. Quite apart from these considerations, it is often almost impossible to interview women who, in most Islamic countries, are not allowed to talk to men without their husbands being present. Mail and telephone surveys are impossible in some countries, either because they are illegal, or because they are impractical. This leaves virtually only personal interviews, often difficult because of geographic and cultural problems.

Published data is less available and often unreliable, whilst different base years and different definitions are often used. Add to this the cost of researching foreign markets, and it will be seen at once that international market research is not just a simple extension of domestic techniques; although it must be said that as far as questionnaire design and sample sizes are concerned, exactly the same rules apply.

SUMMARY

From this brief summary of research methods and techniques in marketing it can be seen that the scope of marketing research can be considerable. Yet, at the same time, we must recognize that even the most carefully designed and conducted studies can at best only provide **imperfect information** of market phenomena. However, that being said, marketing research remains the link between the identification of market

CHAPTER 4

Competitive Analysis and Strategy

$\mathbf{S}$UCCESS in the market place is dependent not only upon identifying and responding to customer needs but also upon our ability to ensure that our response is judged by customers to be superior to that of the competitors. In other words, the development of marketing strategies must be based around both customer satisfaction and competitive differentiation.

Just as we can remember the key components of the marketing mix by the shorthand of the 'four P's', so too can we focus upon the basic elements of competitive strategy by reference to the 'three C's. The three C's in question are: the Customer, the Competition and the Company.

Figure 4.1 illustrates the triangular relationship that exists between the three C's:

Competitive strategy therefore can be seen as a search for differential advantage as perceived by customers. The key here is *perceptions* since the ultimate test question is: How does the customer evaluate our offer compared to competitive offers?' This basic principle is the foundation for market **positioning**. A key component of the strategic process in marketing is the identification of an appropriate competitive 'position' in the market place. In essence the position of a brand or offer is simply the customer's perception of the similarity or dissimilarity of our brand in relation to competitive offerings. As such it will be influenced by the particular marketing mix of product features, promotional appeals, price level and place

Figure 4.1   Marketing & the three C's

(distribution) factors that the company selects.

How do companies achieve this competitive advantage?

Many commentators and academics have investigated this fundamental question and their findings tend to point the same way. Put very simply, successful companies either have a cost advantage or they have a 'value' advantage – or a combination of the two. The cost advantage means that the company can produce and distribute its products at lower cost than the competition, whilst the value advantage means that the company's offer is perceived as providing differentiated benefits to customers – the product has greater 'added values'.

Let us examine briefly these two fundamental sources of competitive advantage.

1. COST ADVANTAGE

In many industries there will typically be one competitor who will be the low cost producer and, more often than not, that competitor will have the greatest sales volume in the sector. There is substantial evidence to suggest that 'big is beautiful' when it comes to cost advantage. This is partly due to economies of scale which enable fixed costs to be spread over a greater output, but more particularly to the impact of the 'experience curve'.

The experience curve is a phenomenon which has its roots in the earlier notion of the 'learning curve'. Researchers discovered during the last war that it was possible to identify and predict improvements in the rate of output of workers as they became more skilled in the processes and tasks on which they were working. Subsequent work by Bruce Henderson, founder of the Boston Consulting Group, extended this concept by demonstrating that *all* costs, not just production costs, would decline at a given rate as volume increased. In fact, to be precise, the relationship that the experience curve describes is between **real unit costs** and **cumulative** volume. Further it is generally recognized that this cost decline applies only to 'value added' i.e. costs other than bought-in supplies.

The experience curve in its general form is shown in Figure 4.2.

There are many implications of this relationship for the

Figure 4.2   The Experience Curve

development of marketing strategy, not least in the determination of pricing strategy. However, its importance in this current discussion is in the fact that if one company's relative market share is greater than that of its competitors then, other things being equal, it should be further down the experience curve. In other words it will have a cost advantage.

Such a cost advantage can either be used to lower price, thus putting the squeeze on competitors, or to earn higher margins at the same price as competitors.

Later in this book it will be suggested that it will generally be preferable to use such a cost advantage to reinvest in the product rather than use it to initiate price wars and thus run the risk of reducing the product to the status of a 'commodity'.

2. VALUE ADVANTAGE

We have already observed that 'customers don't buy products, they buy benefits.' Put another way the product is purchased not for itself but for the promise of what it will 'deliver'. These benefits may be intangible, i.e. they relate not to specific product features but rather to such things as *image* or *reputation*. Alternatively, the delivered offering may be seen to outperform its rivals in some functional aspect.

Unless the product or service we offer can be distinguished in some way from its competitors there is a strong likelihood that the market place will view it as a 'commodity' and so the sale will tend to go to the cheapest supplier. Thus the importance of seeking to attach additional values to our offering to mark it out from the competition.

What are the means by which such value differentiation may be gained?

Essentially the development of strategy based upon additional values will normally require a more segmented approach to the market. When a company scrutinizes markets closely it frequently finds that there are distinct 'value segments'. In other words different groups of customers within the total market attach different importance to different benefits. Market segmentation is discussed in greater detail in Chapter 7 but its importance here lies in the fact that often there are substantial opportunities for creating differentiated appeals for specific segments. Take the motor car as an example. A model such as the Ford Sierra is positioned in the middle range of European cars; within that broad category specific versions are aimed at defined segments. Thus we find the basic, small engine, two-door model at one end of the spectrum and the four-wheel drive, high performance version at the other extreme. In between are a whole variety of options, each of which seeks to satisfy the needs of quite different 'benefit segments'. Adding value through differentiation is a powerful means of achieving a defensible advantage in the market.

In practice what we find is that the successful companies will often seek to achieve a position based upon *both* a cost advantage *and* a value advantage. A useful way of examining the available options is to present them as a simple matrix as in Figure 4.3.

Figure 4.3 The Sources of Competitive Advantage

Let us consider these options in turn.

For companies who find themselves in the bottom left hand corner of our matrix the world is an uncomfortable place. These products are indistinguishable from their competitors' offerings and they have no cost advantage. These are typical 'commodity' market situations and the only ultimate strategy is either to move to the right on the matrix, i.e. to cost leadership, or upwards into a 'niche'. Often the cost leadership route is simply not available. This will be the case particularly in a mature market where substantial market share gains are difficult to achieve. New technology may sometimes provide a window of opportunity for cost reduction but in such situations it is often the case that the same technology is available to competitors.

Cost leadership, if it is to form the basis of a viable long term marketing strategy, should essentially be gained early in the market life cycle. This is why market share is considered to be so important in many industries. The 'experience curve' concept, briefly described earlier, demonstrates the value of early market share gains – the higher your share relative to your competitors, the lower your costs should be. This cost advantage can be used strategically to assume a position of price leader and, if appropriate, to make it impossible for higher-cost competitors to survive. Alternatively price may be maintained enabling above-average profit to be earned which is potentially available to develop further the position of the product in the market.

The other way out of the 'commodity' quadrant of our matrix is to seek a 'niche' or segment where it is possible to meet the needs of customers through offering additional values. Sometimes it may not be through tangible product features that this 'value added' is generated, but through service. For example, a steel stockholder who finds himself in the commodity quadrant may seek to move up to the niche quadrant by offering daily deliveries from stock, by providing additional 'finishing' services for his basic products or by focussing upon the provision of a range of special steels for specific segments.

What does seem to be an established rule is that there is no middle ground between cost leadership and niche marketing. The relationship between size, differentiation and profitability is generally agreed to be as depicted in Figure 4.4. Being caught in the middle (i.e. neither a cost leader nor a niche-based provider of added values) is generally bad news.

Finally, perhaps the most defensible position in the matrix is

Figure 4.4 The Dangers of the Middle Ground

the top right-hand corner. Companies who occupy that position have products that are distinctive in the values they offer and are **also** cost competitive. Arguably, many Japanese products, particularly in consumer markets, have achieved this position. Clearly it is a position of some strength, occupying 'high ground' which is extremely difficult for competitors to attack.

MARKET SHARE STRATEGIES

In discussing the advantages and disadvantages of pursuing niches or volume it is important that the issues surrounding 'market share' be fully understood. That there is a strong relationship between market share and return on investment has been confirmed by the analysis of data from thousands of companies participating in the PIMS study (Profit Impact of Market Strategy). This study, in searching for explanations of variations in profitability between firms, identified a strong correlation between market share and ROI.

However, a warning should be sounded: it may well be that profitable companies have high market shares, but it does not follow that all high market share companies will be profitable. Quite simply this is because market share can be 'bought'. It can be bought through price reductions, increased marketing effort and product development. All of this can be good practice unless it is at the expense of long term profit. Some companies have failed to recognize that investing in market share is really only viable early on in a product/market life cycle. Likewise, other companies have been caught out when the product/market life cycle turns out to be much shorter than was anticipated. In summary, market share strategies are long-term, and in volatile markets such strategies must be pursued with care.

A further issue surrounds the question, 'share of *which* market?' In other words, of what is market share a measure? The answer is that it all depends on how we define the total market. A holiday tour operator specializing in the organization of cultural tours of sites of antiquity, accompanied by a professor of archaeology, is not operating in the same market as a tour operator offering ten days in Majorca for two hundred pounds. Yet they both offer holidays.

The definition problem is helped if we use the concept of the 'served' market. The served market is best described in terms of the specific needs that we seek to meet rather than some generic product category. Some have called market share in this context 'share of mind', meaning that when potential customers are contemplating a purchase to meet a specific need they limit their choice to offerings that they consider competitive. The marketing challenge may thus be seen as one of how to increase 'share of mind' amongst specific target groups.

COMPETITIVE ANALYSIS

As markets mature, as growth rates stabilize or markets enter recession the only way to grow a business faster than the growth of the market is at the expense of the competition. This implies a need to understand in the greatest possible detail the competitive context and the characteristics of specific competitors. Here the work of Michael Porter, a Harvard Business School professor, is particularly valuable in providing a framework for the systematic exploration of the competitive context. Figure 4.5 summarizes the main forces driving industry competition.

Figure 4.5   Forces Driving Industry Competition
Michael E. Porter, *Competitive Strategy*, New York Free Press, 1980.

These key determinants of competitive position are:

► **Market Competition**

Obviously the more numerous or equally balanced the competitors, the more intense will be the rivalry within the market. If this is combined with a slow industry growth rate, and if fixed costs relative to variable costs are high, then the prognosis is for a high level of aggressive competition probably accompanied by severe price cutting. A further influencing factor will be the extent to which the competing products on offer are seen as substitutes by the market place with few switching penalties for buyers.

Of key importance will be the relative cost structures of the major players in the market; these will be determined not just by market share but by capacity utilization and production technology.

► **Threat of New Entrants**

In analysing markets one of the factors to be appraised is the existence, or absence, of 'barriers to entry'. In other words, how easy is it for new entrants to enter the market? Typically barriers might be provided by economies of scale so that without a minimum market share unit costs will be uncompetitive. Similarly heavy start-up costs – whether through the need for capital investment or high levels of marketing expenditure – can provide a barrier. Government regulation, as for example in the telecommunications industry, might also prove an effective barrier.

Conversely markets may be easy for new competitors to enter where product differentiation is low or where technology changes can overcome cost barriers. In the latter case a good example would be the way in which new technology has made it possible for new daily papers to be launched in an industry which previously had high entry barriers.

► **Substitute Products**

One factor that can considerably alter the strategic balance in a market place is the development of products that meet underlying customer needs more cost-effectively than existing products. The development of synthetic fibres had a major impact upon the demand for natural fibres, for example. Similarly, the advent of home video recording through video cameras has virtually eliminated the demand for home movie products.

▶ **Bargaining Power of Buyers**
The competitive climate of a market will clearly be influenced by the extent to which customers wield power through purchasing strength. Thus a market that is dominated by a limited number of buyers, or where a buyer takes a larger proportion of the seller's output, will substantially limit the seller's opportunities for individual action or development. The UK grocery market illustrates this situation well, with a handful of major retail chains being able to exert considerable influence over manufacturing suppliers' marketing policies and thus their profitability. Another source of competitive threat from buyers will exist when opportunities arise for backward integration up the value chain by buyers.

▶ **Bargaining Power of Suppliers**
Many of the threats that potentially exist from buyers can also come from the suppliers to an industry. If the supply of critical materials is controlled by a few suppliers, or if an individual company's purchases from a supplier constitute only a small part of his output, then freedom of manoeuvre may be limited. Again, if opportunities exist for forward integration by suppliers, this constitutes a further source of potential competitive pressure.

COMPETITIVE INFORMATION

Competitive analysis at this level requires access to a wide range of information, necessitating a continued monitoring of all sources of data. The range of competitive intelligence that should be gathered is illustrated in Figure 4.6. Some of the issues listed appear to be obvious and yet it is surprising how often we lack accurate information on them. Ideally a 'data bank' on the competitive environment should be established; use should be made of annual reports; annual statutory returns; Dun and Bradstreet reports or their equivalent; trade press and financial reports; publications from trade associations as well as company catalogues and advertisements.

► WHO ARE THE COMPETITION . . . WHERE?
► WHO ELSE MIGHT BECOME A COMPETITOR?
► THEIR SHARES OF MARKET SEGMENTS AND TRENDS
► THEIR PRODUCT LINE, PERFORMANCE, QUALITY, SERVICE
► THEIR MANAGEMENT, ITS SKILL, PHILOSOPHIES
► SIZE AND DEVELOPMENT OF THEIR SALES FORCE AND HOW THEY ORGANIZE THE SALES EFFORT
► THEIR PROMOTION STRATEGY
► THEIR PRICING POLICY, TERMS, DISCOUNTS
► THEIR TECHNOLOGICAL CAPABILITY
► THEIR FINANCIAL STRENGTH
► THEIR OBJECTIVES

Figure 4.6   Competitive Intelligence

Information can often be gathered from customers and suppliers about competitor's actions or intentions. If personnel are recruited from competitors they should be debriefed as far as professional ethics allow. In fact it is often surprising to see just how much openly available competitive intelligence can be gathered by making use of the sources described above.

Figure 4.7 overleaf gives some indication of the sources of competitor information, most of which is readily accessible. What organizations typically lack is an effective **marketing intelligence system** that collects, interprets and disseminates this information on a regular and systematic basis. This is not so in the case of the Japanese External Trade Organization (JETRO), a subsidiary of the Ministry of International Trade and Industry (MITI), which has eighty offices around the world all of which gather competitive and relevant information for transmission back to Japan. The larger Japanese companies also operate worldwide monitoring systems, which, quite legally, screen and index all material, patents, licences and academic journals in their fields of interest.

To be a viable basis for marketing strategy competitive analysis must be organized and managed as an ongoing activity – not just an *ad hoc* response to a particular circumstance.

COMPETITIVE BENCHMARKING

The ultimate test of the efficiency of any marketing strategy has to be sales – not just measured against volume targets, but rather in terms of profit. Those companies who strive for market share, but who measure market share in terms of volume sales, may be deluding themselves in that volume can be bought at the expense of profit. The only market share measure that counts in the long run is the **sterling share** of the market. In other words, what percentage of the total expenditure made by customers in this market ends up in our sales revenue?

Because market share is an 'after the event' measure we need to utilize continuing indicators of competitive performance; this will highlight areas where improvements in the marketing mix can be made.

In recent years a number of companies have developed a technique for assessing **relative** market place performance, which has come to be known as 'competitive benchmarking'. Originally the idea of competitive benchmarking was literally to

	PUBLIC	TRADE/ PROFESSIONALS	GOVERNMENT	INVESTORS
WHAT COMPETITORS SAY ABOUT THEMSELVES	▶ ADVERTISING ▶ PROMOTIONAL MATERIALS ▶ PRESS RELEASES ▶ SPEECHES ▶ BOOKS ▶ ARTICLES ▶ PERSONNEL CHANGES ▶ RECRUITMENT ADVERTISEMENTS	▶ MANUALS ▶ TECHNICAL PAPERS ▶ LICENCES ▶ PATENTS ▶ COURSES ▶ SEMINARS	▶ COMPANY HOUSE REPORTS ▶ LAWSUITS ▶ OFFICE OF FAIR TRADING AND MONOPOLIES COMMISSION	▶ ANNUAL MEETINGS ▶ ANNUAL REPORTS ▶ PROSPECTUSES ▶ STOCK/BOND ISSUES ▶ SPEECHES TO SECURITY ANALYSTS
WHAT OTHERS SAY ABOUT THEM	▶ BOOKS ▶ ARTICLES ▶ CASE STUDIES ▶ CONSULTANTS ▶ NEWSPAPER REPORTERS ▶ ENVIRONMENTAL GROUPS ▶ UNIONS ▶ EX-EMPLOYEES	▶ SUPPLIERS/ VENDORS ▶ TRADE PRESS ▶ INDUSTRY STUDIES ▶ CUSTOMERS ▶ SUB-CONTRACTORS	▶ LAWSUITS ▶ GOVERNMENT MINISTRIES ▶ NATIONAL PLANS	▶ SECURITY ANALYSIS ▶ REPORTS ▶ INDUSTRY STUDIES ▶ CREDIT REPORTS

Figure 4.7   Sources of Competitor Information

take apart a competitor's product, component by component, and to compare its performance in a value engineering sense with your own product. This approach has often been attributed to the Japanese, but many western companies have also found the value of such detailed comparisons.

However, the idea of benchmarking is capable of extension beyond this simple comparison of technology and cost-effectiveness. Because the battle in the market place for the 'share of mind' that we referred to earlier is essentially concerned with perceptions, it is perceptions that we must measure.

Companies like Rank Xerox have led the way in conducting regular surveys amongst customers, in which they seek to measure exactly how their customers see them as suppliers not just of a product, but of a total service. Not only do Rank Xerox measure the perceptions of customers concerning the relative performance of Xerox copiers compared to other copiers – they also seek to measure the image that customers have of them compared to other groups in the 'office automation' field, like IBM, Digital and NEC.

The measures that are used in this type of benchmarking programme include delivery reliability, ease of ordering, after-sales service, the quality of sales representation and the accuracy of invoices and other documentation. These measures are not chosen at random, but are selected because of their importance to the customer. Market research, often based on in-depth interviews, would typically be employed to identify what these 'key success factors' are. The elements that customers identify as being the most important then form the basis for the benchmark questionnaire. This questionnaire is administered to a sample of customers on a regular basis – for example, British Telecom carry out a daily telephone survey of a random sample of their domestic and business customers to measure customers' perceptions of service. For most companies an annual survey could suffice; in other cases perhaps quarterly, particularly if market conditions were dynamic.

The output of these surveys might typically be presented in the form of a competitive profile as in the example in Figure 4.8.

Importance to customer			Elements	Performance		
Low	Medium	High		Poor	Satisfactory	Good
			Reliable delivery			
			Order cycle time			
			Delivery frequency			
			Stock availability			
			Quality of sales people			
			Technical service			
			Order status information			

●----- Company   ●——— Key competitor

Figure 4.8   Competitive Benchmarking

SUMMARY

In today's environment the ability to present customers with a total offer that is recognized as superior to competitive offerings has become the prime task of marketing. We have seen that it is possible to gain competitive advantage both through lower costs and through greater product and service differentiation.

Knowledge of the competition is as important as knowledge of customers. Increasingly the leading companies are developing information systems that enable a continuing monitor of competitive strategy and performance to be maintained.

In these days, when the phrase 'competitive advantage' has become the rallying cry in so many organizations, it becomes even more crucial to build marketing strategies that explicitly take account of competitive considerations.

CHAPTER 5

The Marketing Audit

THE AUDITING PROCESS

A MARKETING AUDIT is an integral part of the wider **management audit.** In order to explain what a marketing audit is, it is necessary to explain firstly what the audit process is and how it relates to business disciplines other than finance, and secondly to explain what a management audit is.

Auditing as a process is usually associated with the financial side of a business and is conducted according to a tightly-defined set of accounting standards. The conventions of accounting are well documented, easily understood, and consequently lend themselves readily to the auditing process. The total business process, although less formal, more innovative and relying more on judgement than on a set of rules, is still nevertheless capable of being audited.

Basically an audit is the means by which a company can understand how it relates to the environment in which it operates. It can thereby identify its own strengths and weaknesses as they relate to external opportunities and threats. It is thus a way of selecting a position in that environment based on known factors.

Expressed in its simplest form, the purpose of a business plan is to answer three central questions:

1   Where is the company now?
2   Where does the company want to go?
3   How should the company organize its resources to get there?

This being so, the audit is one of the means by which the first of these questions is answered.

Often, the need for an audit doesn't manifest itself until things start going wrong for a company, such as declining sales, falling margins, lost market share and under-utilized production capacity. At times like this, management often attempts to treat the wrong symptoms. For example, changing the product, reorganizing the sales force, reducing prices, and cutting costs are just some of the actions which are often taken by management. But such measures are unlikely to have much effect if there is a much more fundamental problem which has not been identified. Essentially the argument is that the problem has to be properly defined; the audit is a means of helping to define the problem.

Although business problems are far less amenable to the highly structured analytical methods characteristic of the sciences, it is the very complexity of business problems that give rise to the need for some kind of structured procedure to help identify problems. The more complex the problem, the more necessary is a structured approach.

To summarize, the audit is a structured approach to the collection and analysis of information and data in the complex business environment as an essential prerequisite to problem-solving.

THE FORM OF THE AUDIT

So far we have considered what an audit is and why it is relevant to problem-solving in business. Before turning specifically to the larger question of what a management audit is and where the marketing audit fits in, it is necessary to describe the form which is common to both the management audit and the marketing audit.

An auditor will be faced with two kinds of variables. All business variables can be split into two kinds. Firstly, there are variables over which the company has no direct control. These usually take the form of what can be described as **environmental** and **market** variables. Secondly, there are variables over which the company has *complete* control. These we can call **internal,** or **operational** variables.

Key:
White areas: Uncontrollable variables
Tinted area: Controllable variables

Figure 5.1   Internal and external marketing variables

This gives us a clue to the structured way in which an audit should be conducted. That is to say, in two parts:

1   the external audit
2   the internal audit

Figure 5.1 describes in a very simple form the total business process. The white area represents the external variables over which the company has no direct control. The tinted area represents the area over which the company has complete control.

The external audit is concerned with auditing the *uncontrollable* variables, whilst the internal audit is concerned with auditing the *controllable* variables.

A central feature of all audits is the external audit and the internal audit. The purpose of the internal audit is to help assess the relative importance of the organization's internal resources *vis à vis* the external environment, and in particular *vis à vis* the market in which the company operates and the resources of competitors. This means that whether we are talking about a marketing audit, a distribution audit, a production audit, or any kind of audit, internal resources should always be assessed relative to key external factors.

The term *management audit* merely means a company-wide audit which includes an assessment of all internal resources *vis à vis* the external environment. In practice the best way to carry out a management audit is to carry out a separate audit of each major business function. Thus the marketing audit is merely part of a management audit, in the same way that a production audit is part of a management audit.

The following illustrates this point:

Marketing audit
Distribution audit
Personnel audit   } all add up to the
Finance audit   management audit
Purchasing/production audit

THE MANAGEMENT AUDIT

Before going on to describe the Marketing Audit in detail, it is necessary to stress that, although it is easier to carry out a Management Audit by breaking it down into discrete parts based on the major functional areas of a business, it would be completely wrong to imply that this means that each of the constituent audits is mutually exclusive. In practice this can never be the case, because it is obvious that everything that happens in each major business area has an indirect influence on sales and that all are therefore interdependent.

Just as a mark of a good company is the skill with which it succeeds in organizing its total resources in such a way that it achieves a profitable competitive advantage in the process of satisfying market wants, so the mark of a good auditor is the skill with which he is able to understand the relationship between a company's several resources and how they relate to the external environment.

What are these major organizational resources? The major headings to be considered are as follows:

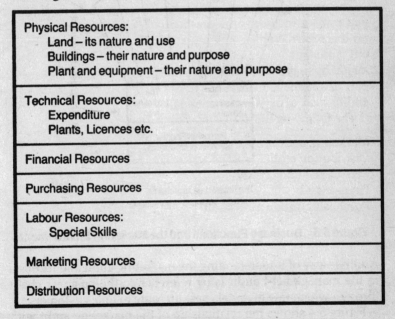

Figure 5.2   The Management Audit: Major Organizational Resources

It will be obvious from what has been said earlier that consideration of each of the items under these major headings will be of value only when compared with similar data for competitive companies.

Whilst this functional categorization could be further subdivided, it will be seen from Figure 5.3 how each of these major business functions fits into the conceptual framework of the total business process given in Figure 5.1.

Key:
The tinted area represents
the total business organisation

Figure 5.3   Business Functions and the Marketing Environment

Another way of understanding the marketing audit and its place in the management audit is by reference to the business chain through which raw materials pass en route to final customers.

Figure 5.4 shows the relationship of the marketing audit with other functional audits.

Figure 5.4   The Marketing Audit in Context

THE MARKETING AUDIT

The external audit starts with an examination of information on the general economy and then moves on to the outlook for the health and growth of the markets served by the company. The competitive environment is also included as part of the external audit.

Whilst the eventual objective of the external audit is to assess the extent to which economic and market factors indicate what the desired course of action should be, the starting point is to consider all possible angles.

Some of the key areas to be included in the external market are shown in Figure 5.5 below.

Economic Environment	The Market Environment	The Competitive Environment
Economic	Total Market Size	Number of Competitors
Fiscal	Segments	Profitability
Social	Channel	Degree of Integration
Business	Products	Cost Structure
Legal	End Use	Products
Technological	Geography	Technology
International	Needs	Sales & Market Shares
Intra Company	Tastes	Marketing Skills
	Habits	Key Success & Failure
	Attitudes	Factors
	Purchasing Ability	
	Stocks	
	Turnover	
	Profits	

Figure 5.5   The marketing audit: The Business Environment (Past, Present, Future)

The internal audit checklist is given in Figure 5.6:

Sales (total, by geographical location, by industrial type, by customer, by product)
Market Shares
Profit Margins

Marketing Mix Variables, as follows:

▶ Market Research	▶ Samples
▶ Product Development	▶ Exhibitions
▶ Product Range	▶ Selling
▶ Product Quality	▶ Sales Aids
▶ Unit of Sale	▶ Point of Sale
▶ Stock Levels	▶ Advertising
▶ Distribution	▶ Sales Promotion
▶ Dealer Support	▶ Public Relations
▶ Pricing, Discounts, Credit	▶ After Sales Service
▶ Packaging	▶ Training

Customer Classification
Customer Buying Power
Customer Problems and Requirements
Customer Methods of Supplier Selection
Marketing Procedures
Marketing Organization
Sales/Marketing Control Data

Figure 5.6   Marketing Operation Variables
(past, present, future)

To complete the picture of the marketing audit, the information in Figures 5.5 and 5.6 will be combined, in Figure 5.7, to show the *external audit* (Fig. 5.5) on the left, and the *internal audit* (Fig. 5.6) on the right:

EXTERNAL AUDIT	INTERNAL AUDIT
The Business Environment (past, present, future)	*Marketing Operational Variables* (past, present, future)

Economic Environment	**Own Company**
Economic	Sales (total, by geographical
Political	location, by industrial type,
Fiscal	by customer, by product)
Social	
Business	Market Shares
Legal	Profit Margins
Technological	Marketing Mix Variables,
International	as follows:
Intra Company	

The Market Environment	▶ Market Research
Total Market Size	▶ Product Development
Segments	▶ Product Range
Channels	▶ Product Quality
Products	▶ Unit of Sale
End Use	▶ Stock Levels
Geography	▶ Distribution
Needs	▶ Dealer Support
Tastes	▶ Pricing, Discounts, Credit
Habits	▶ Packaging
Attitudes	▶ Samples
Purchasing Ability	▶ Exhibitions
Stocks	▶ Selling
Turnover	▶ Sales Aids
Profits	▶ Point of Sale
	▶ Advertising
The Competitive Environment	▶ Sales Promotion
Number of Competitors	▶ Public Relations
Profitability	▶ After Sales Service
Degree of Integration	▶ Training
Cost Structure	
Products	Customer Classification
Technology	Customer Buying Power
Sales & Market Shares	Customer Problems and
Marketing Skills	Requirements
Key Success & Failure Factors	Customer Methods of Supplier
	Selection
	Marketing Procedures
	Marketing Organization
	Sales/Marketing Control Data

Figure 5.7   The Marketing Audit:
External and Internal Variables Combined

WHEN SHOULD THE MARKETING AUDIT BE CARRIED OUT?

A mistaken belief held by some is that the marketing audit should be a last, desperate attempt to define a company's marketing problems in such a way that a solution suggests itself which is within the capability of the firm to implement; or at best something which is carried out by an independent body from time to time to ensure that a company is getting the optimum utilization from its resources.

However, marketing is a complex function, with many interrelating parts which themselves interface with the market place and the actions of competitors. Thus it seems illogical not to carry out a thorough situation analysis at least once a year. This is especially so when it is considered that the rate of technological advance, improved communications and increased competition make it increasingly difficult to retain a secure position in traditional markets.

Fundamentally there is no difference between a situation analysis and a marketing audit except that the actual term *marketing audit* implies a formal, periodic review by an independent body. As such, it is not uncommon for companies to subject themselves to such an audit by an outside firm of consultants from time to time; whereas a situation analysis may be considered to be a continuous, internal process of self-appraisal and evaluation culminating in a summary marking the beginning of a new planning cycle and forming the basis of the next decision-making stage.

In an ongoing situation, a company will constantly review its marketing organization and operating effectiveness and adapt gradually to changing circumstances. Some companies, however, particularly those new to marketing planning, will adopt a more formal, major audit-type approach and then may make a number of far-reaching changes in the organization and policies as a result. The purpose of both the situation analysis and the marketing audit, however, is the same; their purpose in relation to marketing planning is to help the company to understand the dynamics of its business and its markets, and how they inter-relate.

There is much evidence to indicate that many highly success-ful companies, as well as using normal information and control procedures and market research reports throughout the year to adapt to their changing environment, also start their planning cycle each fiscal year with a formal review through an audit type process of everything which has had an important influence on trading activities. Certainly in many leading consumer goods companies the self-audit approach is a tried, tested and thoroughly understood self-discipline which is built into an integrated management process. The recommendation, then, is that the marketing audit should be institutionalized as part of an annual planning system.

This brings us to the more difficult question of who should carry out the marketing audit, for surely it is difficult for any manager to be completely honest and impartial when reviewing his own departmental operations?

It may well be advisable to have someone from outside carry out an audit every so often to check that a company is getting the most out of its resources. However, outside studies often suffer from a lack of internal ownership.

The answer, therefore, is to have the audit carried out by the company's own line managers. Problems usually centre around lack of time and lack of objectivity. The best way to overcome these problems is firstly by institutionalizing auditing pro-cedures in as much detail as possible, and secondly by thorough training in the use of the procedures themselves. However, even this will not result in the achievement of the objectives of an audit unless a rigorous discipline is laid upon management from highest down to the lowest levels involved in the audit. Such a rigorous discipline is usually successful in helping man-agers to avoid the sort of tunnel vision that often results from a lack of critical appraisal.

WHAT HAPPENS TO THE RESULTS OF THE AUDIT?

The major question which remains to be answered centres around what happens to the results of the marketing audit. In the same way that some companies waste considerable time and effort developing marketing plans that cannot be used, so other companies consume valuable resources carrying out audits which bring very little by way of actionable results.

Much of the literature indicates that marketing plans are developed in three major phases, as follows: a searching analysis of the industry and the company (the marketing audit); the formulation of objectives and strategies on the basis of the audit; the development of programmes to implement the strategies.

There is grave danger that at the marketing audit stage, which provides the foundations on which the whole planning edifice is built, insufficient attention is paid to the need to concentrate on analysis which determines which trends and developments will actually affect the company. The list in Figure 5.7 merely demonstrates the completeness and logic of analysis. But whilst the planner should consider every heading, he should discipline himself to omit from the plans that will eventually be prepared all information that is unrelated to the company's specific problems. Inclusion of such things as brand-switching analyses, or over-detailed sales performance histories by company and product which lead to no logical actions whatever, only serve to rob the marketing plan of focus and reduce its relevance. All analysis should be assessed on the basis of what it means in terms of the company's future development.

The next step is to sift and organize the information in a logical manner, followed by a review of the information to identify those factors and conditions that appear to be pertinent to the future of the company. In other words, situations, trends, facts, information and opinions which appear to have a bearing on the problems which face the company in getting and maintaining customers. Judgement has to be used so that anything which is

not relevant is omitted, the end result being a condensed statement
of market information which is pertinent to the company's problems, with all extraneous information removed. Often this end
result is referred to as *intelligence* as opposed to *data* or *information*.

HOW TO ORGANIZE THE FINDINGS OF THE AUDIT

Since the objective of the audit is to help indicate what a company's marketing objectives and strategies should be, it follows
that it would be helpful if some format could be found for
organizing the major findings of the marketing audit. Indeed, the
key to the successful completion of this stage of the marketing
planning process is an ability to organize major findings into a
logical and usable format as an aid to setting objectives, just as at
the audit stage itself the task is made easier by adopting a
structured approach to the task.

It will be recalled that the marketing audit begins with
obtaining information on the general economic environment,
and then goes on to examine the outlook for the growth and
health of the industries served by the company, including a
review of competitive activities. The internal audit of the company's own resources can then be made in the light of this background information on the economy, the market, and competitors.

It has also been stated, however, that merely to record information of this kind is not problem-solving. This requires discovery
of the extent to which these economic and other factors do
actually indicate what the course of the business should be.
Economic indicators *per se* cannot be used in plans in any direct
way. One way of writing down facts, information and conclusions in such a way that the task of reviewing marketing
objectives becomes easier is by summarizing the audit under the
headings **Strengths**, **Weaknesses**, **Opportunities** and **Threats**,
often referred to as a SWOT analysis. Expressed in its simplest
form, this means listing the company's key internal strengths and

weaknesses as they relate to external opportunities and threats.

This is the most difficult phase in the whole auditing process, for it represents the final focusing of attention on what the auditor considers to be the key issues affecting the business. It will be immediately apparent that several items could be included either as strengths or weaknesses, or as opportunities or threats, depending upon the view of the auditor; for what is seen as a threat by one person is often seen as an opportunity by another.

Whilst this will always be so, it must be said that the actual act of carrying out the marketing audit, if done thoroughly according to the structured approach suggested here, will go some considerable way towards giving the auditor a comprehensive knowledge of the business, trends in the market, where value is added by competitors, and so on. This should ensure a more realistic assessment of strengths, weaknesses, opportunities and threats, which will eventually form the basis of realistic marketing objectives and strategies.

An initial format for the SWOT analysis is given in Figure 5.8. This will be expanded on in Chapter 17 on marketing planning.

Strengths (Internal)	Weaknesses (Internal)
Opportunities (External)	Threats (External)

Figure 5.8   Initial Format for a SWOT Analysis

SUMMARY

In summary, however, the main point to bear in mind is that by adopting the kind of structured approach to the auditing process recommended in this text, the persón carrying out the audit stands a much better chance of a reasonable definition of the key problems facing a company than he would if he relied entirely on a more intuitive approach.

Thus there are basically two phases which comprise the auditing process:

1 The identification, measurement, collection and analysis of all the facts and opinions which impinge upon a company's problems;
2 the application of judgement to uncertain areas which are remaining following this analysis.

The first step in the auditing process is, therefore, to list all the facts and opinions relating to the problems facing the company. Analysis of these facts and opinions, and the application of judgement to help isolate those factors that are critical to success and the synthesizing and sorting process, then follows.

CHAPTER 6

Buyer Behaviour

AT ITS MOST simplistic level, business could be described as some kind of popularity contest in which products and services all vie for attention, buyers voting for the winners with their chequebooks.

Since few businesses offer unique products or services, and as few buyers have unlimited finance at their disposal, every purchase decision is, in reality, a **choice** decision.

Should we spend our hard-won savings and buy that dream kitchen? Company A are more expensive than Company B, but they offer more attractive designs, don't they? Might we do better if we bought do-it-yourself kitchen units . . . could save some money that way? How about getting it on credit and paying back by instalments? But what about that exotic holiday we promised ourselves? We couldn't have that and a new kitchen . . . Or could we somehow manage both? And what about the car? It's reaching a state where we ought to think of getting a newer model . . .

Such thinking could typify almost any purchase decision, and we know this to be true because we are all buyers ourselves. In the end we make our choice using a combination of rational judgements, based on facts and previous experience, and subjective feelings which determine our likes and dislikes. Factors such as our upbringing, values, stage of life, situation in which we find ourselves and the pressures we are under can all have some bearing upon our purchase decision.

As man is a thinking, feeling creature, before he takes any

action it has to seem to be logical and to feel right. Both the 'head' and the 'heart' need to sanction any commitment to action. Successful marketers know this to be true and use this knowledge to their advantage.

In this chapter we will look at some of the useful behavioural models that have been developed and can help marketers to understand the very bedrock of the marketing process – the preferences, prejudices, motivations and buying habits of their customers.

We will also consider what different pressures exist if the buyer is buying on his own behalf, or for an organization. Equally we will look at differences in industrial buying decisions and consumer purchases.

BUYERS AND CONSUMERS: KNOW THE DIFFERENCE

Often the person who buys a product or service is also the consumer, but this is not always the case. For example, in an industrial setting a buyer might be ordering vast shipments of raw materials which go to different parts of the organization to be processed. He doesn't use these materials personally. On the domestic front, a housewife might buy articles of food or clothing for her family which she will never use herself.

Clearly it is in the marketer's interest to know all about his buyers *and* consumers. If he has both, then inevitably they may have different needs which have to be satisfied. However, for simplicity's sake, in this chapter we will confine ourselves to talking about buyers only. The lessons we learn about them will in most cases be just as applicable to consumers.

A GENERAL MODEL

Whenever we try to predict human behaviour we must never forget that we are dealing with an extremely complex phenomenon. Many scientists claim that the main challenge facing Man is not to understand and conquer outer space, but to explore inner space; to find out how the brain works, how memory functions and so on. Even experts in this field claim that there are vast grey areas when it comes to understanding the inner working of *Homo sapiens*.

Nevertheless, from the work that has already been done in the behavioural field, we believe it is possible to draw a general model of the influences on consumer behaviour.

In this model we show the influences on the buyer as coming from two sources, personal and external.

The personal influences are those which are characteristics or traits of the buyer as an individual. Thus he will have hopes, fears, ambitions, doubts, perceptions, beliefs, attitudes, values, knowledge and experience. The buyer faces the world with a 'persona' or personality which is his alone, and only he knows how much energy and hard-earned wealth he is prepared to put into the buying transaction.

However, the individual does not operate within a vacuum; there are always external influences which can have a bearing on his behaviour. Is the transaction legal? How will peer groups or the family respond? Is the general economy such that it is wise to buy now? How much is the buyer's behaviour conditioned by his situation, social class or culture? None of us are as free as we might choose to believe.

Figure 6.1 overleaf shows these two sources of influence feeding through 'hoppers' on to the 'pans' of a balance. Clearly, if for a particular type of purchase the personal factors far outweigh the external ones, then the marketer needs to know this – and also what these factors are. If the balance swings the other way, the marketer should be just as interested to understand the reasons why.

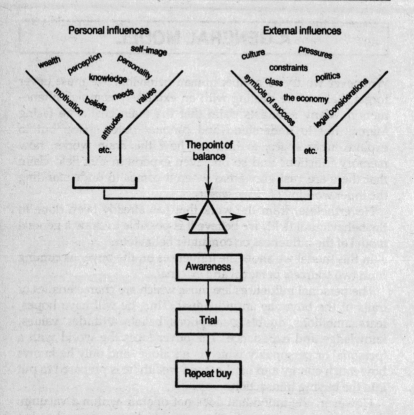

Figure 6.1   Influences on Consumer Behaviour

At the end of the day it is this balance between personal and external forces which characterizes how the buyer interacts with the buying process. In simple terms this process can be described in three stages:

1 **Awareness** – The buyer becomes aware of a product, service or new brand through some sort of communication. This might be in the form of advertising or some other type of promotion controlled by the marketer. Equally, awareness might be established by word of mouth, which is clearly not under his control. The most that can be accomplished at this

stage of the buying process is that the buyer will decide to give the product or service a trial.

2 **Trial** – Here the customer uses and evaluates the item and decides if it performs in a satisfactory way. Whether or not the buyer will decide to repeat the purchase will depend upon how well the product or service met his needs and how far it conferred non-functional benefits on the user. So, for example, a sports car is often bought not just as a means of transportation but for a host of other reasons, not least among them some form of social recognition, self-image enhancement and prestige. The trial is therefore not an entirely rational process because the buyer is making up his own mind using many subjective criteria.

3 **Repeat buying** – The decision to re-buy depends largely upon what happened during the trial phase. Various elements of the marketing mix, especially advertising, can be used to remind the buyer of the benefits he derived from the trial. Obviously, it is extremely difficult to persuade disappointed customers to try the product or service again. Chastened by the experience, they would prefer to seek an alternative source of supply.

This general model helps to provide an overview of buyer behaviour, but before it becomes really useful there has to be a greater understanding of the influencing factors which play such an important part in the scheme of things.

While the perfect explanation of buyer behaviour might never be found, systematic and intelligent study can help us to get closer to understanding the behaviour of our own customers. The trick is to establish which of the many influencing factors are the most potent when it comes to them making the buying decision for a particular product or service.

Let's start by looking in more detail at the personal influencing factors.

PERSONAL INFLUENCES

Knowledge Buyers need information to help them to come to a decision. Witness the growth of consumer associations that conduct independent tests of goods and services and provide their members with the results. However, the completely rational buyer is probably a figment of the imagination, except perhaps for some industrial purchases where technological considerations might well outweigh all other factors, or extremely high investment decisions where the risk of getting it wrong is too high to contemplate. The information we take in and use is generally clouded by what is called selective perception.

In a recent product test in France, two well-established brands of margarine were evaluated by four hundred households. One was the brand leader, the other was much smaller in terms of market share. Half of the sample was provided with the two brands in anonymous wrappers marked simply X and Y, the other half received its margarine in the usual brand wrappers.

When asked to state which brand they preferred, there was approximately a fifty-fifty split between the anonymous brands. Surprisingly, the other half of the customer sample who knew the identity of the product, voted sixty-five to thirty-five in favour of the brand leader.

This illustrates how perhaps the most rational reason for buying food – its taste – can be distorted by other considerations. Selective perception has the effect of getting us to 'massage the facts', or even screen them out, so that the information we receive is what we want to hear. In many ways we are the promoters of self-fulfilling prophesies.

At an American university a guest speaker had been invited to give a talk to the senior students. As an experiment, half of the students about to attend the lecture had been informed that this particular speaker was a last minute stand-in and had a poor reputation in his specialist field. In contrast, the other students were told how lucky they were to have such an eminent authority to come to the university and that they would be witnessing something special. On evaluating the speaker's lecture, those who had been 'conditioned' to expect the worst were highly critical, whereas those going in with high expectations largely found them fulfilled.

What messages might the marketer draw from these stories?

i)   Getting knowledge about our products or services over to customers is not easy;
ii) we need to think about effective learning mechanisms to 'educate' our customers.

It is a fact that many of the things we know today are a result of continued repetition ... just think of poems you know, or multiplication tables! Therefore customers can also learn about our products and services if we continually repeat simple and memorable messages to them, whether from face-to-face salesmen or through advertising. How many of us can honestly say that when we hear the beginning of a jingle on a TV commercial something in our brain doesn't sing along with it?

The second theory about learning is to appeal to as many of the senses as possible. We take in information through sight, sound, touch, taste and smell, and to this list some would add a sixth sense, some form of intuitive process. It can be shown that although we might remember something by seeing it, our chances of recall are enhanced if we can hear it as well. Better still, using it or handling it makes the learning a totally sensory experience.

Motivation   At first sight the field of motivational studies can be quite confusing. For some psychologists words like 'motive', 'drive', 'urge', 'wishes', 'needs' and 'wants' have a particular meaning of their own. For others, they can be used interchangeably. Fortunately there is general agreement on the concept of motivated behaviour, as is the observable response to a felt need.

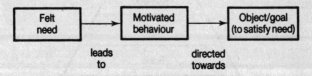

Figure 6.2   The Process of Motivation

The above diagram shows how the 'motivation' process works. A need is said to exist until action has been taken to satisfy it.

One of the most significant figures in the study of motivation is Abraham Maslow. As a result of his studies he saw Man as a perpetually wanting creature. Moreover, he concluded that human needs develop in a sequential way, from what he termed 'lower' needs to 'higher order' ones. He identified five main categories.

At the lowest level, Man's actions are driven to satisfy what Maslow termed 'basic needs'. These are mainly physiological in nature, such as the need to satisfy hunger and thirst, and to stop feeling cold.

Needs at the next level are termed 'safety' or 'security needs' and are largely concerned with protection from physical or psychological loss.

After that are 'belonging needs', the needs for affection and affiliation, to be part of a group and enjoy all the social contact that goes with it.

Next are what he described as 'ego-status' needs, which are concerned with the need to feel important in the eyes of others, to have self-esteem, recognition, success and prestige.

The highest level of needs Maslow described as 'self-actualization'; the need for challenge, personal fulfilment, to be creative and to realize one's own potential.

Conventionally this hierarchy of needs is shown like this:

Figure 6.3   Maslow's Hierarchy of Needs

Maslow claimed that, while an individual is likely to exhibit some needs at all of these levels, there is a tendency that:

1 Needs at the lower levels have to be satisfied before higher-level needs come into play. This can help to explain why to someone living on the breadline, regular meals are of infinitely more worth than striving for, say, a key to the senior executives' washroom (a notable prize for many an aspiring executive with ego-status needs!).

2 This hierarchy of needs is situational, in the sense that if circumstances change, or if one is threatened at one's existing level, it is possible to 'slide' back to a lower level. For example, someone who is a cooperative and sociable team member (satisfying his belonging needs) might become withdrawn and uncommunicative, keeping information to himself, when it is rumoured that there will be some lay-offs in his department. (Safety needs are now paramount.)

3 It is possible that some individuals might be influenced by higher level motives even when lower needs have not been fully satisfied. So, for example, they might cut back on food which they can ill afford in order to sustain an activity which to them is self-actualizing. (The starving artist syndrome.)

Some critics of Maslow have commented that in the western industrialized societies the basic needs are largely covered by the State or by various welfare organizations, as perhaps are many of the safety needs. However, this argument doesn't really invalidate his proposition, it just serves to provide another perspective.

Figure 6.4   Un-met Needs in Developed Markets

For the marketer, the implications of Maslow's work are far-reaching. Imagine that we had to market Bicko Biscuits. These are the various messages we might convey to our customers if we could identify them in the hierarchy of needs:

5. Self-Actualization   'A new experience. Tease your taste buds with our biscuits'

4. Ego-Status   'Not for the *hoi polloi* these Bickos'

3. Belonging   'Join the in-crowd, have a Bicko'

2. Safety   'Our biscuits are pure, through and through'

1. Basic   'Bickos fill you up'

At a more serious level we might note that:

1   At the creature comforts level (because that is what the basic needs might amount to in the industrialized societies) there might be a demand for cheaper commodities or smaller packs, in order to save money and at the same time afford to run a car or buy a video-recorder.

2   Here there will be a preference for the familiar; for life assurance, burglar alarms and so on.

3   These needs might materialize as demands for distinctive styles of clothing, various group activities from holidays to team sports, romantic greetings cards and gifts of all shapes and sizes.

4   This level will be concerned with anything that conveys non-spoken messages about power, prestige, achievement, strength, recognition and importance.

5   The final level is not always easily distinguishable from the previous level, but deep down it is to do with living to one's own standards and aspirations, rather than those imposed as a societal norm.

Some other interesting ideas on motivation came from David

McClelland who came to view achievement as one of the greatest motivators. For him, men are motivated by striving for goals of one kind or another. He concluded that:

1 Ambitions and aspirations are not static, but change over time.

2 The more one achieves, the more ambitious one becomes (the corollary to this being that failure brings with it a decline in aspirations).

3 Ambitions and aspirations are largely influenced by the behaviour and performance of other members of the group to which a person belongs.

Personality There have been many studies about personality and its influence on subsequent behaviour, although not all of these have been adopted by marketers. One of the earliest ways of personality 'typing' was to identify if people were inclined to be **introverts** (inward-looking, quiet, thoughtful, etc.) or **extroverts** (outward looking, gregarious, socially skilled). Using this basic typology it is suggested by some that it is possible to identify differences in life-styles, job preferences, hobbies and so on.

Another way of looking at personality type is to consider the extent to which a person is 'compliant', 'aggressive' or 'detached'.

Compliants like to be needed and appreciated; they seek to avoid conflict and are unlikely to upset others; they are loving and unselfish.

Aggressives believe in the survival of the fittest; they need to be the best and to achieve recognition even if they have to exploit others to do so.

Detacheds tend to be self-sufficient and private; they want minimal interference from others and place high value on their independence.

Some tentative results have been obtained by behavioural researchers using this framework, but the extent to which purchasing behaviour is influenced by personality variables is still not clearly understood.

Some thought-provoking work has been done by Everett Rogers, who was interested in how personality type might influence a person's readiness to buy a new product or service. He identified five 'types' as the diagram shows:

Figure 6.5   The Adoption and Diffusion Process
(After Everett Rogers, *Diffusion of Innovations*, New York Free Press 1962)

For any new product or service, someone somewhere has to be adventurous enough to buy it first. These are the innovators and in any market are likely to comprise about 2.5 per cent of the buying population. What appeals to these people is novelty and a sense of pioneering. To lead fashion, whether in clothes or anything else, is highly attractive to innovators and as a consequence they are not as price-sensitive as other buyers might be.

If the product or service lives up to its expectations it is taken up by the early adopters. These are slightly more cautious than innovators and don't like the idea of being guinea pigs for new ideas. Nevertheless, as soon as they are satisfied that the new product works, they are happy to buy.

Gradually, by this process of people buying, using and talking about the product or service, it reaches all types of buyers – even the late adopters.

This simple model of innovation is of great use to the marketer because it can give him some insights about his customers and the best ways of communicating to them. For example:

Innovators ▷ 'It's new and technologically light years ahead'

Early Adopters ▷ 'Things are changing, catch the wave'

Early Majority ▷ 'Look at the benefits you could gain'

Late Majority ▷ 'Look at the benefits that have been gained'

Late Adopters ▷ 'You can't beat a tried and trusted idea'

Attitude While attitude is not an easy concept to define, there is some agreement that it refers to three elements which are assumed to predetermine behaviour, as summarized in the figure below.

COGNITIVE	Beliefs and perceptions held by an individual about the benefits of the product, service or brand in question.
AFFECTIVE	The individual's overall evaluation of the item in question, expressed as feelings of liking or disliking.
CONATIVE	A tendency to respond in a consistently positive or negative way with respect to the product, brand or service. For example, to reflect one's feelings towards a brand by generally buying it, if one's evaluation of it is positive. The reverse of this situation would also be true. It must be noted that it is possible for individuals to have a favourable attitude to a particular product, but lack the money or need to take any action.

Figure 6.6 Elements of Attitude

Attitudes develop over life as people gain experience and change their responsibilities. While in theory attitudes ought to be very personal and individualistic, in practice they can be similar to those held by many others. This is because attitudes are modified by many societal influences such as interaction with other people or groups, exposure to information, the current values in the environment at large and emerging wants or needs.

Much corporate advertising and image projection is designed to encourage positive attitudes towards the company. In this way, instead of treating each buying decision as a separate evaluation, the customer will more or less automatically approach the supplier to which he is favourably disposed.

While attitude can influence purchasing behaviour, favourable performance of the product or service has the effect of reinforcing the attitude. Equally, many customers seek reassurance that they have done the right thing by making the purchase and so after-sales communication, through personal contact or advertising, will also help to strengthen positive attitudes.

Up until now we have concentrated on the 'personal influences' side of our general model about buyer behaviour. We have looked at some of the key factors which help to determine behaviour – knowledge, motivation, personality and attitude. But, as we have seen, even these factors are affected by some influences external to the buyer. Let us now switch our attention to this other equally important set of factors.

EXTERNAL INFLUENCES

Culture This is one of the most persuasive influences on customer choice; the sum total of social and spiritual beliefs, technologies, values and actions that impinge upon all individual and group behaviour. Culture can have a general effect upon whether or not entire product classes, such as washing machines, are purchased at all in certain societies.

Although there are many superficial similarities between French and Belgian culture, such as the French language, there are significant differences in the ways certain products are purchased. The French prefer to purchase alcohol in the form of wine, for example, whereas Belgians show a greater propensity for drinking beer.

Numbers, colours, symbols, style of dress, body language and methods of greeting may also have quite distinctive meanings in various cultures. If the marketer is unaware of these then his consequent embarrassment will be measured not only in blushes, but in lost sales. There are many examples where multinational marketers have failed to appreciate the effects on customer behaviour of using words that turned out to be either obscene or meaningless.

However, even at the more limited level of marketing at home, one had to be sensitive to the different 'subcultures' which can typify certain regions of the country. For example, in the UK, patterns of family life and social activities can vary tremendously between, say, the south-east and the north-east regions.

Economic Economic factors are of great significance in deciding whether a particular purchase takes place at all, when it occurs, and how payment is made.

Clearly changes in people's incomes have direct consequences for their purchasing behaviour. Therefore national trends and government fiscal policy can be useful in building formal economic models which can help to predict aggregate demands for products and services i.e. the amounts which will be bought throughout the economy.

Marketers must use such models with caution, however, because they often cease to be of value if they are applied too rigidly, except in the most general, commonsense way. As we have seen, individuals and small groups might be driven to behave in quite idiosyncratic ways, as the following example demonstrates.

A company launched a new health-type apple drink, and, because of new manufacturing technology, was able to price it as low as ordinary lemonade. The launch was accompanied by extensive advertising which described the product benefits and stressed its quality. Despite all this the response was very disappointing. Subsequent research showed that potential customers did not believe that the benefit and quality claims could be genuine at such a low price. The company therefore increased the price by 20 per cent and, sure enough, demand rose. In fact, over the following two years the price was increased in stages until it was double the original launch price – and with every increase sales rose too!

Economic theorists would tell you that both buyers and sellers are rational in an economic sense; i.e. producers of goods and services always maximize their profits, while customer choice is determined by the extra utility or satisfaction derived from the purchase compared with the final outlay. Also, it is generally assumed that there is such a thing as a 'demand curve', which dictates that as price goes up, the quantity demanded will fall.

Of course, both of these economic theories hold true in many cases, but in life there are many exceptions to the rule and the apple drink story is one of them. The moral of the story is that economic factors may not explain the totality of customer behaviour. Price carries quality connotations for the customer which the marketer must carefully take into account. It is the customer's perception of price which matters, not the abstract economic notion.

Social Context   In consumer markets we are all familiar with the idea of 'keeping up with the next-door neighbours'. Behaviour in which the individual takes the responses of others into account is in fact not just confined to consumer markets; social context also influences much industrial purchasing. For instance, research in Europe and North America has shown that although an objective cost-benefit analysis, based on economic and technical performance factors, is said to dictate the industrial purchasing process, other notions are also taken into consideration. These include the size of the supplier, the perceived quality of its staff, the marketing policies it pursues and the creativity of the sales contacts.

A British manufacturer of defence equipment selling to the Middle East has found that price is of little importance. Quality is taken for granted. Performance is assumed to be as specified. The crucial determinant of the purchase order is the ability to establish a personal rapport with the buyer. There have been occasions where orders have been awarded to the most expensive tenderer, whose performance levels have been lower, rather than to the cheaper bidder.

Situation Situations exert more specific influences on customer choice than perhaps any other factor. Births, marriages, deaths, unexpected guests, things breaking down or wearing out, sudden illnesses, holidays, hobbies, pastimes – the list is almost endless. Every change of situation can stimulate a new set of needs and generate a new group of potential customers.

At first sight such events appear random and haphazard. Yet astute marketers have noted that many of life's events come to all of us, regardless of the uniqueness of our personal biography. That patterns exist can be illustrated by the concept of the family 'life cycle':

'Life Cycle'

Young dependants	Little purchasing power, but can influence family buying decisions.
Young singles, not living at home	Few financial burdens; fashion opinion leaders; recreation orientation. *Buy:* basic kitchen equipment, basic furniture, cars, holidays.
Young newly-marrieds, no children	Better off financially than they will be when family arrives; high purchasers; above average purchase of durables. *Buy:* cars, refrigerators, cookers, furniture to last, holidays.
Full nest I, youngest child under 6	Home purchases at a peak, financial assets low; few savings; interested in new products; like advertised products. *Buy:* washers, driers, TV, video, baby foods, cough mixture, vitamins, toys.

Full nest II, youngest child over 6	Better off financially; some wives work; less influenced by advertising; buy large size, economy packages. *Buy:* many foods, cleaning materials, bicycles, music lessons, pianos.
Full nest III, older marrieds with dependent children	Financial position improving; more wives work; some children work; hard to influence with advertising; high purchase of durables. *Buy:* new more tasteful furniture, replacement refrigerators, etc., non-essential appliances, magazines.
Empty nest I, married couple, children departed, one partner still working full time	Home ownership at peak; most satisfied with financial situation and money saved; interested in travel, recreation and self-education; make gifts and contributions; less interested in new products. *Buy:* holidays, luxuries, home improvements.
Empty nest II, marrieds, no children at home, retired.	Drastic cut in income, stay at home. *Buy:* medical appliances, health care products which aid sleep and digestion.

Socio-Economic Grouping

A popular way to categorize buyers is by using a combination of social and economic factors. This gives rise to the following general classification:

Class A *(approx 3 per cent of population)*	Usually live in large detached houses or in the better parts of town. The head of the household is likely to be a successful business or professional person, for example a senior civil servant, or have considerable private means.

Class B *(approx 12 per cent* *of population)*	Head of household quite senior, but not top of his or her business or profession. Quite well-to-do, respectable life style without being luxurious. Non-earners will live on modest private incomes or pensions.
Classs C1 *(approx 23 per cent* *of population)*	Head of household will be small tradesperson or non-manual worker carrying out what are usually termed 'white-collar' jobs.
Class C2 *(approx 32 per cent* *of population)*	Head of household will be skilled manual worker who will have served an apprenticeship or equivalent. Typical jobs could be foreman, electrician, plumber, carpenter.
Class D *(approx 21 per cent* *of population)*	Head of the household will be a manual worker, generally semi-skilled or unskilled, such as machinist, bus driver, shop assistant, process worker.
Class E *(approx 9 per cent of* *population)*	Mainly old age pensioners, widows, casual workers and any others who for reasons of illness, disability or unemployment are dependent on social security schemes.

This particular grading system is long-established and, while it has served its purpose and been particularly useful for targeting for advertising, many marketers are looking for ways to improve upon it. In many countries it has been recognized that buying decisions are no longer clearly correlated with social class. Instead the concept of 'life style' has moved to the fore.

Life Style

The concept of life style is based upon the values and aspirations that individuals hold. It is suggested that such factors can provide a better indication of likely purchase behaviour. One such life style typology is shown below:

Self-explorers
(approx 15 per cent of population; this group is forecast to grow slowly)

Motivated by self-expression and self-realization; have broad horizons, high tolerance; see global picture; hold spiritual values (but shun organized religion); reject doctrinaire solutions in favour of holistic, evolutionary growth based on individual awareness.

Social resisters
(14 per cent of population)

Caring group, believing in fairness and quality of life for all; altruistic; concerned about social & ecological issues; can be intolerant and moralistic.

Experimentalists
(11 per cent of population; slowly growing)

Highly individualistic, they are motivated by fast-moving enjoyment; materialistic and pro-technology but against traditional authority (like the self-explorers).

Conspicuous Consumers
(19 per cent of population; slight growth)

Motivated by acquisition, competition and getting ahead. They are traditional, pro-authority and support law and order. Concerned about appearance and position; pushy.

Belongers
(18 per cent of population; shrinking slightly)

Seek quiet, undisturbed, conventional family life; conservative, traditional rule-followers. Tend to be against change; interest in future revolves around the security of the family.

Survivors
(17 per cent of population; shrinking slightly)
Strongly class-conscious and community spirited. If not taken advantage of, will be hardworking, traditional and cheerful. Their motivation is to 'get by'; often active trade unionists.

Aimless
(5 per cent of population; a) will remain stable b) will increase)
a) *Young Unemployed* – motivated by short-term pleasure or 'kicks'; often anti-authority.
b) *The Old* – whose motivation is day-to-day existence, often in trying circumstances.

We have looked at some of the more pertinent factors which act as external influences on the buyer's behaviour; namely culture, economy, social context, situations, 'life cycle', socio-economic factors and life style groupings. From what has been discussed it is clear that to get anything like a perfect understanding of a buyer's behaviour is not easy; at best we get tantalizing insights into elements of behaviour. Indeed, comprehensive models of buyer choice must seek to combine all these elements of behavioural influence if they are to provide a useful base for marketing strategy.

CONSUMER VERSUS INDUSTRIAL PURCHASE DECISION

Earlier we talked about the buying decision process as having three stages; awareness, trial and repeat buying. It is perhaps more accurate to describe this process as being typica' of most consumer purchases. For industrial purchases the buying process can be more complex and involve more stages, as the figure below shows:

Stage	Description of industrial buyer's actions
1.	Recognizes needs or problems, works out general solution.
2.	Works out the characteristics and quantity of what is needed.
3.	Prepares detailed specification.
4.	Searches for and locates potential suppliers.
5.	Analyses and evaluates tenders, proposals, plans, etc.
6.	Selects 'best' supplier.
7.	Places trial order.
8.	Evaluates trial order.
9.	Negotiates main contract subject to trial results.
10.	Monitors deliveries, quality etc.

Figure 6.7   Industrial Buying Process

The need for the purchase invariably starts from within the buyer's organization as some kind of problem or need. The remaining 'buy stages' gradually unfold, sometimes over a period of weeks or even months. This process is clearly very different to walking into a shop and saying 'I'll have one of those please!', paying, and walking out.

What makes the industrial buying decision more complex is the fact that rarely is just one person involved. Because of the technological, production, financial, safety and quality ramifications of buying a new piece of plant or machinery, for example, a number of people have to be satisfied that the correct buying decision is being made.

THE DECISION-MAKING UNIT (DMU)

The individuals who are involved to one extent or another in the decision-making process are known as the DMU. In practice the size of the DMU tends to be in proportion to the size of the buying company as the following figure implies:

Number of employees	Size of DMU	Average number of contacts made by salesman
0–200	3.42	1.72
201–400	4.85	1.75
401–1000	5.81	1.90
1000+	6.5	1.85

Figure 6.8   Decision-making Unit (from McGraw-Hill Research)

Clearly we are talking here about important buying decisions, but what is interesting to note is how salesmen rarely make contact with all those who influence the purchase. In effect they are missing opportunities to explain how their product or service will benefit each person in the DMU – and experience tells us that all members need to feel favourably inclined towards the purchase, especially those with organizational status.

PRESSURES ON THE INDUSTRIAL BUYERS

When we buy things for ourselves, often we have only ourselves to satisfy. At most only our partners or close family are likely to be concerned. For the industrial buyer the situation is very different. He finds himself, as one member of the DMU, perhaps involved with senior executives of higher status to himself; almost certainly working with people who are technically more competent. Sometimes there is not enough, or confused, information about what is required, and some of his colleagues might be trying to score points over others because secretly they would prefer to see another supplier with the contract. Much human interaction and behaviour can be at work in these situations and the official 'buyer' can feel himself pulled this way and that – and on top of all this are all the external factors that we have already discussed.

Little wonder then that those involved like to maintain that they are being strictly rational and analytical in their approach to the buying decision. It certainly helps to keep the decision-making on track, but consider this example.

A pump manufacturer, with a reputation for making robust and reliable pumps, called in an industrial designer to improve their appearance. Engineers at the company were shocked: 'You won't improve our pumps' performance; anyway, who sees them? They're installed underground' was their cry.

'Ah,' said the chief executive, 'but they are not *bought* under-ground, are they?'

SUMMARY

1 All buying decisions are choice decisions.
2 The marketer has to try to understand the buyer's motivations and behaviours if he is going to influence the buyer.
3 The buyer's behaviour is rich and complex and emanates from many sources, some personal to the individual, some external.
4 While every buyer is different, it is possible to establish patterns of 'sameness'.
5 All patterns of behaviour are partly rational, partly emotional, depending upon the nature of the product or service and the buyer's situation.
6 The industrial buying situation is more complex than the typical consumer situation because it has more stages, more people get involved and, as a result, the quality of their interaction can confuse matters.
7 By analysis and creative research it is possible for marketers to get closer to understanding buyers. Knowing how people buy makes it easier to sell to them.

CHAPTER 7

Market Segmentation

W<small>E HAVE SEEN</small> so far that marketing is an attitude of mind concerning customer satisfaction rather than a set of techniques to simply 'sell' products or services. No matter how good the product or service on offer, if there are not enough customers to buy it then there is no business.

Equally, when an organization starts giving customers the consideration they deserve and finds out more about them and their needs, it often discovers that they do not possess the resources or skills to take advantage of *all* market opportunities. In other words, a particular organization may not be as competitive as others when it comes to some *particular types* of customer, whereas it might be very competitive when it comes to others.

For example, we might consider the way in which numerous variations of domestic appliances, such as refrigerators and washing machines, are aimed at different customers and consumers depending upon their needs, motives for buying and social and economic characteristics. In consumer and industrial markets it is increasingly necessary to create and present a different offer to each group of customers, or, in the language of marketing, **market segments**. Therefore the theme for this chapter is the customer – the most important person in the life of any business.

For reasons of clarity we have chosen to talk about customers and their needs throughout this chapter, although, as we have already seen, sometimes the *customers* are not the *consumers* of our products or services. For example, if we ran a small bakery most of the bread might well be bought by the housewife; yet it would be her family who are the main **consumers.**

Similarly, manufacturers of expensive toys will have to understand all about the needs of the consumers – small children – but all the sales will be made to parents or adult relatives, and so *their* motivations must be equally understood.

Having two levels of 'customer' in this way does not invalidate any of the principles outlined in this chapter. It just means that extra thought has to be given to such situations to ensure that the marketing activity is focused in the right place.

CUSTOMERS AS SOURCES OF PROFIT THROUGH SEGMENTATION

It should be stressed that the strength and value of the marketing process hinges on how well we handle the process of customer segmentation. Get it wrong and it is likely that there will be a 'mismatch' between our offer and the needs of the customer.

The concern, therefore, is to seek ways of classifying customers so that, whatever the nature of our business, we will be in a position to offer a product or service to them which will enable us to differentiate ourselves from everyone else. This is the way to increased profitability.

Conceptually, it is easy to grasp that markets don't buy anything – it is people who buy things. It is only when we can identify **groups** of buyers that we can begin to talk about markets. Such markets can be further classified into submarkets, or segments. There are many different ways of approaching segmentation; how can we be sure we are using the best one?

Unfortunately, it is impossible to be prescriptive about this because some creative insight is necessary to provide us with the very method of segmentation which is right for our company. Remember, the purpose of segmentation is to find the best ways to match our capabilities with groups of customers who share similar needs and thereby gain some commercial advantage.

There are, however, some generally accepted criteria concerning what constitutes a viable market segment. These are as follows:

CRITERIA FOR VIABLE MARKET SEGMENTATION

IDENTIFIABILITY AND MEASURABILITY

The segment must be clearly identifiable and measurable in terms of the variable chosen as the basis of segmentation. Marketing managers often get a hunch that their customers belong to groups that have specific attributes, but there may be no objective evidence to support a differentiated marketing programme.

RELEVANCE

The basis of segmentation (age or social status, for example) must be relevant to the purchase or use of the product. Customers of a particular brand might well share all sorts of personal characteristics, but these can only form the basis of effective market segmentation if they can be related to buyers' behaviour.

POTENTIAL

The segment should be of sufficient potential size to ensure that an adequate return can be obtained from any marketing investment made in it. Over-segmenting the market results in trying to serve many small submarkets without being able to reap the advantages of long production runs and distribution economies.

ACCESSIBILITY

An identified market segment can be exploited commercially only if it can be reached. It must be accessible to one or other element of the marketing mix, usually but not exclusively the media. It must also be capable of being serviced through available marketing channels.

Although there are many methods of segmentation, they are basically variations of just two approaches. Both of these need to be considered.

1   Analysis of the way customers respond or behave.
2   Analysis of customer characteristics.

ANALYSIS OF THE WAY CUSTOMERS RESPOND OR BEHAVE

This is essentially a description of the way customers actually behave in the market place, and falls into two parts: firstly, **what** is bought; secondly, **why**.

In respect of **what** is bought, we are talking about the actual structure of markets in the form of the physical characteristics of products – place of purchase and price paid, for example. This information tells us if there are any groups of products (or outlets, or price categories) which are growing, static, or declining, thus indicating where there are opportunities and where we might be faced with problems. Consider the following example.

A very small carpet company whose sales were declining discovered on analysis that, although the market for carpets was rising overall, the outlets to which they had traditionally sold (i.e. specialist carpet shops) were accounting for a declining proportion of sales. Furthermore, the analysis disclosed that demand for higher priced carpets was falling and there was a switch towards fibre types not manufactured by this company.

Knowing this information, the company was able to revise its production plans and change its traditional distribution outlets, which had the effect of reversing the decline in sales and profitability.

Although this example might appear to be elementary, it is surprising to find even today how many companies plan ahead on information which is little more than a crude extrapolation of past sales trends. Clearly, such approaches are fraught with danger and can cause serious commercial problems when market structures change, as in the case of the carpet company.

The second part of analysing customer behaviour is to understand **why** customers behave the way they do. If we can understand the behaviour of our customers we are in a better position to sell to them. However, when it comes to predicting human behaviour, we know from experience that people do not always behave in the expected manner.

One behavioural theory is that customers are rational when it comes to making a purchase and therefore seek to maximize their satisfaction in that purchase or in its utility value when compared to the financial outlay or effort put into the transaction.

However, this theory only helps up to a point. While it might work quite well in some markets, it is well known that other markets can exhibit increase in demand with increase in price. This will be particularly true of goods or services which appeal to the vanity or ego of the purchaser such as cars, beauty care products and clothes.

As we have seen, there are also a number of theories based on the idea that a customer's behaviour is largely conditioned by the psychological or social pressures exerted by those around him or her. Thus their attitudes and behaviour can be influenced by family, work colleagues, cultural patterns, personal aspirations and life style. Such socio-psychological dimensions can provide many opportunities for successful segmentation strategies.

One such strategy that has proved highly successful in consumer markets is the idea of life style segmentation.

LIFE STYLE SEGMENTATION

'We are what we eat' is a point of view that has been around for some time and, in a sense, its extension to 'we are what we consume' is the basis for life style marketing.

Essentially the life style concept relates to individual aspirations, personal role models (and role playing) and statements that people want to make about themselves. Much of modern consumer advertising is based on the principle of life style **aspirations.** Very few of the consumers of Marlboro cigarettes, for example, are going to find themselves on a horse in the Arizona desert rounding up steers! Similarly, most users of certain hair shampoos that are currently advertised are unlikely to live the exotic lives that are featured in those advertisements.

In life style marketing the reality is less important than the aspiration and the self-image. Because different people will have different aspirations and self-images, then it is logical that this should form the basis for a segmentaion of the market.

Thus, in life style segmentation the aim is to group consumers on the basis of 'shared values'. So, for example, one group of potential customers for a financial service may be typified by their traditional, family-oriented life style, in which savings are synonymous with security. Another group however, thinks in terms of consumption, rather than saving, and is concerned to maximize short-term gain from any investment they might make. Clearly such different groups need to be addressed in quite different ways.

Figure 7.1 opposite describes a particular segmentation analysis of life styles in a consumer goods market.

BENEFIT SEGMENTATION

It will be recalled from Chapter 1 that one of marketing's basic principles is: customers don't buy products, they buy benefits. A corollary of this tenet is that not all customers seek the same benefits. In other words, an opportunity might exist to segment the market according to the **benefits** that customers seek.

This is based on the notion that when customers buy a

► THE STATUS SEEKER	A GROUP WHICH IS VERY MUCH CONCERNED WITH THE PRESTIGE OF BRANDS PURCHASED
► THE SWINGER	A GROUP WHICH TRIES TO BE MODERN AND UP TO DATE IN ALL ITS ACTIVITIES
► THE CONSERVATIVE	A GROUP WHICH PREFERS TO STICK TO LARGER SUCCESSFUL COMPANIES AND POPULAR BRANDS
► THE RATIONAL MAN	A GROUP WHICH LOOKS FOR BENEFITS SUCH AS ECONOMY, VALUE, DURABILITY ETC.
► THE INNER-DIRECTED MAN	A GROUP WHICH IS ESPECIALLY CONCERNED WITH SELF-CONCEPT: MEMBERS CONSIDER THEMSELVES TO BE INDEPENDENT
► THE HEDONIST	A GROUP WHICH IS CONCERNED PRIMARILY WITH SENSORY BENEFITS

Figure 7.1   Some Examples of Life Style Segments

product or a service they do so because they wish to acquire the benefits the product or service will bring them. In this sense, the physical features or characteristics of what is purchased do not motivate buyers. What does motivate buyers is what the product will do for them.

The difference between the **features** of a product or service and the **benefits** which that product or service gives to the customer is not just a question of semantics. It is crucial that the company seeking success should be aware of this difference. Too often companies fall into the trap of talking about what their product or service is or does (**features**) instead of what the customer will get out of it (**benefits**).

BENEFIT ANALYSIS

The best starting point for a company is to undertake a detailed analysis to establish the full range of benefits it can offer to its customers. This can be done by listing the major features of the product or service, and then working out what these mean to the customer. However, we will first say a little more about the different kinds of benefits that exist.

1. Standard Benefits

These are basic benefits which accrue from the product or service. They will not be unique because our competitors can, in all probability, claim similar benefits for their goods or services. However, it is important for us to work out the standard benefits because customers are often not as knowledgeable as they appear to be. If we do not communicate the standard benefits, customers might well believe that our offer is in some way inferior to that of our competitors.

The following are examples of standard benefits:

EXAMPLES OF STANDARD BENEFITS

'Our product meets all the Safety Legislation requirements, *which means that* your staff will be at no risk when they use it.'

'Our service has a money-back guarantee, *which means that* if we don't do the job to the standards we claim it doesn't cost you a penny.'

2. Company Benefits

These are the benefits which the customer will receive by dealing with a company. Remember the customer is not just buying your products or services, he is also buying a relationship with a company. The more it is possible to convince him that there are additional benefits to be gained from entering into a business relationship with one particular company, as opposed to with competing ones, the more persuasive becomes the argument. Look at the following examples:

EXAMPLES OF COMPANY BENEFITS

a) 'We've been specializing in this technical field for longer than anyone else in this area, *which means that* you have the best possible expert advice close at hand whenever you need it.'

b) 'We are a small family business, *which means that* you get individual and personal attention when you deal with us.'

3. Differential Benefits

Without doubt, the benefits which offer the greatest prospect of a competitive 'edge' over competitors are **differential** benefits. Here we are looking for benefits that cannot be provided by others. If you think about this for a moment, it is obvious that if a company is offering more or less the same as everyone else in the business, chances are that it can only compete by offering a lower price.

If a company cannot identify any differential benefits, then it is either providing a product or service which is identical in every way to the offerings of the competition (which is most unlikely), or the benefit analysis has not been done thoroughly enough.

Some examples of differential benefits are:

EXAMPLES OF DIFFERENTIAL BENEFITS

1 'We are the only supplier who genuinely provides a round-the-clock service, *which means that* your machinery will never be out of service.'

2 'We use a unique hardening process on our machine tools, for which we have the patent, *which means that* our tools last longer and that saves you money.'

Which Means That . . .'

You will have noticed that all the examples given above state a feature of the product, service, or company and then turn this into a benefit for the customer by using the expression 'which means that . . .'

The 'So What' Test

Sometimes it isn't easy to decide if the product of the expression 'which means that' is genuinely a benefit. In these cases, challenge the supposed benefit with 'so what!' One of two things will happen.

1 The 'so what' test will reveal that the benefit is real and has substance for the customer.
2 The 'so what' test will reveal something with little benefit for the customer, in which case continue with another 'which means that' until a real benefit is reached.

The following example shows the 'so what' test in operation:

AN EXAMPLE OF THE 'SO WHAT' TEST

'Our components are fully tested, which means that every single one will perform to the specification laid down.'

Response: so what!

'. . . which means that they have a guaranteed life of twenty thousand hours and will not let you down.'

Response: so what!

'. . . which means that your production lines can run continuously without the inconvenience of sudden breakdowns, thus giving you savings on both production and maintenance.'

This would seem to be a very worthwhile benefit.

Clearly, to be useful for segmentation a benefit has to appeal to a significant number of customers. The benefit analysis process described here not only enables us to make a comprehensive list of all benefits, but also to see how they relate to what different customers seek. It thus makes it possible to emphasize product benefit with a high level of appeal for any particular customer segment.

So far we have looked at customers in terms of *what* they buy and **why** they buy it. It is also possible to segment markets by the characteristics of customers.

ANALYSIS OF CUSTOMER CHARACTERISTICS

This approach to segmentation seeks to find ways of describing groups of customers in terms of their predominant characteristics. There are a number of different ways of approaching this type of analysis. The most frequently used methods are based on what are called 'demographics'.

(i) CONSUMER MARKETS

For consumer markets, these demographics are likely to be age, sex, education, stage in the family life cycle, and social status in life represented by jobs, residence, and income. The following table summarizes these categories:

▶ Socio-economic: eg. social class, status, income
▶ Psychographic: eg. personality, attitudes, motives
▶ Demographic: eg. age, sex
▶ Geographic: eg. country, region, urban or rural dweller.

By knowing about these characteristics of our customers it is possible, through research, to find out more about what they read, what they watch on television, how they spend their leisure time and how much disposable income they will have. All of this information can assist our choice of methods in reaching various customer groups and influencing the tone of what we wish to say to them.

Some simple examples follow:

1   Retired professional and business people often have a high disposable income and tend to spend more money on specialist services like health care. They will probably spend more on things such as hobbies and holidays. Less well-off retired people will obviously have less disposable income and will devote more of their resources to the basics of life.

2   Young families with one or two young children, particularly those in the managerial classes, will tend to live on private estates. They have an above-average income; they often commute long distances to work and for shopping, and have high expenditure on furniture, entertainment, kitchen equipment and domestic appliances.

3   Often, certain kinds of people tend to be located in certain types of location. For example, our first group (above) would live in private flats, in detached or in semi-detached houses in seaside areas; whereas the second group (above) would probably be found in modern, cheaper, private housing estates. Today it is possible to be very specific about consumer purchasing habits according to the type of accommodation and area in which people live. One such method is known as ACORN (A Classification Of Regional Neighbourhoods) which breaks the whole of the UK down to thirty-eight neighbourhood types, all of which can easily be identified by their post-codes.

(ii) INDUSTRIAL MARKETS

For industrial markets, demographics are likely to be: type of industry, company size (by number of employees), turnover, main production processes, level of technology, purchase quantity/frequency, type of buyer (for example research chemist, production engineer) and level of after-sales service requirements.

Some examples follow:

1   Imagine a small businessman with a specialized reclamation and repair service for machinery. It would obviously be quite useful for him to classify potential customers using what is called the *Standard Industrial Classification*. This is a government publication that analyses industry, forming a number of broad categories and then a number of sub-categories within these broad groups. It is then a comparatively simple task for the businessman to ascertain which categories are likely to have a demand for his particular services.

2   Our small businessman may now be able to classify potential customers by using some, or a combination, of the following:
    – Company size;
    – the nature of the firm's production processes;
    – levels of expenditure on specific areas like distribution, research and development.

SUMMARY

A useful summary of the issues relating to market segmentation is shown in the following table:

Bases for Market Segmentation

What is bought	▷ price categories
	▷ outlets used
	▷ physical characteristics of different products
Who buys	▷ demographic factors
	▷ socio-economic factors
	▷ geography
Why	▷ benefits
	▷ attitudes/beliefs
	▷ personality/lifestyle

To summarize this section on customer segmentation:

Figure 7.2   Market Segmentation

▶ Very few companies can afford to be 'all things to all people'.
▶ Customer segmentation enables the firm to target its limited resources on the most promising opportunities.
▶ What is an opportunity for firm A is not necessarily an opportunity for firm B, since the two companies will have different strengths and weaknesses.
▶ A company needs to develop the customer segments it understands, and for which its offer is best suited.

▶ Segmentation can be based on many factors, but, as we have seen, the segments should be:

(a) large enough to ensure that they are economic to service;

(b) defined in such a way that the company can develop specialized skills in serving them;

(c) described in terms which are relevant to actual purchase behaviour.

When tackled intelligently, customer segmentation will help to determine a company's marketing and sales objectives, and also help to improve decision-making in complex business situations.

CHAPTER 8

Product Management

THE products or services that are offered to the market place are the most visible signs of an enterprise. In all probability they convey to customers more about a company than any other form of marketing activity. Not only are they the source of all revenue and profits today, but they will also be the most important factors in terms of success in the future.

However, continued successful business operations also depend upon the ability of companies to base their products or service offerings on the changing needs of a dynamic market place. Exactly how fast the marketing environment is changing will vary from business to business.

Nonetheless, regardless of its rate, change is a fact of business life and we ignore it at our peril. This means that the product or service element of the marketing mix has to be managed carefully. In turn this means that we have to learn to look at our offering in a new light and begin to understand some of the strategic options open to us if we want to survive and win. Selecting the most suitable strategies for our products or services is what this chapter is all about.

WHAT IS A PRODUCT/SERVICE?

On the surface this might seem to be a naïve question, yet its answer is fundamental to successful marketing.

From the ground covered in earlier chapters we know that what we sell has to match up in some way with what the customer wants. The product or service links the customer to us like this:

Figure 8.1   Linking Customer Needs with Corporate Goals

The customer should need our product or service, either to help solve some current problem he or she is facing, or else to make a contribution in some way to corporate or personal objectives. For our part, we need a viable product or service to help us improve our present position and meet our objectives.

While we should be clear about our own needs and objectives, those of the customers are not always quite so obvious and sometimes we have to make intelligent guesses about them. Even so, we can already see that it will be helpful to look at the product or service we offer through our customer's eyes.

It has been shown that customers buy products or services for many reasons. Different people look for different types of benefits to satisfy their needs. Here are some types of customer benefit.

Possible Customer Benefits

Good value for money/competitive price
Novelty
Availability
Good design
Ease of use
Fashionableness
Safety
Pride of ownership
Economy in use
Efficient performance/end results
Ease of servicing
Quality
Packaging
Prompt delivery
Choice of colours/sizes/etc.
Reliability
Terms available
Discount available
Reputable image (of supplier)
Convenience/minimal disruption of normal routine
Scarcity value
Ease of purchase
After-sales service
Durability
Guarantee/Warranty available
Prestige or status
Labour saving
'Storability'
Space saving
Return on investment
Availability of spares
Range of accessories/peripherals
Easy to follow instructions

Made in this country
Ecologically safe i.e. doesn't damage
    environment
Freedom from artificial additives
Designer labelling

What this should have confirmed is that in the customer's perception a product or service becomes more than just a physical entity, a sum of its component parts. For the customer our offer assumes a whole new range of dimensions, some of which might surprise even us.

When the customer makes a purchase, not only does he buy our product or service, but he buys along with it a whole package of benefits. At the end of the day it will be his perception of these benefits which will influence his decision to buy or not.

Thus the situation is not like this . . .

But more like this . . .

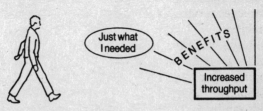

The following process describes how we can arrive at a match between the benefits of our major products and selected market segments. Taking a specific market segment, look at the list of possible customer benefits we generated earlier and:

A
1 Pick out the three major benefits for this customer segment. Identify these in some way on the list.
2 Next, select the four benefits which come after those just selected. Again, mark these in the same way.
3 Finally, identify all the other benefits which are on the list and are valued to a lesser extent by this key market segment.

B Now make a list of all the products or services supplied to this market segment.

C Combine the information just assembled by completing the benefit analysis worksheet on the opposite page.

See notes on page 132

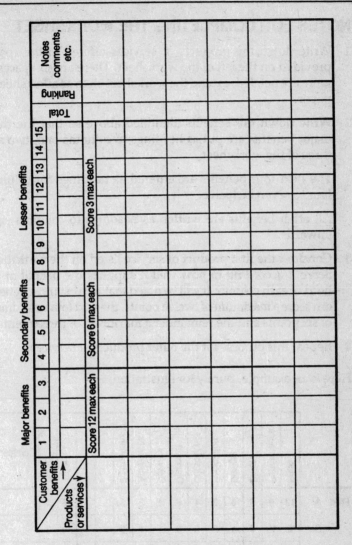

Figure 8.2   Benefit Analysis Worksheet

NOTES FOR COMPLETING THE WORKSHEET

1 Write down the products or services offered in the spaces provided on the left of the worksheet. There are six spaces. If more are needed, extend the worksheet on to another sheet of paper.

2 Write down the benefits identified above so that the three major benefits are put as headings to columns one, two and three of the worksheet.

   The next four benefits are entered as headings for columns four to seven inclusive.

   All other benefits are written as headings to columns eight onwards.

3 Consider the first product or service listed on the worksheet. Score it according to how well it supplies the benefit at the head of each column. It will be noted that the first three benefits can score a maximum of twelve points, the next four a maximum of six points and the remainder a maximum of three points.

4 Repeat this process for the other products or services.

Here is an example, purely for illustration:

	Price	Performance	Safety	Design	Packaging	Durability	Discount	Delivery	After-sales	Instructions			Total	Rank	Comments
Prod A	12	9	9	6	3	4	6	1	3	3			56	1	
B	6	10	7	4	3	6	6	1	1	2			46	3	
C	8	10	10	4	3	3	6	3	3	2			52	2	
D	4	8	12	6	3	6	6	3	1	3			52	2	

Figure 8.3   Benefit Analysis Worksheet Results

INTERPRETATION OF THE WORKSHEET

The 'total' score is an indicator of how many 'benefit points' each product is providing.

In this example, Product A scores the most points and is ranked first, Products C and D come next to rank equal second, while Product B is ranked third.

Not only does this technique enable products or services to be compared and measured against the benefits they supply, it also gives rise to some very pertinent questions. For example:

▶ Why are products B, C and D not competitively priced?
▶ Can the performance of the products, especially A and D, be improved?
▶ Why are the safety scores of B and A so low?
▶ Why is packaging so uniformly poor?
▶ Can the design of B and C be improved?
▶ What are the immediate steps that might be taken to improve the benefits provided to customers?
▶ Taking into account the ranking of the individual products or services (i.e. their total benefit scores), is the correct allocation of energy and resources being made to each? Might their relative importance be reappraised?

Such questions asked of any company can only lead to a search for improvement. This will be just as true for our products or services as it was in the illustration given here. Moreover, since all such improvements are based on providing greater customer benefits, they hold every prospect of bringing about important changes. This process can be repeated for other market segments of our business.

So far we have returned to the idea that the product or service is the most visible thing which connects the supplier to the customer.

We went on to ask a quite fundamental question, 'what is a product or service?' A marketer's response is to define output in terms of how it provides customer benefits. Thus a product or service, as well as being a physical entity, will be perceived by the customer as a 'package' of benefits.

We found that there were a number of sources of potential benefits to customers, but in reality they would not all be equally attractive. Some benefits have more currency than others. Building on this point, we suggested a technique which enables a company to assess its output in terms of the benefits it provides.

THE PRODUCT/SERVICE LIFE CYCLE

The idea of benefit analysis which we have just explored is a very important one. It does have one drawback, however. It is virtually a 'snapshot' of the company's products or services at a given moment, and cannot portray what is happening over a period of time.

Because the product/service life cycle **does** enable us to understand what happens over time, the concept becomes a valuable marketing tool. Like most good ideas, the life cycle concept is extremely simple to grasp. What it tells us is that any product or service exhibits a sales pattern as shown in the following diagram:

Figure 8.4   Product/Service Life Cycle

The early part of the sales curve denotes a struggle to get the product or service known; sales were hard to come by and a lot of time and energy went into developing contacts in order to create awareness and acceptance of it. It is aptly called the **introduction phase.**

Assuming the product or service is acceptable to its target market, then there comes a time when it 'takes off'; everybody seems to want to buy it. This is the **growth phase.** But no market is infinitely expandable, and eventually the rate of growth slows as the product or service moves into the **maturity stage.**

Eventually a point is reached where there are too many firms in the market; price wars break out and some firms drop out of the market. Sales level off or gradually decline as demand has largely been satisfied, if not by us, then by the many competitors who would have been equally attracted by the growth potential of the market for this product/service. This is the **saturation phase.**

After a period of relative stability, the interest in our product/service wanes and sales start to fall more quickly. This is the **decline phase.** Exactly how far sales are allowed to fall is largely a managerial decision, as we will see.

This then is the product/service life cycle and it appears to hold true for all products and services. For fashion items and similar short-lived fads, the life cycle can be quite short; decline is reached perhaps in days. For other items the life cycle can be measured in decades.

What does it tell us?

- ► The life cycle curve can be a predictive device. It can tell us what sales pattern we might expect and allow corrective action to be taken.
- ► It can be a comparative device, in the sense that it can tell us if we are mirroring the total market experience or somehow falling short. The following diagrams illustrate this point!
- ► The life cycle curve can tell us how we might best support and invest in our product or service, as we shall see in a little while.

Diagram A

Here our life cycle curve follows the movement of the market curve, but on a smaller scale.

Diagram B

Here our life cycle curve peaked while the total market curve was still growing. Something must have been going very wrong for this to happen. What was it? Why are we in decline at this stage?

Figure 8.5   Product/Market Strategy and the Product Life Cycle (1)

▶ The life cycle curve can give us important clues about when to use short-term strategies in order to 'distort' the life cycle to our advantage. For example, suppose this curve represented one of our products or services:

Figure 8.6   Product/Market Strategy and the Product Life Cycle (2)

It tells us that we have just passed through the growth phase and appear to be entering the maturity phase. If we take no action, we could expect the sales curve to level out and eventually decline.

However, we could take steps to delay this process.

uct/market strategy and the product life cycle

Figure 8.7   Product/Market Strategy and the Product Life Cycle (3)

We could, as the illustration shows, improve the product or
extend the range and thereby stimulate more sales. When that
initiative has run its course, and sales start to level out again, we
could extend the market or develop a new segment. Again this
stimulates the sales curve and extends the period of growth.

However, these actions all cost money and so they have to be
weighed against the level of increased sales they would expect
to generate. Eventually there comes a time when it becomes
counter-productive to prop up an ailing product or service in
this way. The section on portfolio management in the next
chapter will help us in making the go/no-go decision about
investing in particular products or services.

But, for now, let us concentrate on understanding more about
the life cycle.

LIFE CYCLE – COSTS AND STRATEGIES

As this example has shown, in respect of product management a company must be prepared to vary its strategies as the product or service moves through its life cycle. But it is not only in respect of product management that alternative strategies should be considered. Pricing, distribution and promotional efforts also need to be regularly reviewed. For example, early promotional efforts will almost certainly have to concentrate on creating awareness for the product, especially if it is a completely new product or service concept. Later in the life of the product, when awareness levels are high, it is more likely that a company will need to spend more effort on positioning and imagery in what often turn out to be crowded markets during the high growth phase. Likewise, distribution channels are likely to change, as will pricing. Clearly, it may prove fatal to refuse to bow to price pressures as the market reaches maturity, because if hard-won market share is lost at this crucial stage this could well adversely affect profits as market share is lost.

So, market circumstances change over the life of a product or service and a company's policies should also change accordingly. The following table illustrates a set of guidelines used by one company in the electrical components market to help it determine appropriate marketing strategies at different stages of the life cycle. In this case, the company combined the two stages of maturity and saturation.

	Introduction	Growth	Maturity/ Saturation	Decline
Costs	Can be high, due to in-experience in supplying and the cost of promotion.	Increasing due to increased volume and fighting off competition. High growth requires funding.	Stabilizing/ reducing as experience and reduced competition take effect.	Can be high if not managed due to diseconomies of scale eg. only small runs.
Demand	Unpredictable. Forecasts can vary widely.	Upper limits might be forecast but volatile situation sensitive to prices and competition.	Fairly well defined.	Known and limited.
Com-petition	Largely unknown.	Many new entrants jump on 'bandwagon'. Competition fierce.	Marginal competitors leave. Remainder tend to specialize with particular segments.	New entrants are unlikely. Competition declines.
Customer loyalty	Trial usage, new relationship, little loyalty.	Some loyalty but to ensure supplies many customers might have more than one supplier.	Well-established buying patterns with high customer loyalty.	Extremely stable. Customers are not motivated to seek new suppliers.
Ease of Entry	Relatively easy because market leaders have not yet emerged. Customers feeling their way.	More difficult as some suppliers begin to establish market share and benefit from economies of scale.	Difficult because of established buying patterns. New business has to be won.	Little incentive to enter.

Figure continued overleaf

	Introduction	Growth	Maturity/ Saturation	Decline
Price	Price to capitalize on newness (high) or to penetrate the market (low).	Price competitively.	Price defensively.	Price according to perceived product life eg. high to milk remaining life.
Promotion	Active and aggressive.	Active and aggressive.	Selective and specialized.	Minimal if at all.
Product/ Service Range	Limited and specialized to meet the needs of early customers.	Rapid expansion in order to capitalize on new opportunities.	Range expansion slows down or ceases.	Range narrows as unproductive items are dropped.

Figure 8.8   Life Cycle Stages: Characteristics and Responses

Drawing a product life cycle can be extremely difficult, even given the availability of some form of time series analysis. This is connected with the complex question of market share measurement.

Firstly, let us remind ourselves that a firm needs to be concerned with its share (its proportion of volume or value) of an *actual* market. However, in order to measure an actual market, great care must be taken to ensure that a company is measuring the right things. Take the example of the company manufacturing a nylon carpet for institutional markets. It is clearly nonsense to include concrete in their measurement of the floor-covering market because concrete, although a floor covering, does not satisfy the needs that customers have for warmth and colour and therefore is not a part of their market. Neither, probably, should linoleum nor woollen carpets be included.

To help with this, let us remind ourselves of the following definitions:

PRODUCT CLASS   eg. carpets

PRODUCT **FORM**   eg. nylon rolls

PRODUCT **BRAND**   eg. 'X'

'X' as a brand, for the purpose of measuring market share, is concerned only with the aggregate of all other brands that satisfy the same group of customer wants.

Nevertheless, the manufacturer of 'X' also needs to be aware of the sales trends of other kinds of carpets and floor covering in the institutional market, as well as of carpet sales overall.

So far we have studied the idea of the product or service life cycle. We found that not only do products/services not last forever, but that the pattern of sales over their lifetime is remarkably similar.

The life cycle can be useful in four ways.

1   It can be a predictor of sales performance.
2   It enables us to compare ourselves with our 'industry'.
3   It gives us clues about how and when we might use short-term strategies to extend the life cycle.
4   It provides us with clues about the most appropriate strategies to use at different stages of the life cycle.

The important point to remember at this stage is that the concept of the product life cycle is not an academic figment of the imagination but a hard reality which is ignored at great risk. It is interesting to see how many commercial failures can be traced back to a naïve assumption on the part of managements that what was successful as a policy at one time will continue to be successful in the future.

Let us now broaden the discussion to a consideration of managing a range of products or services and the ways in which they satisfy market needs.

The art of successful product management must be based on a clear view of just *how* the present and future product range will continue to meet these twin goals of customer and corporate objectives.

As a first stage in successful product management it is important to think of the 'product' as a variable in the marketing mix, in the same way that we consider price or promotion as a variable. The extent of freedom to manoeuvre on the product variable will depend largely upon the internal resources of the firm and where its strengths are in relation to the competition. We shall explore the techniques of **strengths and weaknesses analysis**, often called a SWOT analysis, in more detail in Chapter 17. For now it is sufficient to suggest a number of pertinent questions to help us establish the appropriateness of current product strategy:

▶ What benefits do customers seek from this type of product?
▶ Does our product provide these benefits in greater proportion than competitors' products?
▶ What competitive product advantages are causing us to lose market share?
▶ Does our product range still provide 'value-in-use' to the customers in relation to its cost to them?
▶ Does each product in our range still meet the corporate objectives set for it?

The answers to these, and other questions, will provide a firm basis for developing a product/market strategy.

PRODUCT/MARKET STRATEGY

What is product/market strategy? Very simply it is the totality of the decisions taken within the organization concerning its target markets and the products that it offers to those markets. Strategy implies a chosen route to a defined goal and an element of long-term planning. Thus the product/market strategy of the firm represents its commitment to a particular direction in the future.

The effective company is one which plans for growth, and in terms of its product/market strategy seeks to plan its **product portfolio** well in advance – in terms required or determined by product policy. The company must plan for growth, and both product policy and product/market strategy must be growth-oriented; but clearly the growth must have purposeful direction if future profits and cash flows are to be maximized. This direction is provided through appropriate growth policies, indicating the **vectors** (variable directions) along which the firm is intended to move.

One helpful device for considering product/market strategy is the so-called 'Ansoff' matrix, named after its developer. The Ansoff Matrix shown in the figure below depicts the simple concepts employed.

Products/services

		Existing	New
Markets	Existing	Market penetration	Product/service development
	New	Market extension/ development	Diversification

Figure 8.9   The 'Ansoff' Matrix

STRATEGY OPTIONS

Most companies find that the strategy options open to them can be encapsulated in the Ansoff matrix where the axes are 'products/services' and 'markets'. Businesses have the option of staying with their existing products/services or developing new ones. Equally they can choose to remain in existing markets or develop new ones. The combination of these options gives rise to the following broad strategies.

Market Penetration

This will involve keeping existing customers and finding new ones in the same market. Thus pricing and promotion will have to be very competitive, because other suppliers are not just going to sit back and let us take their business. However, there are fewer unknowns and therefore in theory fewer risks.

Product/Service Development

This would involve modification of existing products/services to improve their quality, style, or whatever characteristics are valued by customers. The ultimate goal would be to increase sales or profits, or even reduce costs by taking advantage of new technology.

The implication of this strategy is that the company possesses the technical resources and skills to make it a viable proposition.

Given the failure rate of new products/services and the element of the unknown associated with this strategy, it must be considered as slightly risky.

Market Extension/Development

This involves finding new users for the product/service. This might mean going further afield geographically (even exporting), opening up new market segments, or finding new applications for the products/services.

This strategy implies that the company has marketing strengths and the wherewithal to make inroads into new markets.

Again the element of dealing with the unknown makes this a slightly more risky strategy.

Diversification

The most risky strategy of all, since both markets and products/services will be new. Because of the high risk such a strategy would need very careful evaluation. However, if we develop a brilliant new idea for a product or service, it might be appropriate for us to move in this direction.

The procedures described in the next chapter provide a means of determining the most appropriate product strategy to follow.

SUMMARY

In managing products or services the marketer must pay due regard to the benefits that customers seek as well as to the position in the product life cycle.

Marketing strategies will need to be adjusted as the life cycle changes. The appropriate marketing mix at the point of introduction will not be effective at the maturity stage, for example.

Finally, the Ansoff matric provides a useful framework for identifying the strategies options available to the company as it seeks to develop its product/market base.

CHAPTER 9

Product Strategy

MOST BUSINESSES operate by offering more than one product or service to the market place. They can be said to have a *portfolio* of products or services. Thus, while all the discussion about the life cycle holds true, in reality most companies are managing not one, but a number, of different product/service life cycles.

Ideally these would be managed so that they 'meshed' together in a sensible way, as the following diagrams show:

Today

Figure 9.1(a)

Today

Figure 9.1(b)

A Portfolio of several Product Life Cycles

Not a good pattern. All three products peaked some time ago and are now in decline. There is no new product to offer a promise for the future.

A good pattern. Product A, the earlier breadwinner, is in decline; but product B still holds a prospect of growth and product C is in its introduction stage, offering a bright future.

. A successful business would develop a portfolio more like that in Figure 9.1 (b). In fact, over the years, its growth could be attributed to a number of well-timed and profitable product/service launches like this:

Figure 9.2 Ideal Product Introduction Pattern over Time

Therefore, in order to achieve a successful product/service portfolio, it will be necessary to manage our existing output and bring it into line with our longer-term objectives. At the same time we will have to be capable of generating not only profits, but also sufficient funds to invest in new products and services.

The idea of a product portfolio is for a company to meet its objectives by balancing sales growth, cash flow and risk. As individual products progress or decline, and as markets grow or shrink, then the overall nature of the company's product portfolio will change. It is essential, therefore, that the whole portfolio is regularly reviewed and that an active policy towards new product development and divestment of old products is pursued. In this respect, the work of the Boston Consulting Group over the past decade has had a profound effect on the way managements think about this subject and about their product/market strategy.

In many respects the idea of the product portfolio is similar to the investor's portfolio of stocks and shares. The investor, for example, may wish to achieve a balance between yield or income and capital growth; some shares might produce more of the latter and less of the former and vice versa. Again, the investor might attempt to achieve a balance in terms of risk – some shares having a higher risk of capital loss attached, against which must be balanced the prospect of higher returns.

Cash flow is a key determinant of the firm's ability to develop its product portfolio. To emphasize this, the Boston Consulting Group developed a means of classifying products within the firm's portfolio according to their cash generation and cash usage.

THE BOSTON MATRIX

In the Boston Consulting Group's simple matrix, products are classified according to their positions on two dimensions: one is concerned with **relative market share** and the other with **market growth rate**.

Market share is used because it indicates the extent to which the products should be capable of generating cash. **Market growth** is used as an indicator of the product's cash requirements.

The measure of market share used is the product's share relative to the largest competitor. This is important because it reflects the degree of dominance enjoyed by the product in the market. For example, if company A has 20 per cent market share, and its biggest competitor has 20 per cent market share also, this position is usually less favourable than if company A had 20 per cent market share and its biggest competitor had only 10 per cent market share. The relative ratios would be 1:1 compared with 2:1. It is this ratio, or measure of market dominance, that the horizontal axis measures. The definition of high relative market share is generally taken to be a ratio of 1.5 or more.

The cut-off point for high as opposed to low market growth should be defined according to the prevailing circumstances in the industry, but this is often taken as 10 per cent. The somewhat picturesque labels attached to each of the four categories or products give some indication of the prospects for products in each quadrant.

Figure 9.3   The Boston Matrix

The Question Mark is a product which had not yet achieved a dominant market position and thus has a high cash flow; or perhaps it once had such a position and has slipped back. It will be a high user of cash because it is in a growth market. This is also sometimes referred to as a *wildcat*, or *problem child*.

The Star is probably a newish product that has achieved a high market share and which is probably on balance more or less self-financing in cash terms.

The Cash Cows are leaders in markets where there is little additional growth, but a lot of stability. These are excellent generators of cash.

Dogs have little future and are often a cash drain on the company. They are probably candidates for divestment, although often such products fall into a category aptly described by Peter Drucker as 'investments in managerial ego'.

Since the 'Cash Cow' is the only quadrant which actually generates cash, some very clear messages come from the Boston matrix:

1 To manage the product/service portfolio effectively the cash
   generated by 'cash cows' must be used to invest in 'stars' and
   selected 'question marks'.
2 Investing in 'question marks' with good prospects should
   lead to them developing into 'stars'.
3 Investing in 'stars' should develop them into tomorrow's
   'cash cows'.
4 The higher the relative market share of a 'star', the better are
   its prospects as a 'cash cow'.
5 High investment in a 'cash cow' should never be necessary.
6 Investment in 'dogs' is generally money wasted.

The Boston matrix can be used to forecast the market position of
our products, say, five years from now if we continue to pursue
our current policies. The following diagram illustrates this process for a manufacturer of plastic valves. The area of each circle
is proportional to each product's contribution to total company
sales volume.

Figure 9.4 The Product Portfolio, Current and Projected

THE DIRECTIONAL POLICY MATRIX

As a further aid to product strategy, Shell, General Electric, McKinsey and others developed a multi-factor approach to portfolio management. They used **industry attractiveness** and **business strengths** as the two main axes and built up these dimensions from a number of variables. Using these variables, and some scheme for weighting them according to their importance, products (or businesses) are classified into one of nine cells in a 3×3 matrix. So the same purpose is served as in the Boston matrix, i.e. comparing investment opportunities among products or businesses. The difference is that multiple criteria are used.

The matrix is constructed in a similar way to the Boston matrix except it should be noticed that the axes have changed. For the sake of simplicity the labels attaching to each of the Boston boxes have been retained.

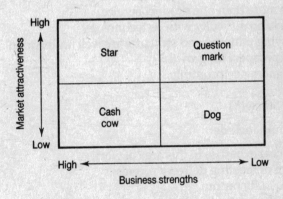

Now we are dealing in terms that can be more easily understood. How 'attractive' are the various markets or market segments for each of our products or services and to what degree are we playing to our 'business strengths' when we supply them?

The question is:

What characteristics would a particular company be looking for to describe a market that would be attractive to it?

It is impossible to be precise in answering this question because the answer should be different for every company. Therefore the lists that follow are just some general headings that might be considered.

Market Attractiveness

This could involve:

- The size of the market(s)
- Its 'reachability'
- The number and quality of the competitors
- The level of prices that can be charged
- The profits to be made, versus effort put in
- High customer loyalty
- A supportive business environment
- Has needs that can easily be satisfied
- Takes more than one product/service
- There is no difficulty with its technology
- Its buying patterns and structure are well understood
- Good prospect for growth
- Customers pay promptly

Business Strengths

These could include:

- Technical expertise in this area of work
- Record of meeting delivery promises
- High quality output
- Flexibility i.e. to changing requests
- Good reputation/image
- Creative i.e. solutions to customers' problems
- Have a bank of loyal customers
- Room to grow
- High quality/loyal staff

▸ Some successful products/services
▸ Good at small/medium/large production runs

Having established the criteria for market attractiveness and business strengths, it is now possible to construct a portfolio matrix for the business. However, before doing so, let us look at an example of how a small company set about this task.

SEALITT LTD.

This small company makes various types of seals and gaskets. Its original product was rubber trim for fitting motor vehicle windows. These are supplied to motor factors, replacement windscreen specialists and van/caravan converters.

It then developed door trim rubber strips for draught and weather sealing, essentially for motor factors. This venture led to producing draught-excluder strips for DIY outlets. Its latest ideas are to provide seals for double glazing units and also gaskets of all shapes, sizes and application, mainly for engineering companies.

The company buys in most of its materials. Its strengths are the expertise it has developed for buying judiciously, and the ability to cut and shape materials economically but to high standards.

Its portfolio matrix looks like this:

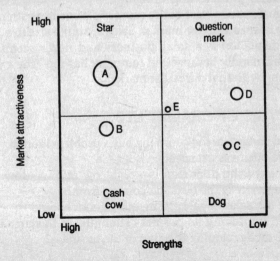

The key to the diagram is:

A = window trim (vehicles)
B = door seal strip
C = glazing seals
D = gaskets
E = DIY

The size of each circle approximates to the level of sales for that item.

The company's strengths are geared up to supplying the 'motor trade'; the demand for window trim makes it an attractive market. Similar strengths apply to door seals, but the market is less attractive since there is a smaller demand for replacements. (It would not have the capacity to supply the OEM – (Original Equipment Manufacturer – market eg. Ford, Rover.)

Double glazing seals looked on the surface a good proposition for Sealitt Ltd., but it was found that there was some new expertise to acquire; also several customers went out of business without paying. The well-established double glazing companies either produced their own seals or had approved suppliers. Thus this item, which started as a 'question mark', went almost immediately into the 'dog' quadrant.

The gaskets use least of the company's business strengths but seem to be an attractive market. Sales are quite sizeable.

DIY insulation is a small business and never seems to have taken off, mainly because the company has too little experience in dealing with that particular market.

ANALYSIS OF SEALITT LTD.

It would seem that the company has a problem looming in terms of future business prospects.

At present the door trim is a cash cow and window trim is a star, but where is the next star coming from?

Since the sales of gaskets are quite good, should the company invest in improving its business strengths in this area and concentrate on developing this part of the business?

Can the DIY insulation find more attractive markets?

Is a new question mark required with better 'credentials'?

The double glazing sealing appears to be a flop and should be discontinued, as it is only getting in the way.

These are serious questions which have to be answered. To help answer these questions, here are some strategy options suggested by the Directional Policy Analysis.

STAR	QUESTION MARK	
Invest for Growth	**Opportunistic Development**	
▶ penetrate market	▶ be critical of prospects	
▶ accept moderate short-term profits	▶ invest heavily in selective products/services	
▶ sell and promote aggresively		
▶ expand ▷ geographically ▷ product line		
▶ differentiate product/service		
CASH COW	**CASH DOG**	**GENUINE DOG**
Maintain Market Position and Manage for Earnings	▶ live with low growth	▶ prune aggressively
▶ maintain market position with successful products/services	▶ improve productivity	▶ maximize cash flow
▶ differentiate products/services to keep share of key segments	▶ reduce costs	▶ raise prices at expense of volume
▶ prune less successful products or services	▶ look for 'easy' growth segments	▶ minimize expenditure
▶ stabilize prices, except where temporary aggressive stance is required to deter competitors		

Figure 9.5   Directional Policy Analysis for Sealitt Ltd.

THE DIRECTIONAL POLICY MATRIX AS A PREDICTIVE DEVICE

So far we have just looked at the portfolio matrix as a static 'snapshot' of the company. However, it is possible to make even greater use of it, as we shall see.

Let's go back to our example of Sealitt Ltd. This time the manager has added more information to the matrix by indicating the trends he expects for each part of the business. His two-year forward projections are shown as dotted lines and again the circles represent sales levels.

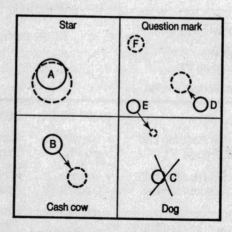

Figure 9.6   Portfolio Matrix showing Current and Forecast Positions

We can see that overall the sales from the star are going to increase, but that the market growth will slow down slightly.

The cash cow is planned to maintain the same level of sales, but the market is certainly becoming less attractive and matches with fewer of the company's strengths.

Product C, the double glazing seal, will be scrapped. The DIY insulation E is seen to be fading away and is likely to be withdrawn.

Gaskets (D) are planned to generate more sales, but the product is still short of being a star.

A new product F is scheduled to provide the lost revenue from C and E. This product, with the right investment, looks to have a prospect of becoming a future star. It certainly plays to more of the company's strengths than the gaskets business.

It is essential for the company to get a new star as the window trim sinks into the cash cow quadrant.

DEVELOPING NEW PRODUCTS AND SERVICES

So far in this book we have tended to focus on existing products and services. However, experience tells us that nothing lasts forever. Eventually today's breadwinners fall into decline and something else has to be found to take their place.

In practice most new products and services emerge gradually from modifications of existing ideas and technology – from putting together familiar things in a slightly different way. It is this interplay between existing products or services and the search for improvement and innovation that provides the dynamism for the growth-orientated company.

However, the search for growth, prosperity and market opportunity is not without risk. A high proportion of new products and services finish up on the scrapheap without anyone mourning their passing. The road to success is strewn with the smouldering remains of erstwhile 'world beating' ideas developed by bright, intelligent managers.

Some businesses stake their all in a new product or service; failure, when it occurs, is often total.

RESISTANCE TO CHANGE

As if getting the right quality of innovative ideas were not problem enough, there is also the issue of resistance to change which occurs in all walks of life, the company being no exception.

This resistance can derive from a number of factors:

► The desire to maximize returns from existing capacity products and services;
► the desire to defend current patterns of behaviour, systems and procedures;
► the desire to minimize losses on existing plant and equipment (and people) through enforced obsolescence;
► the desire to protect status derived from past experience;
► the desire to avoid risk consequences;
► fear of the unknown.

However, by personal leadership and demonstrating an openness to change themselves, managers can create the right climate for innovation. In this way the company can capitalize on its strengths by being able to respond to new situations. It is such a flexible approach that at the end of the day is the hidden strength of the small company.

STRATEGY OF MINIMAL RISK

The least risky way of dealing with the development of new products and services is not to innovate but to copy others.

By taking this stance the company avoids all the costs associated with developing new ideas and creating the markets for them. Instead, it takes the ideas and modifies them according to its capacity. It then 'surf-tides' the wave in the market place created by the innovator.

The key to success with this strategy is **timing**. To get into the market too early, before the new idea becomes accepted, can put a company in the position of a trailblazer with all the attendant costs. But if a company arrives too late, the market for the idea may have been monopolized by others.

Nevertheless, it does seem that a risk/reward 'rule' appears to operate along a continuum as shown:

Low risk

High risk

Low rewards

High rewards

Although this may seem a little prescriptive, such a 'rule' is endorsed by proverbs and sayings such as: 'Luck favours the brave' and 'Who dares wins'.

It will therefore be useful to look at other options towards the right-hand end of the risk/reward line.

CREATIVE IDEAS

The potential sources of new ideas for products and services are virtually boundless. They can range from the sudden insight, the 'eureka' kind of invention, through to some very analytical techniques.

Here are just some sources of ideas for new products or services. There is no significance in the order which follows.

▶ Brainstorming – a technique which involves a group of people 'free thinking' about the new uses to which a product or service can be put. The key to brainstorming is that *all* ideas are listed and judgement about their feasibility is suspended. Only when a large number of ideas are generated are they considered in terms of feasibility

▶ Talking and listening to customers or intermediaries

▶ Monitoring technological developments

▶ Monitoring new legislation, for example that which has impact on safety, the environment or crime reduction. These can be potent sources for new products or services

▶ Running an ideas scheme among staff

▶ Attribute listing – This involves listing the attributes of a

product or service and then modifying them in the search for
an improved version.

▶ Carrying out market gap analysis

▶ Monitoring imports to the country

▶ Keeping in touch with what competitors are doing

▶ Setting up a 'think tank' with staff and/or appropriate out-
siders

▶ Analysing past sales figures for significant trends

▶ Making forced relationships – new ideas are listed and then
worked at in pairs. Sometimes interesting products or services can emerge from this process. For example, separate
gramophone turntable, tape deck, amplifier and tuner were
put together as a 'music centre'. More recently a TV and video
recorder have been integrated into one single unit

▶ Conducting specific market research

▶ Monitoring customer queries or complaints

▶ Lateral thinking – looking at familiar ideas and turning them
back to front. For example, a small company made glass fibre
boats but needed to diversify. It could have looked at other
types of craft, but equally it decided that if its expertise was
making structures to 'keep water out' then it also had the
expertise to 'keep water in'. By developing this line of thinking the company expanded into making storage tanks and
reservoirs, essentially using its existing technology

▶ Applying new ideas stemming from the availability or application of new materials. For example, new plastic materials
are being developed which can make them ideal substitutes
for more expensive metal products

Irrespective of **how** we generate new ideas for products or
services, there seem to be three universal 'laws' of which we
should be aware:

1 Successful innovators have a much better understanding of user-needs than their less successful contemporaries;

2 the odds against a new product or service being successful are very high, in the order of thirty to one against. Therefore to have one good idea it is likely that we would need to have considered about thirty. In other words, the quality ideas come from quantity;

3 the key sources of new product ideas are likely to be based on research and development and market research. Attractive though they might seem, successful ideas generated by creative thinking techniques have been fairly limited, because they are likely to be product- rather than market-focused.

OTHER CONSIDERATIONS

Perhaps giving birth to the new idea for a product or service is the most difficult part of the process of innovation, but there are clearly many other factors to take into account before we rush to the market place.

The following are the kinds of factors that need to be taken into account:

- Is there a need for the new product or service?
- What sort of demand will there be?
- Are the customers likely to be new or existing ones?
- Can I reach the new customers?
- Will the new product/service fit in with the existing range?
- Do we have the resources and expertise to provide it?
- What does the competition provide? How does it compare?
- What will be the costs of providing this new product/service?
- What will be the result if we don't provide it?
- Will it make money?
- Is it what we want to make, or like making?
- Is it consistent with the image of our company?
- What life could we expect from the new product/service?

A SCREENING PROCEDURE FOR IDEAS FOR NEW PRODUCTS OR SERVICES

All the considerations we have just raised make it essential that new ideas for products or services are rigorously screened to ensure they will be viable.

The screening procedure should look something like the illustration opposite:

We have seen that new products are the life blood of a company in its attempt to survive in a dynamic and competitive marketing environment. The search for viable and profitable new products must be a continuing task of marketing management but it is a task which is fraught with risk.

For the majority of companies the introduction of a new product involves a great deal of investment, both in the development process and in the initial introductory stage when market acceptance has to be won if the product is to succeed. This investment can represent a considerable slice of a company's resources, not only financial but also physical and managerial; yet there can be no fail-safe guarantee that the investment will yield the sort of return that the company would consider acceptable. In some cases a single new product failure could bring disaster to a company, especially if it had pinned all its hopes on the new product only to find that the outcome fell far short of expectations.

Consider the case some years ago of the Rolls-Royce RB211 engine. Here the company had committed major resources to an engine which, whilst technically unimpeachable, did not match the wants of a large enough section of the market to recoup the tremendous development costs. Hindsight would suggest that this was an unwise step to take. As it was, it almost led to the collapse of the company.

Another example occurred in the consumer goods market, when a major food manufacturer invested heavily in developing a new dessert. Careful testing indicated that the product would be acceptable to potential customers. However, when the

Figure 9.7 Screening Procedure for New Products

company proceeded to launch the product it found that retailers were unwilling to stock it as the type of packaging developed for the product led to problems of stacking.

These examples can be matched with many others in the consumer, industrial and service markets. Research has indicated that, in some product areas, up to 80 per cent of all new product launches fail, in the sense that they do not meet marketing targets and are withdrawn soon after their introduction. Some product fields, such as grocery or cosmetics, are more prone to early failure than others but, whatever the context, all the evidence seems to suggest a high failure rate for new product introductions.

What then should marketing managers do in attempting to reduce the uncertainty that surrounds the new product launch? There are no crystal-ball revelations about prospects for success or failure in this area, but some procedures can be very helpful in quantifying the risks implicit in a new product launch. We shall now go on to explore some of these methods, but, before we do so, we should first look more closely at some other factors involved in the new product-testing decision.

TESTING PROCEDURES

Let us consider the means of testing available to a European manufacturer of sisal-based floor coverings who markets his products to the 'contract' market; that is, a market where an intermediary, often either an architect or a purchasing agent, buys the product for use in offices, hospitals and schools.

This is a fairly complex market where various types of floor covering are available. It is a highly competitive market and, frequently, the floor covering is specified on the basis of some total, overall scheme for interior decoration.

On the advice of marketing consultants, this company was attempting to formalize its new product-testing procedures. Previously, they had tried to identify trends in styles and colours on the basis of past sales. There had always been an attempt to perform a 'break-even' analysis on the basis of projected costs and prices. Beyond this, new product testing was more a matter of technical assessment or product quality.

The consultants suggested a process of testing which involved several stages. (This process, which we shall examine in detail shortly, indicates activities which should take place, in one form or another, in all new product testing.) Each stage in the analysis provided the opportunity to pause and make one of three decisions: launch the product now; collect further information; or abandon the product now. The three decisions were given the shorthand of GO (launch the product), GO ON (carry on testing) and NO GO (reject).

In the case of the floor covering manufacturer, the sequence started with a test designed to give a broad picture of how acceptable the product concept was to its potential market. (This was accompanied by an initial appraisal of how the product might fit into the company's product portfolio.)

Figure 9.8   Stages of New Product Development

Concept Test   This was administered by means of a dozen interviews conducted by trained interviewers, with architects and purchasing agents representative of the target market. The purpose of the test was to expose them to details of the technical specification, possible colour range and recommended uses of the product. Sometimes artists' impressions of designs and colours were shown. The results of this stage of the test sequence were entirely qualitative but they served to eliminate all those products which were complete non-starters. It was scarcely possible to make a decision to launch the product at this stage.

Qualitative Screen This was the next stage, and formed a screening process which posed two basic questions:

(a) Is the product concept compatible with company objectives?

   Issues involved were for example:
   ► Does the concept complement our existing market offering?
   ► Is it compatible with the image that we seek and the segment of the market with which we identify?

(b) Is the product concept compatible with company resources?

   Issues involved here were:
   ► Does the company have the capital to get this product to market and to develop an initial level of sales?
   ► Does the company have the necessary know-how and adequate physical facilities to handle the product successfully?

Economic Analysis If the product concept survived this screening process it was subjected to this next stage in the testing sequence. This analysis was designed to examine the economics of the project under differing assumptions of costs incurred and revenue achieved.

It was conducted at a fairly simple level as the company at that time had only a limited knowledge of how the market would react to products priced outside the narrow band with which the company was familiar. It was acknowledged that this stage of the testing sequence could be made considerably more sophisticated by applying the methods of investment appraisal that were in common use in other companies.

Once this stage of the testing had been successfully concluded, the company might feel sufficiently confident of the viability of the concept to move ahead to a full-scale market launch. Such a decision would have to be based on some highly positive results from the initial stages of the test sequence since the cost of setting up a promotional programme would be substantial. More often a decision would be taken to go on to the next, and more expensive, stage of the analysis.

Product Test In this case the product test was designed to gain impressions from a relatively large number of potential customers of how they would react to the physical product when it was compared with competing products. The expense of product testing lies in the fact that considerable quantities of the physical product must be provided. The aim of the test is to identify a representative sample of the target market and to interpret the reactions relative to the competing products. Aspects of the product tested at this stage would be physical characteristics, the range available, the suggested usage, price and image connotations. This company recruited a panel of architects and purchasing agents who were invited to compare, according to a number of appropriate criteria, the proposed new products with selected competitive products.

The analysis of these results enabled a picture to be built up of how the proposed new product compared with existing products in a number of key dimensions.

It was at this stage that the company normally made the final decision as to whether or not to launch the new product. Clearly there would still be some uncertainty about the new product's success, but the sequential testing had enabled this uncertainty to be reduced to an acceptable level. The company could have gone on, as many do, to the next test.

Test Market This, as the name implies, is an attempt to reproduce the conditions of a full-scale launch but on a much smaller scale. Often a town, or geographical area, is chosen as representing the ultimate market; the product is launched in that town or area alone and its progress observed. As a test of this kind is very much an 'experiment', it is necessary to ensure that conditions within the test market would be such that they could be reproduced on a national scale. For example, no extra promotional effort should be expended other than an amount proportional to the total to be spent in the proposed full-scale launch.

It should be noted, however, that test markets can never be completely reliable indicators of ultimate market performance. Quite apart from the problems of 'grossing up' small-scale test market results to provide a global picture, there is always the possibility of unusual competitive activities which distort the results.

While we have portrayed these stages of testing as a sequence, it should be clear that some of the stages could be conducted concurrently, as with the qualitative screen and the economic analysis. Whatever the sequence, the purpose of new product testing remains the same:

▶ to reduce uncertainty surrounding the new product to a level acceptable to the company whilst still enabling the launch to be made at the earliest possible time.

The methods of product testing might vary from marketing situation to marketing situation but, whether the product be a new airline service, heavy-duty transformers or a vinyl wallpaper, the principles are universal and the benefits considerable.

SUMMARY

The key to successful product strategy is a balanced portfolio of products which includes both established products and a steady flow of new products. The use of the Boston matrix can be helpful in analysing the options for product strategy and in highlighting gaps in the portfolio.

Because the chance of failure is high in new product launches the use of formalized methods of appraisal is advocated, including market research as well as economic analysis.

CHAPTER 10

Distribution and Logistics Strategy

DISTRIBUTION AND THE MARKETING MIX

MAKING SURE that products reach customers cannot be regarded by marketing managers as simply the concern of someone else. The distribution activity is as much part of the company's marketing mix as are product, pricing and promotion decisions. In fact in some markets, the impact of the distribution element on sales can exceed that of the other mix elements. Seen in this light, the means whereby the product reaches the customer assumes a vital importance in marketing strategy. The implications of this view of distribution's marketing role are therefore far-reaching, and can involve a considerable reappraisal of attitudes as well as of the means of distribution used. Moreover, as studies have estimated that the average European manufacturing company spends 15 per cent of its sales revenue on distribution-related activities, it is not difficult to contemplate the benefits of such a reappraisal.

Although *place* is a convenient shorthand description used to define one of the quartet of 'P's' which go to make up the marketing mix, it represents the means whereby the needs of the market and the offering of the company are physically matched. As such it provides the addition of time- and place-utility to the product. Without this added value the product is worthless.

AN OVERVIEW

Many of the issues we need to address as marketers can be demonstrated by considering the following example:

Fruit Farms Ltd. is a small company based in the South Midlands which grows and sells its fruit produce. In getting its fruit to the customer it has a number of quite different options. It can:

► Advertise and get people to come and pick their own fruit;
► sell the produce at its own farm shop;
► sell to local fruiterers;
► sell to supermarket chains;
► sell to local restaurants and hotels;
► sell to manufacturers of, for example, jams, pies, or frozen foods;
► transform its product into jams, pies or frozen packs and sell these direct through retail outlets and mail order catalogues;
► use a combination of some of the above.

Which is the best distribution channel to select? The short and easy answer is the one which helps to make the business most profitable – but which one would that be?

If the company wanted to keep its costs down it could let customers pick their own fruit. Would it sell enough?

If it sold through intermediaries it would then have to provide them with a profit margin and this could represent lost profits for the company. Then again, it would cost money to staff and run its own farm shop.

If it sold to local restaurants and hotels would it have to deliver, or would they collect? More cost considerations.

If it sold to supermarkets then it would have to package the fruit in their containers and to their standards. Could it do this? At what cost?

If it sold to manufacturers it could sell in bulk orders, but they would probably demand a lower unit price – so would the company be better off?

As we can see, it is easier to come up with the questions than it is the answers.

As more and more companies take a new look at the role of distribution in their marketing effort they also are coming to similar conclusions. While there is considerable scope for profit enhancement through distribution improvement, it isn't always immediately obvious where to make the improvements. Nor is it always a cost-saving benefit which pays off. Sometimes profitability can be improved by spending more on some aspects of distribution, rather than less.

For example, Rank Xerox have found that it pays to ship high-value spares to European customers by air express, rather than by less expensive surface transport. Although some savings are made on packaging and insurance, the main benefit is that faster deliveries mean lower inventory carrying costs for goods in transit. In addition, this means that customers can be involved more quickly, which has the effect of improving cash flow and of course, enhancing service levels to customers.

This example shows how important it is for the marketer to have an overview of the whole distribution process and not to see it merely as a means of transporting the product from A to B in the cheapest possible way. Indeed, in many companies the marketing department is seen to be responsible only for demand *creation* rather than demand *satisfaction*. The costs of distribution are often pushed into someone else's cost centre. Not surprisingly in such circumstances, it becomes exceedingly difficult to achieve a situation in which marketing and distribution work closely together.

To overcome these problems of compartmentalization of the company's effort, a new integrative approach to marketing and distribution has been introduced.

THE LOGISTICS CONCEPT

The emphasis behind this approach is to view the movement of products, as they pass through the manufacturing process and eventually to the customer, as a total system. Thus instead of marketing, production, distribution and purchasing – all working away oblivious to the others and each trying to optimize their individual efforts – the logistics concept suggests that it may be necessary for some or all of these areas to operate sub-optimally in order that the whole system may be more effective.

So, for example, the marketing manager might have to be prepared to accept a lower level of customer service than he would like; or alternatively the production manager might have to schedule shorter runs with more frequent tool changes if the overall effectiveness of the system is to be maximized.

In practice there are five areas of concern which have to be addressed in logistics management. These key decision areas constitute the logistics mix.

LOGISTICS MIX

This comprises **facility, inventory, communication, unitization** and **transport decisions.** Let us look at each of these decision areas in turn.

Facility Decisions   These are concerned with how many warehouses and plants we should have, and with where they should be located in order to optimize the customer service/cost equation. For a majority of companies it is necessary to take the location of existing facilities as a *fait accompli* in the short term. However, taking a longer-term perspective, companies often have alternative options and opportunities opening up from them regarding how they plan their facilities.

Inventory Decisions   The cost of holding stock can be a major element in many companies' total distribution costs. Decisions about how much stock to hold, where to hold it and what quantities to order therefore become vital in the logistics mix. Inventory levels, as we shall see later, are also instrumental in determining the level of service that a company can offer its customers.

Communication Decisions   Logistics is not only about the flow of materials or products through the distribution system; it is also about the efficient flow of information. Here we are concerned with the order-processing system, the invoicing system and the demand forecasting system. Without effective communications support the logistics system will never be capable of sustaining a satisfactory customer service at an acceptable cost.

'Unitization' Decisions   The way in which goods are individually packaged and then subsequently assembled in larger batches can have a major bearing on logistics economics. For example, two competing companies made fertilizer for sale to farmers. Traditionally the product was supplied in plastic sacks, but farmers found these to be very labour-intensive to load, unload and transport around their farms. Company A responded to the farmers' criticism by supplying multiple bags on wooden pallets which, incidentally, reduced their own handling costs in their factory and warehouses. Company B responded by packaging the fertilizer in a 'Jumbo Bag', equivalent to many ordinary sacks. A key feature of this giant bag was the provision of a loop which enabled it to be carried by a hook on a tractor arm.

Company B increased its sales because its new bulk packaging could be easily handled by farmers with tractors; in contrast fewer farmers had fork-lift trucks to handle the pallets of Company A. Moreover, fork-lift trucks with heavy loads could be unstable when on uneven terrain, and the farm environment was very different to the flat concrete floors of the factory and warehouse.

Transport Decisions These are the decisions surrounding the transport function of the company. They are likely to be concerned about such issues as: 'What mode of transport should be used? Should we use our own vehicles or use an outside contractor? How should we route our deliveries? How frequently should we deliver?'

Of the five decision areas, the transport decision has received perhaps the greatest attention in most companies, in that it is one of the more obvious facets of the distribution task. Certainly in recent years there have been many changes in this area, some of which are just gathering momentum. One of the most significant has been the growth of the specialist carrier, to replace the company's own transport service. However, we must remember that, taken in the total logistics context, transport might only account for a small proportion of the total costs.

Together, these five areas constitute the total costs of distribution within a company. Furthermore, it is frequently the case that a decision made in one area will have an effect on the other four. Thus it may be that a decision to open or close a depot will affect transport costs (longer or shorter travelling distances), inventory (stock levels at factory and other depots have to change) and possibly data-processing costs (for installing and operating new system requirements). This is the idea of a *cost trade-off*. Managing the logistics function involves a continuous search for such trade-offs, the intention being to secure a reduction in total costs by changing the cost structure in one or more areas. Alternatively, investment in one of the logistic decision areas might be vindicated if it can be shown to differentiate the product from its competitors in a way that can bring increased sales revenue or improve the market share through better service.

THE SERVICE-LEVEL DECISION

One of the fundamental cost trade-offs in logistics that has an impact upon marketing performance is the question of **service levels**. The level of service is a measure of the extent to which the organization plans to make the product available and to support it in use, for example with the provision of after-sales service.

The simplest measure of service is stock availability, usually measured as the percentage of demand that can be met from stock. Clearly there is more to service than this, as we shall explore in Chapter 12. However, it can be regarded as the foundation of the service 'package'.

Naturally the customer seeks maximum availability and the company will normally endeavour to supply it. However, the problem is that as we increase the planned level of availability, the necessary investment in inventory rises more than proportionately. Figure 10.1 highlights the relationship between inventory and service levels.

Figure 10.1   The Cost of 'Availability'

The reason the curve rises so steeply as the planned level of availability increases is that, even though the chance of a stock-out may be remote, additional safety stock must be held to cover for that possibility.

Many companies frequently underestimate the true costs of holding stock. It is a fair estimate to account for a 25 per cent per annum holding cost for inventory (i.e. 25 per cent of the book value of stock) if we include the cost of capital, storage, obsolescence and insurance. Since most medium-to-large organizations carry millions of pounds of stock at any time, the annual cost at 25 per cent is clearly substantial.

The trade-off that has to be considered therefore is: 'What is the cost of holding stock compared to the cost of a stock-out situation?'

If stock-outs occur too frequently the outcome can be a substantial fall in sales revenue. At best, the company will forfeit the immediate contribution to its cash flow, whilst at the same time incurring some degree of customer hostility. At worst, the customer will not delay his purchase but will buy from a competitor instead. Clearly the cost of stock-outs will vary from product to product and will to some extent be dependent upon the nature and availability of competing products.

Poor stock availability also antagonizes channel intermediaries. In a recent survey carried out in the USA, it was estimated that if a supplier decreased his stock availability by 5 per cent nearly a quarter of intermediaries indicated that they would purchase elsewhere. Oblivious of this reaction, supplying companies estimated that such a reduction of service would at worst lose them 'only about 9 per cent' of their outlets!

ESTABLISHING THE PROFIT CONSEQUENCES OF A STOCK-OUT

Because we are dealing with aspects of human behaviour as well as economics when faced with an out-of-stock situation, there is no precise way of measuring the impact on profit. Instead we have to evaluate the probabilities of stock-out consequences, estimate the frequency at which each of these consequences is likely to occur and make a weighted judgement about the financial consequences. Here is an example of how this might be done:

Consequence of Service	Failure Profit Penalty
Loss of sale to competitor	Gross margin of item
Customer re-ordering	Order-processing cost
Loss of sale on related items	Gross margin on all items
Shipment of goods from other depots	Expediting and transport cost
Expediting of rush orders at factory	Non-standard procedure cost
Customer's ill-will	Possible lost customer

Ideally, a market experiment should be conducted to measure more precisely the effect of non-availability on market share. There have been a number of reported studies which suggest that over a certain range of service improvement there can be a significant impact on sales, however – once a certain 'saturation' level is reached – the customer may find it difficult to distinguish between small improvements in stock availability. Thus, as in Figure 10.2, it is suggested that there comes a point where diminishing returns to service improvement are encountered.

Figure 10.2   The Market Response to Service

The task of marketing management when seeking to develop appropriate levels of stock availability is to balance the known cost of service against the estimated market response. Figure 10.3 depicts the basic trade-off between the cost function and the response function.

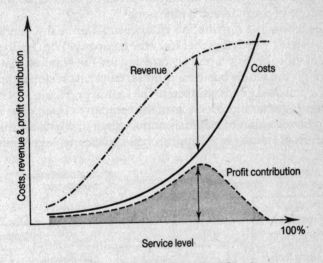

Figure 10.3   The Cost/Benefit of Service

BRINGING THE LOGISTICS MIX TOGETHER

One of the major problems with conventional approaches to distribution is that responsibility for it is spread over too many discrete functional areas; that is, there is a high degree of 'compartmentalization'.

In one engineering company, responsibility for stock levels throughout the system was in the hands of the production department. Yet, *at the same time*, the purchasing manager was pursuing policies which conflicted with the production policy and the distribution manager operated an inflexible delivery system. Little wonder the marketing manager was driven to despair by the erratic service levels customers received.

The acceptance of an integrated systems-based approach lies at the very heart of the logistics concept. This, together with the recognition that the interrelationship of the component parts of the mix makes them mutually dependent, should be the cornerstone of the marketer's philosophy.

Somehow the distribution planner must unite the interlinked subsystems which together form the company. With his logistics orientation he must be concerned with the flow of materials through the whole business process, from raw material through to the finished goods shipped to the customer. Figure 10.4 below brings together those aspects of the company's operations involving flows, either of materials or information, which are the core concern of an integrated approach to logistics management.

Figure 10.4   The Logistics Systems Concept

As we can see, in the traditional model, physical distribution management is concerned only with flows at the end of the production process – getting goods to the customer. In contrast the integrated approach to logistics encompasses the total flow of materials and information into, through and out of the corporate system.

SUMMARY

There is now a much greater recognition of the importance of distribution and logistics in the overall marketing strategy of the business. Not only does the material flow through the firm attract substantial costs (for example, inventory holding charges, transport and storage) but the way in which the flow is managed can have a considerable impact upon customer service. Thus there is a need for a complex trade-off between the costs and benefits attached to different market strategies.

CHAPTER 11

Marketing Channel Strategy

CHANNELS OF DISTRIBUTION

WHERE OUR CUSTOMERS buy our products is logically determined by the outlets at which those products are made available. Typically, many companies will not give too much attention to the question of channel choice; it is not seen as being a variable in the marketing mix. More often than not the distribution channel will have taken its current form as a result of unplanned and haphazard development.

Such a disregard for this vital area of marketing discretion means that many opportunities for profitable market potential are passed over. For example, an international chemical company selling into Europe, using their own sales force to sell direct to customers, found that by using a chemical merchant, or middleman, they could reduce their own sales costs and take advantage of a ready-made sales organization with a host of local contacts.

Another company, a British shoe manufacturer producing good quality shoes, found it possible to open up a new and profitable market segment in the catalogue of a national mail-order firm. This gave the company the facility to reach a wider audience without compromising on its traditional channels – up-market, speciality shoe shops.

Another British company, a carpet manufacturer, was perplexed by its falling sales even though total carpet sales in the UK remained at a high level. It was felt that somehow the quality or the pricing must be wrong to achieve the poor results they were getting. In fact, a deeper examination of the company situation showed that it had continued to sell through the small, traditional High Street carpet shops. The new growth outlets were the edge-of-town carpet warehouses, often selling at a discount. These now accounted for the lion's share of carpet sales and the manufacturer had missed a wonderful opportunity by failing to recognize the change in distribution patterns.

These three examples demonstrate the benefits of taking a fresh look at marketing channels. They each involved a reappraisal of the route by which the customer acquired the product and a comparison of the costs and benefits of the alternative options.

Many companies do not rely on a single channel of distribution but prefer instead to use multiple channels. They may choose different channels to reach each different market segment, or alternatively they may approach a single market via a dual distribution channel. Whatever the situation, it is a necessary and valuable exercise to weigh up the costs and benefits accruing through the use of specific channels of distribution. As the following diagram shows, each channel can have distinctly different costs and revenue profiles.

Figure 11.1   Alternative Channels of Distribution

The range of options here are not unlike those faced by Fruit Farms Ltd., described earlier in Chapter 10. The company can distribute direct to the customer, work through one or more intermediaries, reach the customer by mail or even, in some instances, have the customer come to the factory to purchase and take away the product.

The channel decision has to be undertaken in the widest possible context. It needs to consider questions about the company's overall marketing strategy, the appropriateness of the channel to the product and its image, and customer requirements and preferences. These can be every bit as important as the comparative costs of selling and distribution.

CHOOSING THE CHANNEL

The underlying purpose of the marketing channel is to reach the customer in the most appropriate way. Whilst the requirements of the customer might vary from market to market, it is possible to generalize customer objectives relating to the decision of where to buy the product.

PRICE/VALUE

This dimension is present to a greater or lesser extent in all markets. It implies that the customer is seeking a certain level of value or utility from the product or service, but there is an implicit trade-off between that value and the price charged. In this way shoppers in the UK have a wide choice before them. At one end of the spectrum they can buy their groceries at Harrods; at the other end they can choose the no-frills approach of Kwik-Save or Price-Rite.

In industrial service markets the same principles of price/value optimization apply; the only difference is that professional buyers are likely to use formalized evaluation techniques, such as **value analysis** to help them to reach their purchase decision.

CONVENIENCE/AVAILABILITY

It has long been recognized that these factors can play a key role in competitive markets. For example, in the UK, estate agents, who traditionally played the role of a 'marriage broker' between seller and buyer, now offer a complete range of ancillary services. The prospective property buyer can now literally complete his transaction by convenient 'one-stop shopping'. The recognition of this simple truth has led to many major financial service companies buying into estate agencies as distribution outlets for their products.

On the industrial front, manufacturers of high density polyurethane foam plastic which is used extensively in furniture upholstery often set up plants where there is a high concentration of furniture manufacturers. Not only does this reduce the high transport costs of shipping 'bubbles of air' around the country, which would be the case if they were to move blocks of plastic foam great distances, but it also virtually guarantees supplies 'on tap' for the furniture companies.

COMPANY OBJECTIVES

The selection of marketing channels must fit the requirements and capabilities of the company in addition to meeting the objectives of the customer. Essentially, we can look at two major aspects of the firm's viewpoint on its channel decision. The first is the **market** and the second is **institutional considerations**.

Here is an example of how market considerations might influence the choice of channel. Suppose we were marketing financial services to individuals in the high tax bracket. It would not be appropriate to set up a network of door-to-door salesmen and women. Instead we would be likely to choose an indirect channel of distribution which might rely upon intermediaries such as accountants and bank managers to connect us with our target customers. Clearly we would also be faced with making decisions regarding geographical coverage and penetration of our market, but these decisions are far less difficult to make once we are clear about our distribution channels.

Institutionally, we should be concerned with issues such as image and appropriateness of the channel. For example, if we produced top quality goods with a somewhat élitist image, then we would be obliged to seek distribution channels which would be consistent with this image. It would be counter-productive to do anything less.

MARKETING STRATEGIES

Let us consider a simple distribution channel as shown below:

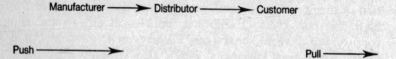

The manufacturer has two main marketing strategies open to him if he wants to maximize the flow of his goods through the channel.

Push Strategy   Here the manufacturer would focus his attention on the distributor and use an armoury of different approaches to 'sell-in' more of his products. He might use his field sales force, advertising and special promotions aimed at the distributor and his special incentive schemes. The use of 'trade marketing' whereby the manufacturer works closely with the distributor in developing joint marketing programmes, has become widespread in recent years.

Pull Strategy   Here the focus of attention would be the customer, and the objective of the strategy would be to stimulate the level of demand so that the distributor would be encouraged to stock the product. Marketing techniques used could include TV advertising, national press advertising and promotions, and in-store demonstrations and exhibitions.

In practice, most manufacturers would probably use a combination of push and pull strategies consistent with their marketing objectives and their capabilities.

WORKING WITH INTERMEDIARIES

One of the problems with indirect marketing channels – that is, those which involve intermediaries – is that they generally lead to a loss of close contact with the market place and some loss of control over key areas such as customer service policy. Also, by implication, there is a loss of margin for the firm in that intermediaries absorb some of the margin that otherwise could have been available to either the company or the customer.

On the other hand, intermediaries are often the only means of providing wider distribution without incurring the considerable costs of maintaining a direct marketing channel. The middleman performs a very necessary function in many markets by consolidating what might be many small shipments, comprising the products of several producers, to multiple customers. This important role is illustrated in Figure 11.2.

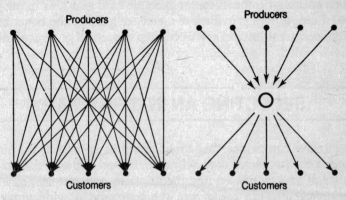

Figure A   Direct distribution   Figure B   Indirect distribution

**Figure 11.2   Direct Distribution and Indirect Distribution.
Direct and Indirect Modes of Shipments**

Figure 11.2(A) represents a 'nightmare' in terms of transport costs alone, regardless of the additional administrative costs for handling a multitude of paperwork. In contrast, Figure 11.2(B) provides a more economic model. Moreover, the intermediary can often generate extra sales. He could, for example, be an electrical wholesaler who buys in cable of all types and ratings, plugs and sockets, electrical fittings, tools and accessories – everything in fact, that the local electrical contractors could require. When the customer orders he specifies a job lot – the requirements to rewire a row of houses, for example – and the wholesaler assembles this 'package', in doing so adds value. This is the concept of a 'value-added distributor'. Another example would be an office furnishings distributor who buys in cupboards and desks as 'flat-pack' units and assembles them before delivery to his customers. Clearly the manufacturer is saved the costs of running an assembly department and he can ship flat-packs far more economically than he could assembled furniture. By taking over assembly functions and reducing transport costs the intermediary can justify a larger margin on his transactions with the manufacturer.

The intermediary is not always a wholesaler, and sometimes this function is performed by a distribution service company. Such specialist companies, for example NFC and TNT in the UK and Europe, will provide the means of gaining the benefits of large-scale distribution at a fraction of the cost of going it alone.

SELECTING AN INTERMEDIARY

For many companies this could prove to be one of the most important decisions they will ever make. Without doubt, an efficient and motivated intermediary can be a priceless asset; a lacklustre also-ran could ruin the company. A wide range of factors could influence the choice decision. Figure 11.3 below shows the result of a recent survey that was conducted in a sample of UK firms, regarding what influenced their choice of intermediary. These factors are listed in order of rank, with the most important at the top of the list:

Criteria	Ranking UK
Knowledge of the market	1
Market coverage	2
Enthusiasm for the product	3
Number and quality of sales personnel	4
Knowledge of product	5
Frequency of sales calls	6
Previous success/track record	7
Costs involved	8
Extent of dealing with competitors	9
Service and stocking facilities	10
Quality of service staff	11
Executive's career history	12

Figure 11.3   Intermediary Selection Criteria

Clearly, these results underline that many of the key selection criteria relate to the intermediaries' marketing expertise and strength 'on the ground'. However, others would add these further considerations to this list and suggest that they should also figure in any selection process:

▶ Is the intermediary creditworthy?
▶ Does he create the right image?
▶ Are his policies regarding inventory and customer service compatible with ours?
▶ Are his total promotion activities and budgets what we would expect for success?
▶ Is his location consistent with our overall distribution strategy?

And perhaps the most important of all:

▶ Is he someone we can trust and with whom we could develop a good working relationship?

If the answer to the last question is negative then all the other criteria are largely redundant, because the secret of success is to select intermediaries who in effect become business partners. Implicit in this is that the relationship between the parties be conducted in an open and mature manner.

RELATIONSHIPS WITH INTERMEDIARIES

At a recent in-company conference, to which, for the first time, a manufacturer's overseas agents had been invited, discussion focused on communications. It is sad to report that the agents, to a man, claimed that the only time they ever had a visit from representatives of the British company was 'when things went wrong'. Not only that, they also felt that they were kept 'in the dark' regarding future plans and new products.

The company in question was to be commended for taking such a bold step in organizing this conference as a means of integrating the agents more fully into the organization. Before they could begin to improve relationships they had to discover how they were perceived by the agents. The impression created by the company was not what they intended and, by seeming to focus on negative parts of the relationship, they had caused the agents to develop a defensive attitude. Instead of trust, they had bred distrust.

The conference did in fact provide both the company and the agents with the opportunity to bring many issues into the open and to work through them amicably. Indeed, the event proved to be a watershed in the company's relationship with its overseas representatives.

So how can a company build a good relationship with an intermediary? Here are some tried and tested suggestions:

▶ **Understand the distributor's needs and problems** – this means getting out and talking to them, and not just when things go wrong. One company insists that its own sales representatives spend a set number of days 'working on the counter' in the distributors.

▶ **Learn from distributors' experiences** – monitor and feed back the information about common problems, market information, current trends and so on.

▶ **Conduct market research studies** – get distributors to provide annual appraisals of the service you provide them with and make recommendations about improvements. Alternatively, conduct customer surveys and share results with distributors to enable them to increase sales.

▶ **Create a distributor panel** – have a small group of specially selected distributors meet at regular intervals to use as a sounding board for future policies and to get feedback on current issues.

▶ **Involve distributors in inputs to company's marketing plan** – this is likely to get them committed to those parts of the plan that make an impact upon distribution.

▶ **Establish two-way communications** – at many different levels, for example director to director, salesman to salesman, clerk to clerk.

▶ **Demonstrate commitment to distributor** – refer customer enquiries and requests to the distributor and don't open up competing distributorships in his territory.

EFFECTIVENESS OF CHANNEL INTERMEDIARIES

Since the success of the manufacturer is heavily dependent on the effective performance of the intermediary, it is necessary to have a general framework against which to asses performance. In recent years the concept of *performance auditing* of distributors has been increasingly used by marketers. One way of doing this is to monitor outlets on a day-to-day basis, keeping check of their sales, either in total or through the range. This information can be useful as a rough control mechanism for management, but a detailed performance audit will go further than this. Here are some of the elements which should be reviewed:

1. SALES PERFORMANCE

i)   Current sales compared with historical sales
ii)   Sales compared with other channel members
iii) Sales compared with target sales
iv)   Sales growth trends

2. INVENTORY MAINTENANCE

i)   Levels compared to contractual (if any) arrangements
ii)   Levels through the range
iii)   Levels compared with market trends
iv)   Number of 'stock-out' situations
v)   Levels of competing stocks
vi)   Condition of inventory and facilities
vii)   Old stock on hand/attempts to shift it
viii) Stockkeeping records/control efficiency

3. ATTITUDE

i)   Enthusiasm/motivation of staff
ii)   General housekeeping
iii) Displays of products/sales material
iv)   Number of suggestions/queries initiated by distributor

4. COMPETITION

i)   Competition from other intermediaries compared with sales figures
ii)   Competition from other product lines stocked by intermediary

5. GENERAL GROWTH PROSPECTS

i)   Does track record indicate future growth? In pace with that projected for region, trade area, etc?

ii)   How does current performance compare with local yard-sticks?

iii) Is intermediary's organization expanding/shrinking? Why?

iv)   What record of investment in his business does intermediary have?

v)   What are the qualifications/experience of his staff?

vi)   What continuity is likely? For example, through management succession plans and health of key staff members.

vii) What evidence of adaptability to change?

viii) What are the intermediary's own business plans? How does he see the future outlook?

Having developed a set of criteria like these, it ought to be possible to evaluate the performance and longer-term prospects of any distributor. More accurate assessment, for comparative purposes, can be attained by weighting the individual criteria according to their importance. Also 'point-scoring' techniques can be used in conjunction with the weighting if they serve a clear purpose.

The performance audit not only provides the marketer with valuable information about the current effectiveness of the distribution channel, but it also establishes the basis upon which a distributor development strategy can be formed.

DEALER DEVELOPMENT STRATEGY

Too often a manufacturer sees himself as *selling to* rather than *selling through* the intermediary. No small wonder then that, with this perception, manufacturers are frequently dissatisfied with distributor performance.

Four areas have been identified as being sources and symptoms of problems common amongst various types of intermediaries. These should be closely monitored by the manufacturer, and are as follows:

1 **Diversification** – the intermediary is spreading his limited resources over too wide a range of products or markets.
2 **Capitalization** – there is inadequate funding/cash flow to sustain the business unless tough management decisions are made.
3 **Market Share** – falling market share can be a valuable pointer to the fact that the intermediary is failing to be competitive.
4 **Attitude** – how positive is the attitude of the intermediary to our company and its products?

In addition, field sales personnel should monitor the dealer's performance in:

- Financial management
- Sales personnel training
- Planning
- Network management
- Market development
- Sales management

It is in these areas that huge strides can be made in terms of dealer development. However, few manufacturers have a sales force of sufficient calibre to play this role, either to identify needs or to provide business counselling.

Some enlightened manufacturers have set up separate specialist teams of advisers to fulfil the dealer development role, thereby overcoming what might be seen in some quarters as a dilution of the field sales activity. The results stemming from this type of investment indicate that distributors become more flexible, adaptive and successful, thus safeguarding the manufacturer's longer term strategic interests. In addition, considerable goodwill can be generated by this approach to dealer development.

It must be remembered that dealer development can be costly, and the decisions regarding the depth and breadth of such improvement activities should not be taken lightly. However, there is an alternative approach to securing more effective control of a distribution channel and this is through a process called **vertical integration**.

VERTICAL INTEGRATION

This is a common phenomenon in marketing channels. Such integration could involve a company merging with or absorbing those firms who are its sources of supply (**backward** integration), or taking similar steps to gain control of those intermediaries closer to its markets (**forward** integration). Such a movement, either forward or backward, can sometimes be accomplished without taking over the ownership of the firms involved.

For example, Marks and Spencer, the retail organization in the UK, can, through its massive buying power, exert considerable control over its suppliers. When you sell 100 per cent of your output to one customer, you are to all intents and purposes owned by them. The motor-car industry has a similar relationship with some of its component suppliers.

Even where integration through ownership or control does not exist, institutional pressures within the channel can be considerable. Who should hold the inventory? In what quantities? How should the available margin be split? Can intermediaries lower down the chain be relied upon to follow through on the desired marketing strategy and promotional plans? The possibilities for conflict are considerable, and prospects are very much enhanced if each level of the channel attempts to maximize its own return. In situations like this, maximization of one's return can only be achieved at the expense of others.

Conflict, and the resulting likelihood of a reduced return being experienced by all, can to a large extent be eliminated if someone within the distribution chain exercises a leadership role. It can therefore be in the manufacturer's interest to set out deliberately to take the initiative and strive for channel leadership, thereby bringing a sense of order and fairness to what could be a volatile and mutually destructive situation. However, leadership can only be sustained if the manufacturer can back up his stance with economic power, or with a unique, highly desirable product which is in great demand.

It is quite conceivable that channel leadership can pass to anyone else in the chain. The example of Marks and Spencer mentioned above demonstrates how a retailer can take the leadership role. Similarly wholesalers, distributors or agents can, if they exploit their power according to their circumstances, influence the channel 'politics' to their advantage.

SUMMARY

Getting products or services to the market is a regulated dimension of the marketing mix. It is vital for the success of the company that customers should have access to the product or service through channels that meet their requirements as well as the company's.

Development relationships with channel intermediaries based on partnership can be a powerful means of building competitive advantage. The aim should be to develop marketing programmes which are attractive to all members of the distribution channel and not just to end users.

CHAPTER 12

Customer Service Strategy

ONE OF THE BEST-SELLING management books of recent years, *In Search of Excellence* by T. J. Peters and R. H. Waterman (Harper & Row 1982) has alerted managers and others to the simple truth that customers create sales, and that the most successful companies are those which create the most customers *and keep them*. It may seem strange that such obvious axioms should provide the basis for a book that appears on executives' shelves around the world. Nevertheless, it has taken a major recession to focus many organizations' attention upon the customer more sharply than was often the case in the past. The lessons of *In Search of Excellence* extend beyond a concern for customer relations, but it is perhaps in this field that the greatest scope for improvement lies for the 'non-excellent' company.

Two factors have perhaps contributed more than anything else to the growing importance of customer service as a competitive weapon. One is the continual development of customer expectations: in almost every market the customer is now more demanding, more 'sophisticated' than he or she was, say, thirty years ago. Likewise in industrial purchasing situations we find that buyers expect higher levels of service from vendors, particularly as more manufacturers convert to 'Just-in-Time' manufacturing systems.

The second factor is the slow but inexorable transition towards 'commodity' type markets. By this we mean that the power of the 'brand' is increasingly diminishing as technologies of competing products converge, thus making product differences difficult to perceive – at least to the average buyer. Take for example the current state of the personal computer market. There are so many competing models which in reality are substitutable as far as most would-be purchasers are concerned. Unless one is particularly expert it is difficult to use product features as the basis for choice.

Faced with a situation such as this, the customer may be influenced by price or by 'image' perceptions, but overriding these aspects may well be 'availability' – in other words, 'Is the product in stock; can I have it now?' Since availability is clearly one aspect of customer service, we are in effect saying that the power of customer service is paramount in a situation such as this. Nor is it only in consumer markets that we are encountering the force of customer service as a determinant of purchase; as we shall note shortly, there is much evidence from industrial markets of the same phenomenon. On top of all this we have seen the growth of the 'service' sector in many western economies. Over 50 per cent of the GNP of the United Kingdom is derived from the non-manufacturing sector and every year the percentage increases. The marketing of services should not call for any different philosophy from that underlying the marketing of physical products. Rather it calls for an even greater emphasis upon availability, particularly given the 'perishability' of the service product. Nevertheless, both service and tangible products are increasingly dependent for their success upon the suppliers' ability to enhance their appeal through the 'added value' of customer service.

WHAT IS CUSTOMER SERVICE?

It is sometimes suggested that the role of customer service is to provide 'time and place utility' in the transfer of goods and services between buyer and seller. Put another way, there is no value in a product or service until it is in the hands of the customer or consumer. It follows that making the product or service 'available' is what, in essence, the distribution function of the business in all about. **Availability** is in itself a complex concept, affected by a galaxy of factors which together constitute customer service. For example, these factors might include delivery frequency and reliability, stock levels and order cycle time as they have an impact upon availability. Indeed, it could be said that customer service is ultimately determined by the interaction of all those factors that affect the process of making products and services available to the buyer.

In practice, many companies have varying views of customer service. A major study of customer service practices found that, in the industries surveyed, a range of views existed as to what constituted 'customer service'. Some of the definitions of service they encountered are shown below.

'All activities required to accept, process, deliver and bill customer orders and to follow up on any activity that erred'

'Timeliness and reliability of getting materials to customers in accordance with the customer's expectation'

'A complex of activities involving all areas of the business which combine to deliver and invoice the company's products in a fashion that is perceived as satisfactory by the customer and which advances our company's objectives'

'Total order entry, all communications with customers, all shipping, all freight, all invoicing and total control of repair of products'

'Timely and accurate delivery of products ordered by customers with accurate follow-up and inquiry response, including timely delivery of invoice'

What all these definitions have in common is that they are concerned with relationships at the buyer/seller interface. This same study suggested that customer service could be examined under three headings:

(1)   Pre-transaction elements;
(2)   transaction elements;
(3)   post-transaction elements.

The *pre-transaction* elements of customer service relate to corporate policies or programmes; for example, written statements
of service policy, adequacy of organizational structure and system flexibility. The *transaction* elements are those customer service variables directly involved in performing the physical
distribution function: for example, product availability, order
cycle time, order status information and delivery reliability. The
post-transaction elements of customer service are generally supportive of the product while in use: for instance, product war-
ranty, parts and repair service, procedures for customer
complaints and product replacement.

Many commentators have defined various elements of customer service, but the most commonly occurring seem to be:

Order Cycle Time
Consistency and Reliability of Delivery
Inventory Availability
Order-size Constraints
Ordering Convenience
Delivery Times and Flexibility
Invoicing Procedures and Accuracy
Claims Procedure
Condition of Goods
Salesman's Visits
Order Status Information

In any particular product/market situation some of these elements will be more important than others, and there may be
factors other than those listed above which have a significance
in a specific market. Indeed, it is essential to understand customer service in terms of the differing requirements of different
market segments and to recognize that no universally appropriate list of elements exists; each market serviced by the company
will attach different importance to different service elements.

It is because of the multivariate nature of customer service and because of the widely differing requirements of specific markets that it is essential for any business to have a clearly identified policy towards customer service. It is surprising perhaps that so few companies have defined policies on customer service – let alone an organization flexible enough to manage and control that service – when it is considered that service can be the most important element in the company's marketing mix. A considerable body of evidence exists which supports the view that if the product or service is not available at the time the customer requires it, and a close substitute is available, then the sale will be lost to the competition. Even in markets where brand loyalty is strong a stock-out might be sufficient to trigger off brand switching. In industrial markets, too, the same pressures on purchasing source loyalty seem to be at work. One survey of industrial purchasing officers found that distribution service was considered second in importance only to product quality as a deciding criterion for vendor selection. Moreover, more than one-third of these purchasing officers indicated that they would cancel the order if it were not available for shipment when ordered.

In the light of this and other evidence it is suggested that there are three basic requirements for the management of customer service:

(1) Define an overall company philosophy of customer service in terms of attitude, organization and responsibilities;

(2) develop internal standards for customer service based on careful studies that have explored the quantitative trade-offs between various levels of customer service and the costs of achieving such levels, so as to identify the most profitable policy for each customer segment;

(3) inform customers what they might expect by way of customer service (perhaps in more general terms than the company defines its policies internally).

To achieve the most effective deployment of corporate resources in developing a customer service policy along the lines broadly defined above, a number of prerequisites exist:

(1)   The differing perceptions of the various parties to the pur-
      chasing decision in terms of customer service must be
      recognized;
(2)   the trade-off potential between the various components of
      the customer service mix must be evaluated;
(3)   the unique customer service requirement of each product/
      channel/market segment must be identified.

If cost-effective customer service policies are to be successfully
developed and implemented within the firm it is imperative that
a formalized logic is adopted and closely followed. Customer
service is too important and too costly to be left to chance.

THE COMPONENTS OF CUSTOMER SERVICE

It is a common fault in marketing to fail to realize that customers
do not always attach the same importance to product attributes
as the vendor. Thus it sometimes happens that products are
promoted on attributes or features that in reality are less important to the customer than other aspects. A floor cleaner that is
sold on its ease of application, for example, will not succeed
unless 'ease of application' is a salient benefit sought by the
customer. If 'shine' or the need for less frequent cleaning are
important to the customer then we might be better advised to
feature those aspects in our promotion. The same principle
applies in customer service: which aspects of service are rated
most highly by the customer? If a company places its emphasis
upon stock availability, but the customer regards delivery
reliability more highly, it may not be allocating its resources in a
way likely to maximize sales. Alternatively, a company that
realizes that its customers place a higher value on completeness
of orders than they do on, say, regular scheduled deliveries
could develop this to its advantage.

Thus there is a great premium to be placed on gaining an

insight into the factors that influence buyer behaviour and, in the context of customer service, which particular elements are seen by the customer to be the most important. The use of market research techniques in customer service has lagged behind their application in such areas as product testing and advertising research, yet the importance of researching the service needs of customers is just as great as, for example, the need to understand the market reaction to price. In fact, it is possible to apply standard, proven market research methods to gain considerable insight into the ways that customers will react to customer service.

The first step in research of this type is to identify the relative source of influence on the purchase decision. If we are selling components to a manufacturer, for example, who will make the decision on the source of supply? This is not always an easy question to answer as, in many cases, there will be several people involved. The purchasing manager of the company to whom we are selling may only be acting as an agent for others within the firm. In other cases his influence will be much greater. Alternatively, if we are manufacturing products for sale through retail outlets, is the decision to stock made centrally by a retail chain or by individual store managers? The answers to these questions can often by supplied by the sales force. The sales representative should know from experience who the decision-makers are.

Given that a clear indication of the source of decision-making power can be gained, the customer service researcher at least knows *who* to research. The question still remains, however: which elements of the vendor's total marketing offering have what effect on the purchase decision? Ideally, once the decision-making unit in a specific market has been identified, an initial, small-scale research programme should be initiated which would be based on personal interviews with a representative sample of buyers. The purpose of these interviews is to elicit *in the language of the customer* first, the importance they attach to customer service *vis-à-vis* the other marketing mix elements such as price, product quality and promotion and second, the specific importance they attach to the individual components of customer service.

CUSTOMER SERVICE TRADE-OFFS

Given that through research we can identify the appropriate elements of the customer service mix for the specific market segments we are targetting, how do we decide on where to place the emphasis?

Whilst ideally the customer would like to have the best of everything, for example 100 per cent availability from stock, twenty-four-hour delivery, reliable on-time deliveries and emergency ordering, it will probably not be cost-effective for the supplier to offer such a service.

In the customer service decision therefore we are forced to make **trade-offs**. The question is what elements of service to trade off against each other? A simple analogy is the decision to buy a car. One person might ideally like a car with the appearance of a Lamborghini and the performance of a Ferrari, but with the miles-per-gallon of a Fiat, the spaciousness of a Volvo estate and perhaps at the price of a Nissan! Clearly not all these things are achievable in one car. The actual purchase decision has to be based upon a trade-off, or a series of trade-offs. The final purchase decision can be viewed therefore as a reflection of the importance that an individual attaches to each aspect of the purchase, i.e. appearance, performance and price.

The technique of trade-off measurement is discussed more fully in Chapter 13 where pricing decisions are discussed. However, the analogy with the customer service decision is a good one. The marketing decision-maker needs to research the service priorities of the company's target markets and to assemble a customer service package which is optimal for that market and for the company.

DESIGNING THE CUSTOMER SERVICE PACKAGE

To compete effectively in any market requires the ability to develop some differential advantage over competing companies and their product or service offerings. Sometimes the differential advantage may be in terms of distinctive product attributes or related benefits as perceived by the customer. On other occasions it may be price or, alternatively, the product may be promoted in such a way that it acquires a distinctive image in the eyes of the market. In just the same way, customer service can be used to develop a differential advantage and, indeed, there can be a major benefit to the company in using customer service in this way. For example in competitive markets, where real product differentiation may be difficult to establish and where to compete on price would only lead to profit erosion, it makes sense to switch the marketing emphasis to customer service.

The current battle in the office copier market provides a case in point. Xerox, the early leaders in this field, have found that competition has become increasingly severe from products which, to the potential customer at least, seem to offer the same product benefits. Pressure on margins is considerable and price cutting would not provide a lasting solution for Xerox. Instead, they have switched the emphasis to service. Their advertisements underline this point. A recent advertisement in the business press for Xerox copiers stated:

'Because the best way to get new customers is to keep your current ones happy, Xerox offers the largest service force in the business. Over 30,000 men and women worldwide.

'Parts inventories and parts distribution systems are all part of our job. That's why we have distribution centres around the globe.

'So, chances are, our technical representatives will always

have what you need where you need it. Whenever possible, we standardize parts so that they're interchangeable from country to country. That way we can take better care of our copiers and our customers.'

Similar use of service as a marketing tool has been made by companies such as Digital Equipment and Caterpillar who have built up commanding positions in their markets and maintained them through the effective use of customer service.

Earlier it was stressed that it is important to establish those components of the total customer service mix which have the greatest impact on the buyer's perception of us as a supplier. This thinking needs to be carried right through into design of the customer service offering. This offering can best be described as the customer service 'package', for it will most likely contain more than one component.

The design of the package will need to take account of the differing needs of different market segments so that the resources allocated to customer service can be used in the most cost-effective way. Too often a uniform, blanket approach to service is adopted by companies, which does not distinguish between the real requirements of different customer types. This can lead to customers being offered too little service or too much.

The precise composition of the customer service package for any market segment should depend on the results of the market research described earlier. It will be determined by budgetary and cost constraints. If alternative packages can be identified which seem to be equally acceptable to the buyer, it makes sense to choose the least costly alternative. For example, it may be possible to identify a highly acceptable customer service package which enables the emphasis to be switched away from a high level of inventory availability towards improved customer communication. Once a cost-effective package has been identified in this way it should become a major part of the company's marketing mix – 'using service to sell' is the message here. If the market segments we serve are sensitive to service, then the service package must be actively promoted. One way in which this can be achieved with great effect is by stressing the impact on the *customer's* costs of the improved service package: for example, what improved reliability will do for his own stock planning; what shorter lead times will do for his inventory levels and how improved ordering and invoicing systems will lead to fewer errors. All too often the customer will not appreciate the impact that improved service offered by the supplier can have on his, the customer's, 'bottom line'.

STRATEGIES FOR SERVICE

Beyond the simple presentation of a marketing message based around an improved customer service package lies the opportunity to develop tailor-made service offerings, particularly to key accounts, based on 'negotiated' service levels. The idea here is that no two customers are alike, either in terms of their requirements or, specifically, in terms of their profitability to the supplier. One UK-based company in the consumer electronics field identified that whilst three of its major customers were roughly equivalent in terms of their annual sales value, there were considerable differences in the costs generated by each. For example, one customer required delivery to each of its 300-plus retail outlets, whilst the others took delivery at one central warehouse. Similarly, one company paid within thirty days of receiving the invoice; the others took nearer to forty days to pay. Again, one of the three was found to place twice as many 'emergency' orders as the others. Careful analysis of the true costs showed that the profitability of the three customers differed by over 20 per cent. Yet each customer received the same value-related discounts and the same level of customer service!

Conducting such a 'customer account profitability' analysis can provide the supplier with not only the basis on which to negotiate price but also a basis for 'negotiating' service. Whilst companies in the United States tend to be familiar with the importance of relating price discounts to customer-related costs, because of the Robinson-Patman legislation, it is rarely used elsewhere in a positive way. Thus, whilst the concept of paying more for an airmail letter than a surface letter is well established, it is less common to find a supplier offering different 'qualities' of service at different prices. Interestingly enough, the business manager who accepts the difference between First Class, Business Class and Tourist Class on the plane he takes to see his customer might never think of how that same principle could be applied to his own business!

DEVELOPING A CUSTOMER SERVICE CULTURE

In our eagerness to develop a customer service strategy it would be a mistake to focus exclusively on the 'external' dimension of service, i.e. customer perceptions. Of equal importance is the 'internal' dimension, i.e. how do our own people, our managers and workforce, view service? What is their attitude to customers? Do they share the same concept and definition of service as our customers?

It would be a truism to suggest that ultimately a company's performance is limited more by the vision and the quality of its people than it is by market factors or competitive forces. However it is perhaps only belatedly that we have come to recognize this.

Much has been written and spoken about 'corporate culture'. We have come to recognize that the shared values held throughout the organization can provide a powerful driving force and focus for all its actions. More often than not, though, we have to admit that most organizations lack a cohesive and communicated culture. Even if there is a defined philosophy of the business, it may be little understood. This lack of shared values can have an impact upon the company in many ways and particularly upon its approach to customer service.

One viable way to assess the customer 'climate' within the

firm is to take the temperature by means of an employee survey. One such approach that has been developed begins with identifying all those personnel who have a direct or indirect impact upon customer service. A useful device here is to consider the complete 'order to cash' cycle and to ensure that we have identified all those people involved in all the different departments that influence the order flow. The focus of the survey should be upon these key people's perceptions of service: what do **they** think is important to the customers? And how do they think we perform, service-wise?

What quite often emerges from these internal surveys is that different employees hold quite different views as to what constitutes customer service. Similarly, they may often overrate the company's actual performance compared with the customer's own rating. Making such comparisons between customers' perceptions and the employees' perceptions can provide a powerful means of identifying customer service problems and their sources.

This 'audit' of internal perceptions and attitudes towards service can form the basis of a programme of action aimed at developing a customer service culture. However, such a process, which almost inevitably will involve a major reorientation within the firm, cannot work without the total commitment of top management. The service culture must grow outwards from the boardroom and the chief executive must be its greatest champion.

Within the customer service function one very practical step is to set up the equivalent of a 'quality circle'. Such a scheme might involve looking at the total order-processing and invoicing cycle and selecting individuals from all the departments or sections involved. This group would meet at least once a week with the expressed objective of seeking improvements to customer service from whatever possible source. A further task that might usefully be given to this group is the handling of all customer complaints that relate to service.

Underpinning all of these initiatives should be a company-wide education programme. Increasingly, more and more organizations have come to recognize the key role that in-company education can have in developing a sense of shared values. Furthermore, because it is a basic tenet of psychology that attitude change must precede behaviour change, education can lead to a measurably improved performance. One of the best examples recently has come from British Airways, whose 'Putting People First' campaign has resulted in a significant change in employee behaviour and thus in the company's performance in the market place.

SUMMARY

Customer service is perhaps the most powerful dimension in the marketing mix of any company. In one sense the development of targetted customer service strategies is only the logical extension of the marketing concept. In other words customer service is about recognizing the specific needs of the customer and developing a strategy that focuses the resources of the organization towards meeting those needs.

As such, the development of a customer service strategy requires a corporate culture that extends beyond slogans and involves all levels of the organization in working together to ensure that, for customers, doing business with your company becomes a regular habit.

CHAPTER 13

Pricing Strategy

T HE PRICING DECISION is one of the most important issues that
the marketing executive has to face. Its impact will usually be
reflected in the quantity of the product sold, the contribution to
profits that the product will make and, even more crucially, the
strategic position of the product in the market place. In addition,
in a multi-product company it is frequently the case that a
decision taken on the price of one product will have implications
for other products in the range. It is not surprising, therefore,
that much has been written and discussed on the subject of
pricing and that it has created considerable controversy as to
how the price decision should be made.

Frequently this controversy has centred around the role that
costs should play in determining price. Traditionally, the price
of a product is based upon the identification of the costs associated with manufacturing, marketing and distributing the product with the subsequent addition of a mark-up to reflect the
desired profitability. Such an approach has been criticized on a
number of counts. Firstly, it can prove to be extremely difficult
in practice to identify the true costs of a product. In so many
cases the company will have joint costs and fixed costs which
can only be allocated to a specific product on an arbitrary basis.
Secondly, such a cost-plus approach to pricing ignores the
demand sensitivity of the market place. It may be that a price
determined on a cost-plus basis is higher than the market place
will accept or perhaps it may even be lower than the price that

the market can bear. Attempts have been made to overcome these problems by using a **marginal cost** approach rather than a **full cost** approach so that the pricing decision becomes one of attempting to maximize the contribution that the product will make – i.e. the difference between the *price* and the direct and attributable *costs*.

The basic problem with any cost-based approach to pricing is that it implicitly assumes that the customer is interested in **our** costs, whereas in reality the customer is only concerned with **his own** costs. This can be expressed another way – the customer seeks to acquire benefits and it is in order to acquire those benefits that he is prepared to pay a certain price. Seen from this perspective, the company making the price decision is faced with the need to identify the value – in the customer's eyes – of the benefits inherent in their product. The costs of that product thus become irrelevant to the pricing decision even though they are highly pertinent to the profitability of that decision. In other words *costs determine profits*, not price.

BENEFITS AND PRICE

Throughout this book we have suggested that in any purchase decision the customer is seeking to acquire 'benefits'. A product must bring with it the promise of performing certain tasks, of solving identified problems, or even of providing specific gratifications. Thus the product is not bought for the particular components or materials that go into its manufacture *per se* but rather it is bought for what, as an entity, it can do.

The implication of the benefit concept from a pricing point of view is that the company must first identify the benefits that the customer perceives the product to offer and then attempt to ascertain the value that the customer places upon them. The key issue here is that it is the customer **perception** that is important. It may be, for example, that two competing companies offer products which are technically identical to all intents and purposes and yet one company can command a premium price. Why should this be? It may be that additional benefits offered by one company in the way of technical advice or after-sales service are perceived to be superior to those offered by another. Or it may just be that the 'image' of that company is seen as superior. Whatever the reason, there are many cases of this type of 'differential advantage' which cannot be explained simply in technical or quality terms. One study looked at the price advantage that IBM have traditionally had in computers and found that IBM machines are priced substantially above competing machines of equal performance; this price differential appears to be independent of machine size. Since a substantial percentage of users are still willing to buy IBM machines even though their relative price is high, the implication is that IBM offers customers something to induce them to pay a substantial premium for an IBM machine.

The study identified that this price premium was achieved not through superior hardware or technology, but rather through the image that IBM had for quality, reliability and customer support.

Another way to look at this price advantage is to think of the maximum price at which the product could be sold as being the sum of two elements. Firstly there is the 'commodity price' element; this is the base price for the generic product which would be determined by supply and demand in the market place. On top of this should then be added the 'premium price differential', which reflects the totality of the benefits that the customer perceives will be acquired through purchase of that product. Figure 13.1 shows this concept diagramatically overleaf.

The existence of this 'premium price differential' can only be explained in terms of perceived benefits. The task of the pricing decision-maker therefore becomes one of identifying these benefits and placing a customer value upon them. It is in reality a 'bundle' of benefits and so the first step in this suggested approach to pricing is to 'unbundle' the product and identify the individual benefit components which together constitute the totality.

Figure 13.1   The Components of Price

PRICE AND VALUE

Every purchase by a customer is a 'trade-off'. The trade-off is
between the value that the customer places on the acquisition of
the product versus the costs that are involved in that acquisition,
plus any subsequent costs that might be involved, for example
maintenance or upgrading costs.

There is nothing new in this idea. Economists have long talked
about the concept of 'utility'. Whilst some of their ideas on the
relationship between price and demand may seem naïve there is
nevertheless an important message for the pricing decision-
maker in the recognition that price must be seen in terms of
value.

The Victorian economist Alfred Marshall was the first really to
articulate the idea of price as a reflection of the value placed on a
product or service by the consumer. He developed the concept of
the **demand curve** which simply stated that the higher the price
charged for a product the lower will be the demand for it as
potential consumers see the price exceed the product's perceived

value to them. It is interesting to note that this concept suggests that the price charged for a product may be lower than the value placed upon it by some customers. This is the notion of a 'consumer surplus'. In Figure 13.2 a demand curve for a particular product is represented and the price currently prevailing in the market place is P_1.

Figure 13.2   The Demand Curve

It can be seen from the diagram that there are some consumers, albeit fewer in number, who would actually be prepared to pay a higher price. The number of such consumers obviously declines the higher the price that is charged. The consumers who fall into this category are actually paying a price less than the value they perceive they are gaining through purchasing the product. They are enjoying a consumer surplus. At the same time, it can be seen from the same diagram that the price P_1 is actually higher than the supplier's long-run marginal cost. In other words in this case there is a 'surplus' accruing to the supplier as well. This analysis is an over-simplification of the real world but it might be a useful focus for the price decision-maker to think of his problem along the lines suggested by Figure 13.3 overleaf.

The pricing problem can be seen in this way as an attempt by the supplier to achieve the greatest possible 'surplus' over long-run marginal cost whilst still pricing no higher than the perceived value placed on the product by potential customers.

Figure 13.3   Consumer and Supplier Surplus

An alternative way of looking at this is to see the problem in terms of the need to identify what value the target market places upon the product and then to convert that value into a market price. The first step to solving this problem is to recognize that there will be different groupings of customers with different perceptions of a product's value. These groupings are in effect **market segments**. Thus we might identify a specific segment of the market that seeks certain benefits from a product and values them at a particular level.

However, it is not sufficient just to identify the perceived value of a product to the customers and then set a price equal to that value. Frequently there will be costs other than price that face the customer in acquiring that product. These additional costs over and above purchase price could include freight, installation, training, maintenance, service, spares support and other 'life cycle costs', as they are sometimes termed. In addition there may be perceived costs in terms of risk of product failure or, particularly in the case of consumer products, social and psychological risk.

From the customer's point of view therefore it can be argued that the decision to purchase is a trade-off between all costs involved on the one hand and the perceived benefits resulting from acquisition on the other. This relationship may be expressed as follows:

Highest Price The Customer Will Pay =
                        Perceived Benefits-Costs Other Than Price

Thus it can be seen that in the pricing decision it is as important to understand the cost structure of our potential customer as it is to know our own! It is essential to the pricing decision to recognize the total cost impact on the customer of the acquisition of our product. Even though the customer may not himself have fully evaluated the implication of the acquisition, the supplier will be better positioned to sell to the customer if these costs are known. The appropriate concept here is that of 'life cycle costs', which refers to all the customer costs that will be incurred by the customer from the acquisition of the product through to the end of its useful life. For example, in pricing a piece of numerical control equipment the manufacturer should identify the effects that the equipment will have on the customer's manufacturing economics, its likely life, any maintenance and upgrading costs and its disposal value if any.

Given a full analysis of the life cycle cost implications of the product, the pricing decision-maker can now focus attention upon the identification and quantification of the product's perceived benefits.

BENEFIT EVALUATION

One of the first attempts to break loose from the constraints of cost-oriented pricing and to seek instead to incorporate some recognition of perceived value was the technique developed by the Glacier Metal Company which they termed 'product-analysing pricing'. This attempted to build up a final price by identifying the physical features that go into the product and then to value these features in customer terms. The method was based upon a statistical analysis of previous prices obtained for similar products to provide quantified estimates of the relative contribution of each physical component to the final price. The analysis was limited as such to the physical attributes of the product and did not quantify non-physical benefits other than by talking loosely about the 'product surround'. Because of these limitations it did not provide the pricing decision-maker with the crucial information on customer evaluation of perceived product benefits – both physical and intangible. To do this we need to seek an alternative approach to benefit evaluation.

TRADE-OFF ANALYSIS

In recent years a number of developments have taken place in the fields of mathematical psychology and psychometrics which have great value in quantifying the relative importance that potential customers place upon the various attributes of a product. These techniques are based upon a type of trade-off analysis called 'conjoint measurement', a powerful device for quantifying the intangible as well as the physical benefits present in a product. The 'trade-off' approach to pricing follows a sequence of logical steps:

STEP 1:   IDENTIFICATION OF BENEFIT COMPONENTS

It is important to recognize that the potential customer for a product will have his/her own perceptions of the benefits contained within that product. To identify these perceived benefits it is necessary to conduct a limited, small-scale survey of potential and/or actual customers. The purpose of this study is to elicit the key features or benefits that are expected to be acquired as a result of using the product. Direct questioning can be used, such as, 'What is it that makes Brand X different from Brand Y?' More sophisticated procedures for elicitation of benefits exist but essentially they all have the same purpose: to draw from consumers their own perceptions of product features rather than the manufacturers'. So, in a study of customers for a new chemical compound, the following attributes might emerge:

Quality
Availability
Impact on customer's production economics
Storage conditions necessary
Technical assistance

The question is then: 'What relative value is placed upon each of these components?'

STEP 2: QUANTIFYING BENEFIT VALUES

Because a product is in effect the totality of its component attributes, a way must be found of separating these and measuring their individual value to the customer. It is here that conjoint analysis becomes particularly useful. Using the attributes identified in Step 1, the researcher presents to the sample of customers a variety of hypothetical products which contain different configurations of the previously identified attributes, each configuration having a different price. Thus, for the example of the chemical compound, the following hypothetical product configurations might be constructed:

Attribute	Product 1	Product 2
Quality	Impurities less than one part per million	Impurities less than ten parts per million
Availability	Make to order	Available from stock
Impact on customer's production economics	No impact	Improves usable output by 10 per cent
Storage conditions	Stable product, long shelf life	Requires high level storage environment
Technical assistance	Manufacturer provides high level technical advice	Weak
Price	£5 a pound	£5.50 a pound

Clearly there are many different combinations of attribute levels. Only two examples are given here but they will be sufficient to demonstrate the concept of trade-off. The question put to the survey respondents is: 'Given that the two alternative products above are available, which would you prefer?' Both products have their advantages and their disadvantages and the final choice will be based upon the trade-off of the plusses and minuses. By extending the questioning to include other configurations of the same attributes it is possible, using conjoint analysis, to produce a numerical 'weight' for each attribute which reflects the relative importance attached to each of the attributes in question. More specifically it enables the researcher to identify for each attribute the weight given to different **levels** of that attribute. Thus for 'quality' it will be possible to determine the extent by which 'impurities less than one part per million' is preferred over 'impurities less than ten parts per million' – or any level of impurity in the range under consideration.

However, the greatest advantage of using conjoint analysis in this context is that it also provides the researcher with **the relative utility of different price levels**. Thus we have a means of interpreting the price equivalence of differences in the perceived values of different combinations of product attributes. Step 3 describes this procedure.

STEP 3: DETERMINING THE PRICE EQUIVALENCE OF VALUE

The output of the conjoint analysis of the data collected in Step 2 might typically appear as in Figure 13.4 overleaf.

For each level of each attribute a 'utility' is computed and this can be graphed to give a visual indication of the importance of that attribute. More importantly, though, it enables the value of this arbitrary 'utility' measure to be given a price equivalence. It will be seen from Figure 13.4 that the difference in utility between a price of £5 and £5.50 is 0.25 (i.e. 1.00–0.75); thus the price equivalence of one unit of 'utility' is (£5.50–£5)/0.25, that is, £2.

Using this information we can say, for example, that a 10 per cent improvement in saleable output is worth a price difference of £1 per pound (£2 (1.00–0.5)). Again we can say that the benefit of a stable product with a long shelf life is worth an additional £0.5 per pound (£2 (0.75–0.5)) over a product requiring a high-level storage environment.

Given this information it is clear that the price decision-maker has a very powerful insight into the components of value in the customer's mind. The decision-maker can now also identify which product attributes have the biggest influence on value perception. In the case examined here, for example, availability and quality are seen as the two major components of value. A change from Level 2 to Level 1 in availability brings an increase in utility of 1.0 and a change from Level 2 to Level 1 in quality produces an increase in utility of 0.75 (worth £2 and £1.50 per pound respectively).

This information on the 'price-equivalence' of customer values can provide a basis for price determination which reflects the worth the market places upon our offer. Perhaps one of the most important features of the value-in-use approach which has been advocated here is that it focuses our attention upon

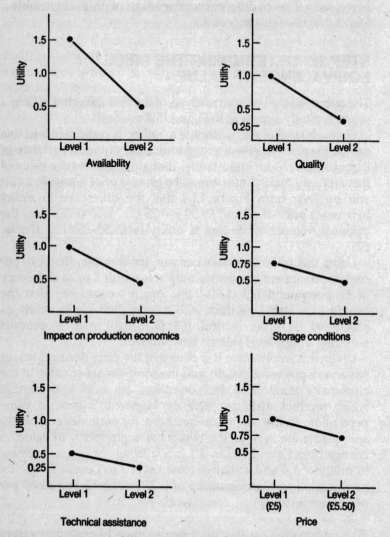

N.B. Level 1 corresponds to the lowest level identified in the study for each attribute;
      Level 2 corresponds to the highest level.

Figure 13.4   Graphical Output of Conjoint Analysis

customer perceptions of product attributes and away from the more narrow production-orientation of suppliers' costs. In this sense it is very much a market-oriented approach to pricing.

There are also certain strategic issues raised by this approach to pricing, particularly with regard to marketing communications. It is well known that in many product/market fields there is a definite relationship between the price obtained and the perception of quality on the part of the customer. In other words, where there is a perception of 'added values' then the demand/price relationship can be radically altered. Where added values are perceived to exist by the customer, the demand curve is, in effect, shifted to the right, as in Figure 13.5:

Key: D1D1   Original demand curve   Q1   Original demand
       D2D2   New demand curve   P2   New price
       P1   Original price   Q2   New demand

Figure 13.5   The Effect of Perceived Added-Values on the Demand Curve

So in this particular case the effect of these heightened perceptions of customer values has been to stimulate greater demand but at a higher price.

To make use of this fundamental model for profit improvement we must recognize two basic factors:

- ▶ **Perception** – to what extent does the customer/potential customer perceive that our product embodies certain attributes?
- ▶ **Value/utility** – to what extent does the customer/potential customer consider these attributes to be important in the purchase decision?

In the first case, if the perception of product performance falls below that of competitive products, what can be done? It may be that the problem is largely one of communication. Perhaps we have not been forceful enough in our attempts to inform the market about the strengths of our product or, if we have, the message still has not come across. Alternatively, it may be that our product is deficient in these attributes and it may thus be desirable to institute a programme of product improvement.

If, on the other hand, we identify that our product scores highly, but on attributes that are perhaps given less weight by the customer (i.e. their value/utility is lower), then we could downgrade the product on these attributes to improve overall profitability, or indeed reduce the price if appropriate. Likewise, recognizing the value/utility placed upon the various product attributes should be of great help in designing and introducing new products or in re-formulating old ones.

From the point of view of marketing strategy value-in-use can become the basis of a more effective segmentation strategy. Because different customers will have different perceptions of a product's attributes and also will differ in the value/utility that they place upon those attributes, it will often be possible to target products to specific groups, or segments, in the market. Price is one of the simplest ways of segmenting markets but price segmentation can become far more effective when based upon value-in-use.

COMPETITIVE PRICING STRATEGY

Most marketing activity takes place within the context of some level of competitive activity. Thus pricing decisions must clearly reflect competitive positioning and the customer's perception of any differential values that are embodied in competitive offerings.

At one extreme is a market with one dominant supplier – say 40 per cent market share to the nearest rival with 15 per cent – and where that dominant supplier has an offer which is high in perceived added values then it is likely that a substantial price differential should be obtained. On the other hand if there is no one dominant player in market share terms, and the market is effectively a 'commodity' market with no perceived product differences, then it is highly unlikely that any one supplier could command a higher price.

In any competitive market place the following relationship will normally hold:

$$\frac{\text{Perceived benefits (market leader)}}{\text{Price (market leader)}} \geq \frac{\text{Perceived benefits (competitor)}}{\text{Price (competitor)}}$$

In other words to maintain a position of market share leadership the ratio of price to perceived benefits must exceed that of the competition. Using this relationship it will be recognized that it is not sufficient to have a high level of perceived benefits if the competition has a substantially lower price. It will sometimes be the case that a supplier may develop an offer with substantial added values and sell it at a high price, but in so doing will provide competitors with a price umbrella under which they can shelter whilst developing 'me too' products. The success of the so-called IBM-PC clones in the personal computer market provides a testament to this.

The position of the product in relation to the market life cycle will also be important in determining pricing strategy. Given the importance of maintaining or increasing market share in the early stages of the life cycle as a means of increasing the speed of movement down the experience curve – to ensure both higher profitability and cash flow as the market matures – careful attention must be paid to the benefit/price ratio.

In the past, marketing authors have distinguished between **skimming** strategies and **penetration** strategies, particularly in the context of pricing new products. It has been suggested that a penetration strategy (i.e. a low relative price) is a route to early gains in market share if:

▶ Demand is price sensitive
▶ Economies of scale exist
▶ Competitive imitation is not difficult

An example of such a pricing strategy might be the low price established initially for the sale of domestic TV satellite dishes.

Alternatively a skimming strategy (i.e. a high relative price) could be appropriate, it is argued, where:

▶ Demand is not particularly price sensitive
▶ There is a relatively flat cost curve (i.e. unit costs at low volumes are not so much higher than unit costs at higher volumes)
▶ There is limited danger of competitive imitation

The pricing policy adopted by Rolex watches is perhaps an example of this approach.

Figure 13.6 suggests the possible pricing strategies that may be appropriate given the opportunities for value enhancement or cost reduction. Value enhancement is a strategy based upon building perceived benefits, whilst cost reduction can provide the basis for successful price competition.

The rationale behind each of these options can be demonstrated by the use of the experience curve concept. As we have seen, it is usually the case that penetration strategies are more appropriate where the opportunity for cost reduction is greatest, i.e. rapid movement down a steeply sloping experience curve can be achieved.

On the other hand a skimming strategy is more likely to be appropriate where rapid cost reductions are unlikely, i.e. the

Figure 13.6   Appropriate Pricing Strategies

experience curve is less steep. Figure 13.7 overleaf outlines the logic of each of the four pricing options.

Ultimately, however, neither a skimming nor a penetration policy will lead to a position of substantial market leadership unless the benefit price ratio is maintained at a higher level than that of the competition. The achievement of a favourite ratio is obviously not down to pricing strategy alone, but can only come about through a total focus of the marketing mix upon differentiation whilst managing the operations of the business to provide a cost advantage.

SUMMARY

The pricing decision is one of the most important issues to be faced by the marketing manager. Almost every market is influenced to some extent or another by the relative price of the products that compete in that market.

When customers buy products they are making choices based upon their perception of the relative value of competing offers.

(1) Follow my leader

In this situation the industry price will follow costs and, in particular, the costs of the price leader

(2) Penetration strategy

Here price is set low by the early entrant to gain advantage of the price sensitive market and thus gain market share and hence lower costs

(3) Skimming strategy

Under a skimming strategy it is assumed that the cost reduction opportunities are low, hence the less steep experience curve

(4) Price leadership

Through a combination of high added value plus low cost, these companies are able to bring down the price 'umbrella' and shake out the less innovative or higher cost competitors

NB All the above charts assume logarithmic scales, hence the experience 'curve' is shown as a straight line

Figure 13.7   Price and the Experience Curve

The maximum price at which a product or service can be sold can be no greater than its perceived value.

In this chapter we have proposed that price should be related to the value of benefits that our product or service delivers. Techniques such as trade-off analysis can be utilized to assist in the pricing decisions, particularly in the valuation of benefits.

CHAPTER 14

Communications Strategy

OPEN ANY newspaper or magazine and you are confronted with advertisements of all shapes, sizes and colours exhorting you to buy this, try that, save money with this product or win a free holiday with that product. Switch on the radio or TV and the story is much the same. Go to the cinema or drive down the High Street and you are bombarded by similar messages, be they off the screen or from billboards.

What is going on? What is it all about? Clearly hundreds of very intelligent people are spending millions of pounds trying to make contact with us. Are they getting value for money?

'I know half the money I spend on advertising is wasted; but I can never find out which half.' This poignant 'cri de coeur', attributed to the first Lord Leverhulme, aptly sums up the feelings of many marketers.

In this chapter, we will examine the various ways that potential and current customers and/or consumers receive communications about our products or services. We will also look at how best to develop a communications mix which will help us to achieve our marketing objectives. Finally, we will consider how the communications mix can be planned and managed. At the end of the day we want to ensure that, as marketers, we get good value from the money, energy, time and brainpower which is devoted to this important aspect of marketing.

COMMUNICATION METHODS

Companies have at their disposal an armoury of communication techniques which might be used singly, or in a combination which we call the *communications mix*. Those with acknowledged expertise in the area of communicating with customers are continually experimenting with the communications mix they employ as they strive to become more cost-effective in this area. The techniques which they use fall under two broad headings: personal communications and impersonal communications.

Personal communications mean just that: they are addressed to the individual, generally in a face-to-face situation such as a salesman's visit or a demonstration. Impersonal communications cover such topics as advertising, point-of-sale displays, various types of sales promotions and public relations, although with the advent of word processors and desktop publishing many companies are now attempting to personalize what were previously impersonal communications – mailshots, for example.

Here then are some of the communication mechanisms by which information, beliefs and intentions can be sown in the customer's mind.

WORD OF MOUTH

Most customers and consumers will readily agree that word of mouth is one of the most influential of all communication channels. Human nature being what it is, we know we will hear the tales of woe from friends and acquaintances who have had bad experiences with certain products or services. Conversely, they may be enthusiastic about their bargains and good experiences.

'I was really pleased with the work the garage did on my car', 'If I were you, I'd try that shop in the High Street, they are always so helpful'; 'Don't buy any of these, it's the biggest mistake I've ever made' – all these are persuasive marketing communications.

Good or bad, such comments have tremendous impact on us

because we value their independent origin and we believe that the supplying company trying to influence us has no control over these messages.

But is the marketer impotent to influence these word of mouth messages? We believe not, for when a company develops a communications strategy all the different audiences that it should address can contribute to a positive image of the company. Figure 14.1 shows some of the communication channels which might have an effect on word of mouth.

By genuinely striving to provide and communicate its intentions to each audience group, the organization can expect to earn a positive response in terms of word of mouth.

ADVERTISING

Advertising is an integral part of the marketing effort and must never be seen as an isolated activity. Its effectiveness will depend not only upon the persuasiveness of the message being conveyed to customers and consumers but also on the accuracy with which the target audience has been selected. Clearly any product or service can offer several different benefits; for example, it can be newer, safer, cheaper, more efficient or unique. Each of these benefits will have more, or less, appeal to different customer groups. Targetting the right message to the right people is the key to successful advertising.

However, the most impressive, elaborate and indulgent campaign will not convince customers and consumers to buy again if the product or service, whose virtues the advertising extols, is non-competitive. Advertising alone rarely produces long-lasting market success. Whilst it will encourage, reinforce a message and perhaps even help to develop a loyalty to a particular product or service, it will be no substitute for an offering which fails to bestow the necessary benefits on a customer.

It must be remembered also that advertising can be subject to controls or constraints from one country to another. For example, in the Netherlands confectionery advertisements must be followed by exhortations to brush one's teeth. Cigarette advertising is banned in many countries. In the wake of AIDS

Figure 14.1   Communication Relationships of an Organization

the advertising of condoms is only beginning to be allowed in some countries and even so there are considerable differences in what is permissible. In the UK the product is not seen and the message is conveyed by implication. In contrast, in Sweden the message is more overt. Clearly cultural mores and sensitivities have a part to play concerning what is and is not acceptable.

EXHIBITIONS

Exhibitions are becoming increasingly expensive to mount and so it follows that companies have to ensure they are going to get good value for their investment. The main attraction is that an exhibition offers the prospect of many potential customers making contact with us without us having to go out looking for them.

But this will not happen by chance; the stand will have to be designed so that it attracts attention and is interesting to visit. Also, the stand staff will have to show high levels of skill and ask questions to ensure that they are using their valuable time with genuine prospects, not with mere sightseers or, as is often the case, staff from competing companies. There will have to be suitable sales aids and supporting material available, together with back-up systems to ensure all prospects receive the appropriate follow-up.

PUBLIC RELATIONS AND SPONSORSHIP

This can be conveyed through several channels, such as through the national and regional press, trade and professional magazines, direct mail, exhibition and seminars. Increasingly the public relations function is becoming as much a part of the impersonal communications function as it is a personal communications function. Nowadays as many publicity and public relations activities are used as opportunities for stimulating personal contact with customers as they are for attracting an impersonal response.

The company which sponsors a golf tournament does so primarily to be able to invite key customers to meet its executives in unusual and interesting circumstances. Both parties should be aware of this underlying purpose. However, it is also the intention of the sponsor to attract as many people as possible to the golf tournament, even if many of the visitors will not be potential customers.

Many companies are moving away from the traditional techniques of press releases and conferences as a means of communicating their marketing message to clients. They are beginning to explore new channels, as the growth in sponsorship in sport, the arts and inner city renewal projects indicates.

PERSONAL CONTACT

For many years salesmen and women have been criticized by some as being 'people who spend their time trying to get others to buy things that they do not really need'. The classic example is perhaps the door-to-door insurance sales representative who, it is alleged, persuades the gullible to sink their savings into a policy they do not fully understand.

Perhaps such salesmen do exist, but which profession doesn't have the occasional, unscrupulous 'rotten apple'? Today many safeguards help to protect us from such unsavoury characters, but what about all the other salespeople who are proudly and legitimately going about their business? What are they doing?

When we stop and think about it, we learn a tremendous amount about products and services from personal contact with sales representatives. We find out how the product works; how it has been modified to give even greater efficiency; how and when it has to be serviced and what back-up services are available. It is quite possible that some of this information could be found in brochures and information sheets, but tracking it down takes time and we are all busy people. The sales representative can make it easy for us; he can respond to all our queries and more. He or she can encourage us, overcome our doubts and uncertainties, widen our horizons and steer us towards that purchase decision. Little wonder personal contact can play such an important role in the communications mix.

SALES PROMOTIONS

As we shall see, these can take many different shapes and forms: for example, two for the price of one; coupons to get a price reduction on the next purchase; purchase of product or service gives you a free entry in a prize draw. Sales promotions are essentially short-lived, aimed to achieve a particular objective which will contribute to the overall marketing objectives. As with advertising, sales promotions need careful planning and monitoring.

POINT OF SALE DISPLAYS

Sometimes called 'the silent salesman'. With suitably designed packaging and attractive dispensers in strategic locations, point of sale displays can communicate valuable marketing information and also contribute to sales.

DIRECT MAIL

Modern technology makes direct mailing less haphazard than it once was. However, any campaign has to be carefully thought out to stand any chance of being successful. Traditionally, direct approaches through the post have had very low response rates but, in recent years, companies have become more and more successful in targetting their mailshots. One of the reasons for this is the fact that more sophisticated techniques have been used to analyse the location of target prospects.

Geo-demographic classifications, as they are called, can be made available through specialist organizations. The best known and probably widest used classification in the UK is ACORN (A Classification Of Residential Neighbourhoods), which was developed in the mid-seventies. This works by segmenting the country, street by street, into eleven distinct housing groups, subdivided into thirty-eight different sociodemographic types. For instance, J36 refers to affluent detached housing in exclusive suburbs where occupants have a high level of disposable income.

A more recent classification is PIN (Pinpoint Identified Neighbourhoods). This system uses the raw ingredients of census data and postal codes from which it is able to produce revealing maps of any neighbourhood, complete with a profile of the inhabitants.

Other data bases exist to enable industrial marketing companies to target their messages in a highly effective way by direct mail. It is therefore not surprising that direct marketing has become one of the most powerful weapons in the communications mix in many countries today.

BRAND MANAGEMENT AND COMPANY IMAGE

Increasingly, corporate and brand image is being recognized as a major influence on sales. In the commercial world, where it is becoming increasingly easy from a technical point of view to duplicate a competitor's offering, the creation of a favourable or different image may give the company a competitive advantage.

The concept of brand management was created in the 1930s by Procter and Gamble, the giant Cincinnati soap and toiletries company. It came about as a result of the failure to launch successfully a new soap at that time, Camay. P & G's original market strength had been founded on a soap brand called Ivory and it was felt that the sales failure of the company was due to 'too much Ivory thinking'.

In a revolutionary step at that time, the Camay advertising account was switched from the agency that handled Ivory and the two brands were encouraged to compete. The brand management system was introduced slightly later and, far from being the disaster some P & G executives thought it would be, the company was soon reaping the rewards.

A strong brand reassures the customer; it gives confidence in terms of the quality and satisfaction that can be anticipated from buying it. From all of this comes the possibility of long-term profits. Many brands are household names today, but the concept of brand management has moved beyond the household goods categories.

People with brand-management experience in fast moving

consumer goods companies are now in demand by financial institutions, service organizations, retailers and new technology-based companies. Their marketing skills are being applied to 'own label' brands. For example, the Midland Bank have introduced new brands of accounts, with names such as Vector and Orchard, which have been strongly promoted. The Halifax Building Society is moving along similar lines with its 'Contents Xtra' insurance scheme.

Without a doubt, the concept of branding can fit in very well with the idea of the corporate image. Take British Airways, for example. Once they were organized on the basis of a number of 'marketing centres', which were essentially geographical areas such as North America, Europe and Australia. With such an organization, it was very difficult to get a focus on customer service and to track down the real needs of customers.

There is now an 'umbrella' or 'master brand', which is British Airways itself. Under this are seven 'pillar' brands: Concorde, First Class, Club World, Club Europe, World Traveller, Euro-traveller and Super Shuttle, each run by a brand manager and a group brand manager. Customer service and profitability have both improved under the new system.

CORPORATE COMMUNICATIONS AUDIT

This technique provides a system whereby the image of the company as perceived by the management can be compared with that held by the public or a specified target group. Often there is a divergence and, as a result of the audit, detailed recommendations can be made for bringing the differing views more closely into line with each other.

The audit also produces secondary advantages. By inter-viewing a cross-section of staff within the company, it soon becomes apparent if there are different perspectives on funda-mental issues. Clearly it is to the company's advantage to take corrective action to clear up any real or imagined misunderstandings. When it comes to analysing the views held about the company by its external audiences, the divergencies of opinion are usually greater than internal differences. The audit therefore not only helps to identify inconsistencies, but, equally importantly, provides the clues for an improvement plan.

A powerful element in the corporate communications audit is the publications audit. This is a technique used to assess the effectiveness of printed material emanating from different parts of the company. The overall graphics layout and content are analysed in the light of their individual purposes and the overall communications strategies of the company.

THE COMMUNICATION PROCESS

Essentially the marketer is faced with the same communication problems as those experienced by any two people talking. Figure 14.2 illustrates such a process:

Figure 14.2   The Communication Process

The sender's message is determined largely by his or her values, knowledge, attitude and vocabulary. It could therefore be claimed to be worded in the sender's personal code. If the receiver is 'tuned in' to the sender's code, because he or she shares similar values and attitudes, then the 'decoding' process is relatively straightforward. If he or she is not attuned to the sender's wavelength then it is very difficult for the message to get through.

The communication process is further complicated by the 'interference' that can come between the two parties. For the marketer this can mean that the receiver's attention is focussed on other matters, for example, or perhaps that the receiver is confused by getting conflicting messages from competing suppliers of products or services.

The lessons for the marketer which stem from this simple communication model are fourfold:

1 Keep the marketing message relatively simple;
2 word it in the receiver's language;
3 choose a medium/mechanism for transmitting the message which gives minimal distortion and interference;
4 know the target audience.

THE RECEIVER'S VIEWPOINT

In the analysis of the communications process we must be concerned to understand the process from the receiver's point of view. What mental processes take place in the receiver's mind on receipt of the message? There is evidence to suggest that the potential buyer goes through a thinking process something like this:

1 Becoming aware and developing understanding and know-ledge (about product or service);
2 developing interest, feelings, beliefs and preferences;
3 developing intentions, convictions and preparedness to try.

In other words the buyer goes through the 'thinking', 'feeling', 'acting' cycle that we mentioned earlier in the chapter on buyer behaviour.

A somewhat similar model of the buyer's thinking process is as given below – the AIDA model.

A   Attention. Something has to happen to capture the buyer's attention from all other possible distractions.

I   Interest. The buyer's interest must now be hooked in order to progress to the next stage.

D   Desire. A desire to own or use the product or service is generated in the buyer.

A   Action. This is required on the buyer's part to ensure that the desire becomes reality.

It is a relatively small step to combine these ideas and come up with a fairly comprehensive model which provides some useful clues about appropriate marketing communication methods. Figure 14.3 overleaf provides a generalized model of the communications and purchase decision process.

DEVELOPING COMMUNICATION OBJECTIVES

We have seen that not only is there a wide choice of communication techniques available to the marketer but also that some might be more effective at conveying certain types of messages than others. Their appropriateness depends to a large extent on the potential purchaser's frame of mind and the stage in the buying decision process he or she is at. We also observed that the choice of communication media had some bearing on the 'interference level' from extraneous 'noise'.

What we now have to decide is **what** we want to communicate and how best to do it. There are a number of possible communication objectives, as indicated in Figure 14.4 on page 243.

Marketing communication objectives should be a concise statement of exactly what we wish to convey to the intended recipients. It will be seen that these objectives are highly

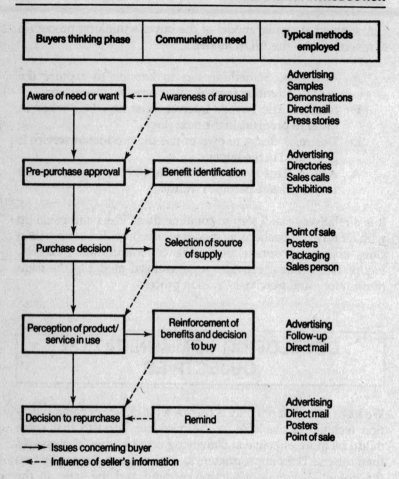

| Buyers thinking phase | Communication need | Typical methods employed |

Aware of need or want ←--- Awareness of arousal
Advertising
Samples
Demonstrations
Direct mail
Press stories

Pre-purchase approval → Benefit identification
Advertising
Directories
Sales calls
Exhibitions

Purchase decision → Selection of source of supply
Point of sale
Posters
Packaging
Sales person

Perception of product/ service in use → Reinforcement of benefits and decision to buy
Advertising
Follow-up
Direct mail

Decision to repurchase ←--- Remind
Advertising
Direct mail
Posters
Point of sale

→ Issues concerning buyer
←-- Influence of seller's information

Figure 14.3   The Purchase Decision and Marketing Communications

	To	
Education and information	Create awareness Inform Generate enquiries	⎫
Branding and image building	Build recognition of company name Create favourable image Reach personnel inaccessible to salesmen	The chosen communication objective(s) must contribute towards a total marketing programme, the objective of which is to achieve profitable sales
Affecting attitudes	Create desire Ease the selling task Achieve positive editorial coverage Overcome prejudices	
Loyalty and reminding	Remind about benefits Endorse the original choice decision (reassurance) Retain customer loyalty	⎭

Figure 14.4   Some Communication Objectives

specific, and are not expressed in terms of sales results, which are themselves influenced by the combined effects of the marketing mix and not just by the communications programme.

THE COMMUNICATIONS PLAN

A major theme throughout this book has been the need to plan and integrate the marketing mix elements against defined objectives.

Nowhere is this more important than in the context of the **communications plan.** Figure 14.5 overleaf shows the logical relationship between the communications plan and overall marketing objectives. It indicates that the communications plan is the blueprint for integrating the various components of the communications mix (or, in the language of the four P's, the promotional mix).

In fact the communications plan comprises three components: the **sales plan**, the **sales promotion plan** and the **advertising**

Figure 14.5   The Communications Plan

plan. The two former components are dealt with in later chapters and we will deal here only with the advertising plan.

ADVERTISING PLAN

As with any plan, the advertising plan should be based around a clearly defined set of objectives. However, there can be a wide range of objectives for advertising. Naturally, we might hope that advertising will have an important influence on sales levels, but it would be wrong to set objectives solely in terms of sales increases since so many other factors also influence sales. Having said this, what objectives should be set for advertising? We may start by agreeing that we need to set objectives for advertising for the following reasons:

1   We need to set a budget for advertising.
2   We need to determine who our target audience is.
3   We need to determine the content of advertisements.

4   We need to decide on what media to use.
5   We need to decide on the frequency of advertising.
6   We need to decide how to measure the effectiveness of our advertising.

These decisions can be summarized like this:
1   Why (Objectives)
2   Who (Target)
3   What (Message-copy platform)
4   Where (Media)
5   How (Creative platform)
6   When (Timing)
7   How much (Budget)
8   Schedule (Putting it all together)
9   Response (How will it be measured?)
10 Evaluation (Did it work?)

Research has shown that many companies set advertising objectives which advertising by itself cannot achieve. A helpful starting point in setting an advertising objective is to ask the question: 'Is it possible to achieve this objective through advertising alone?' If the answer is no, then it cannot be a suitable objective. Try again until the answer is in the affirmative. All other steps in the process of putting an advertising plan together stem naturally from this beginning, as the following list shows:

Steps in the Process of Putting Together an Advertising Plan

WHO   . . . is the target audience?

            ▷ What sort of people are they?

            ▷ How would we describe/identify them?

            ▷ What do they already know, feel or believe about us and our product/services?

            ▷ What do they know, feel or believe about the competition?

WHAT   . . . response do we wish to evoke from the target audience(s)?

. . . are these specific communication objectives?

. . . do we want to say, make them feel, believe, understand or know about buying our product or service?

. . . are we offering?

. . . are the priorities in terms of importance of our objectives?

. . . are our objectives? Can they be written down and agreed by ourselves and the advertising department or agency?

HOW   . . . will our objectives be embodied in an appealing form?

. . . is our creative strategy/platform going to look?

. . . do we know – what firm evidence is there – that this is acceptable and appropriate to our audience(s)?

WHERE   . . . is(are) the most cost-effective place(s) to expose our communications (in cost terms *vis-à-vis* our audience(s))?

. . . is(are) the most beneficial place(s) for our communications (in expected response terms *vis-à-vis* the 'quality' of channels available)?

WHEN   . . . are our communications to be displayed/conveyed to our audience(s)?

▷ What reasoning is behind our scheduling of advertisements/communications over the planning period?

▷ What constraints limit our freedom of choice?

▷ Do we have to fit in with other promotional activity on:
... other products/services supplied by our company?
... competitors' products/services?
... seasonal trends?
... special events in the market? e.g. trade shows?

RESULTS
... What results do we expect?
... What will be our measures of success?

▷ If we are to measure results, is there anything we need to do beforehand (for example, measure starting position or organize a data collection system)?

▷ If we cannot say how we would measure precise results then:
... are our objectives not sufficiently specific?
... are they really communications objectives?

▷ How will we judge the *relative* success of our communications activities (good/bad/indifferent)?

▷ Should we have some intermediate 'milestones' so that corrective action can be taken if it looks as though the expected results will not be achieved?

BUDGET
... How much money do the intended activities need?
... How much money can we afford/make available?
... How will we control expenditure?

SCHEDULE   . . . Who is to do what and when?
                . . . What is being spent on what, where and
                when?

It must be remembered that the role of advertising is never static. As we have seen, the recipient needs to receive new messages as his or her thought processes engage different phases of the buying sequence. Similarly, as the product or service moves through different stages in the life cycle, so too must the advertising objectives reflect the changed priorities.

SELECTING THE RIGHT MEDIA

In choosing the most appropriate medium for your advertising message the company will need to take four main factors into account:

1. *The Characteristic of the Medium:* This describes the geographical coverage the medium gives; the types of audience it reaches; the frequency of publication or screening; its physical possibilities (such as colour, sound and movement) and its power to reach special groups.

2. *The 'Atmosphere' of the Medium:* The consistency with the image an organization wishes to project. For example, an up-market beauty salon might choose to post a glossy brochure to potential clients rather than have cheap leaflets stuffed through all the letterboxes in the neighbourhood along with the newspaper delivery. Thus images can be of quality, élitism, popularity, fun – whatever the requirement, some media will convey the required image more effectively than others.

3. *The Coverage of the Medium:* The number of people exposed to the medium in terms of being aware of the content of the message. For example, a newspaper might be read by just

two or three members of the family, whereas a technical journal might be circulated to a large number of specialists within a company or read in libraries. In contrast, a poster might be passed by thousands of people and yet only be noticed by a few.

4. *The Comparative Cost:* How much it will cost to reach a specific audience size. Cost per 1000 viewers/readers is often used as a comparative yardstick.

SUMMARY

We began this chapter by observing that, as customers and consumers, we are being bombarded incessantly with marketing communications. The 'noise' is at times almost overpowering. However, looking at the communication problem from the company's viewpoint, we can see that there is, or at least there ought to be, a logic behind what this noise is attempting to achieve.

In reality, the company has an armoury of communication techniques which it can 'blend' together into an effective and persuasive communications mix. Essentially, the communications strategy can be summed up in a few words:

▶ What do we want to say?
▶ To whom do we want to say it?
▶ Why do we want to say it?
▶ How do we choose to say it?
▶ Where shall we communicate our message?
▶ When shall we say it?

Although these questions are deceptively simple, the skilled marketer doesn't fall into the trap of believing that the answers are equally easy. As we have seen, many important decisions and choices have to be made, sometimes affecting the organization at all levels.

CHAPTER 15

Sales Force Strategy

IN THIS chapter we shall explore the role of direct selling in the marketing mix, and the sales process itself. We shall also discuss the role of sales promotion.

HOW IMPORTANT IS PERSONAL SELLING?

Most companies had an organized sales force long before they introduced a formal marketing activity of the kind described throughout this book. In spite of this, sales force management has been traditionally a neglected area of marketing management.

There are several possible reasons for this. One is that not all marketing and product managers have had experience in a personal selling or sales management role. Consequently, these managers often underestimate the importance of efficient personal selling.

Another reason for neglect of sales force management is that sales personnel themselves sometimes encourage an unhelpful distinction between sales and marketing by depicting themselves as 'the sharp end'. After all, isn't there something slightly daring about dealing with real live customers as opposed to sitting in an office surrounded by marketing surveys, charts and plans? Such reasoning is dangerous, because unless a good deal of careful marketing planning has taken place before the sales-man makes his effort to persuade the customer to place an order, the probability of a successful sale is much reduced. The suggested distinction between marketing 'theory' and sales 'practice' is further invalidated when we consider that profitable sales depend not just on individual customers and individual products, but on groups of customers (that is, market segments) and on the supportive relationship of products to each other (that is, a carefully planned product portfolio). Another factor to be taken into account in this context is the constant need for the organization to think in terms of where future sales will be coming from rather than to concentrate solely on present pro-ducts, customers and problems.

Investigation of many European sales forces over the last decade has provided evidence that there remains an alarming lack of planning and professionalism in many cases. Frequently, salesmen have little idea of which products and which groups of customers to concentrate on, have too little knowledge about competitive activity, do not plan presentations well, rarely talk to customers in terms of **benefits**, make too little effort to close the sale and make many calls without any clear objectives. Even worse, marketing management is rarely aware that this impor-tant and expensive element of the marketing mix is not being managed effectively. The fact that many organizations have separate departments and directors for the marketing and sales activities increases the likelihood of such failures of communi-cation.

Although its importance varies according to circumstances, in many businesses the sales force is the most important element of the marketing mix. In industrial goods companies, for example, it is not unusual to find very small amounts of money being spent on other forms of communication and very large sums being spent on the sales force in the form of salaries, cars and associated costs. Personal selling is also widely used in many service industries where customers are looking for very specific benefits. Insurance companies, for example, do use media advertising but rely for most of their sales on personal selling. Customers for insurance policies almost invariably need to discuss which policy would best fit their particular needs and circumstances. It is the task of the salesman to explain the choices available and to suggest the most appropriate policy.

Recent surveys show that more money is being spent by companies on their sales forces than on advertising and sales promotion combined. Personal selling, then, is a vital and expensive element in the marketing mix.

The solution to the problem of poor sales force management can only be found in the recognition that personal selling is indeed a crucial part of the marketing process and that it must be planned and considered as carefully as any other element. Indeed, it is an excellent idea for the manager responsible for marketing to go out into the territory for a few days each year and himself attempt to persuade customers to place orders. It is a good way of finding out what customers really think of the organization's marketing policies!

THE ROLE OF PERSONAL SELLING

Personal selling can most usefully be seen as part of the **communications mix**. (Other common elements of the communications mix, it will be remembered, are advertising, sales promotion, public relations, direct mail and exhibitions.) In order to determine the precise role of personal selling in its communications mix, the company must identify the major influences in each purchase decision and find out what information they are likely to need at different stages of the buying process. Most institutional buying decisions can involve a large number of people and take a considerable amount of time. It is possible to split this decision-making process into a number of distinct steps which are known as 'buy phases'.

1 A problem (or need) is anticipated or recognized and a

general solution worked out. For example, designers working on plans for a new plant or machine may decide a special component must be incorporated in the design.

2   The characteristics and quantity of the required items are worked out. This, in the case of the machine component, would indicate the function and required performance of the component and any special design features (weight and size for example).

3   The specification and required quantity of the necessary items is determined.

4   A search is made for potential sources of supply.

5   Potential suppliers' tenders and design specifications are taken and scrutinized.

6   Proposals are evaluated and a supplier selected.

7   Orders are then placed.

8   The supplier's components are subsequently monitored for such things as performance to specification and promptness of delivery.

Different people and different numbers of people are involved in each buy phase. A useful way of identifying who is likely to be involved in the purchase decision, and at what stages, is to look at the decision in terms of its 'newness' to the buying organization. This 'newness' can be broken down into two parts:

1   The complexity of the product;

2   the degree of commercial risk or uncertainty surrounding the outcome of the purchase.

The higher the 'newness' in both these dimensions, the more people tend to be involved and the higher their status. If product complexity is high, but commercial uncertainty is low, then the design engineer and technologists have the more important role. If newness is low in both dimensions, purchasing officers tend to dominate the process. The higher the newness, the more activity is concentrated in the early phases and the more important it is for the salesman to involve himself at an early stage if he is to influence the outcome effectively. This is because a growing commitment operates throughout the decision process. Thus, early decisions are reinforced and become successively more and more difficult to change. The industrial salesman therefore needs to know the degree of newness involved so that he can direct his efforts to the appropriate people.

BUY CLASSES

In using this concept of newness in the purchase decision, the salesman can divide the decision-making process of his prospects into what are called **buy classes**:

- new buy
- straight re-buy
- modified re-buy

NEW BUY

When the need results from a new task, all the buy phases will normally be followed. Several functional departments of the organization will usually be involved: for example manufacturing, design, finance, the company board and the purchasing department. People in all these departments can be influenced during the decision-making process which, in the new buy context, takes the longest time to come to a conclusion.

STRAIGHT RE-BUY

On the other hand, when the need arises for a straight re-buy – for example, re-ordering standard items for stock – the situation is quite different. Only one of two functional departments such as the user and purchasing department may be involved. The other buy phases do still apply in that they will have been followed in the initial purchase routine but, since the technical specification of the product is now known and unchanging, no further technical involvement is needed in the buying process. The only factors likely to worry the buyer, provided that quality is maintained, are price and delivery and these therefore become important negotiating points.

MODIFIED RE-BUY

Sometimes a change in the specification or some other parameter may be necessary; this gives rise to a modified re-buy. Changes in the specification may be initiated by a salesman (for example, an offer of improved performance or a reduction in price) or by the purchasing company itself. The design and manufacturing functions may therefore become involved and most of the buy phases will once more apply.

The industrial salesman should always endeavour to change a straight re-buy situation into a modified re-buy. When he succeeds, the commitment of existing customers may be strengthened and opportunities may be created to open new accounts with companies which have been using the products and services of competitors.

PRESSURE ON THE INDIVIDUAL BUYER

We know from our own personal experience how difficult it can be to agree on the colour of a new wallpaper; partners, friends and even what the neighbours possess all bring pressures to bear which may influence our personal decision. The buying decision-makers in the average company are subjected to many more pressures.

PRESSURES FROM OUTSIDE THE COMPANY

Buyers are subjected to a number of external pressures such as:

▶ **The economic situation**   Is it the best time for investment in new projects? What is the cost of credit? Can the company afford to proceed?

▶ **Political considerations**   Is it the time to embark on new projects, when demand is perhaps being squeezed and government expenditure being cut back?

▶ **Technology**   Does the necessary technology exist for the project? Will the proposed product be overtaken by new technology in the foreseeable future?

▶ **Environmental considerations**   Will the new project be acceptable or will conservationists' interests or pollution controls prevent us from going ahead?

▶ **The business climate**   How will profit levels, interest rates and the cost of labour, for example, influence the decision of whether or not to proceed?

PRESSURES FROM WITHIN THE COMPANY

The way the buying department is organized and the number of people within it will affect the decision process. 'Internal politics', personal rivalries and vested interests will all put pressures on the buyer.

Individual status within the organization will also affect the way in which the decision is reached and the degree to which other people within the company influence it.

There are further pressures from other parts of the organization. The buyer may have to try to reconcile conflicting advice, resist pressure from vested interests and perhaps even act as referee in the final decision.

INDIVIDUAL PRESSURES

Even the buyer's own personality and past experience will influence the decision.

Past purchases will prejudice the buyer. For example, good experiences will be used to justify staying with a particular supplier even if a salesman can show that his product offers benefits which prove that a change would make good sense.

Similarly, habit acts against the industrial salesman who is trying to win a new order. Many buyers prefer to stay with known suppliers rather than risk the disruption of changing to another.

The buyer's perception of the situation may be different from that of other people. Other managers may rate a particular feature of a new product very highly, but the buyer may be obsessed with price, for example, and may therefore resist change, whatever the evidence of its desirability.

Allied to the perception 'barrier', there may be the difficulty of persuading the buyer to change because it takes him a long time to absorb new information.

WHAT DOES ALL THIS MEAN TO THE SALESMAN?

The way the buying process operates in different circumstances has several implications for the industrial salesman. He has to:

▶ Recognize the buying situation he faces, and the stage it is at, and determine how he will handle it;
▶ identify those people in the organization who are likely to be able to influence the purchase decision at that moment and during subsequent phases;
▶ decide what benefits his product and his company can offer to each of these people and what technical help he can give in an attempt to influence the decision;
▶ attempt to convert straight re-buys into modified re-buys by

demonstrating that his product has additional benefits over those used at present.

It can be seen, then, that the large number of people to be influenced, and the extended time this process might take, means that the industrial salesman has to adopt a much wider role than that of merely selling to this customers. Unlike in other forms of selling, he is as much a consultant as a salesman. In industry, selling is a focal point in the dissemination of information (unlike in the consumer field, where advertising plays the major role). Many industrial salesmen have technical qualifications in chemistry, engineering, electronics or management, and most have considerable product knowledge. The industrial salesman is thus able to help his customers in many ways – in fact, he will find that some customers rely on him to solve problems for them to help keep them up to date technically. Without the advice and guidance of industrial salesmen, many manufacturing projects would run into severe difficulties and would be considerably delayed.

UNDERSTANDING THE SALESMAN'S ROLE

The Consultant   When acting as a consultant, a salesman must understand the nature of this role and the way in which it must be performed. It is not necessarily difficult. The key to a successful relationship between consultant and consulted is mutual trust and respect. To perform this role the salesman will have to show (perhaps over a period of time) that his advice is reliable and given in the best interests of his client. To do this effectively he needs to listen to what the client wants, analyse his needs and recommend the best solution. He must be careful not to damage his company's reputation by giving bad advice to gain a quick sale. Above all he has to have an excellent understanding of his company's products.

However, this very knowledge causes problems if it is used incorrectly. Many industrial salesmen make the mistake of dulling the buyer's senses with sophisticated technical jargon. Years of training might have given the salesman a deep understanding of chemistry, electronics or engineering every word of which, he believes, must be used to impress and to demonstrate to the buyer his complete grasp of his subject. Such displays can cause more problems than they solve. Buyers do not like to feel inferior in knowledge, even if they are, and when this happens at best they become bored and at worst annoyed. In either case, the sale is in danger.

Nevertheless, the industrial salesman can play an important part in helping his customers. He might work with design engineers to overcome problems associated with incorporating his product in the overall design, or with systems engineers in setting up procedures for using his product. In this way he is able to influence the decision-making process and build on the growing commitment which develops as time goes by.

The Salesman The industrial salesman may believe that his value to buyers lies in his specialist knowledge rather than in his ability as a salesman. If he thinks in this way he is wrong. Only a few of today's salesmen will experience a seller's market. It is normally a buyer's market and there is plenty of competition from firms at home and abroad. This is the golden rule of selling:

'When all things are equal, the orders usually go to the salesman with the greatest SELLING skills.'

Much of the rest of this chapter is concerned with selling skills, and these are indeed vital to the salesman. However, selling ability is rarely enough to clinch a deal with the modern industrial buyer. Buyers today are better-equipped than ever before. They are better educated and have information about the market which is as accurate as the supplier's own information; they also understand finance – margins, liquidity, cash flows and returns on investment capital. Armed with this knowledge, the buyer will be in a position to negotiate every aspect of the proposed deal. Furthermore, in times of recession, buyers have power to back their demands.

The Negotiator   Faced with such knowledgeable buyers, the industrial salesman must therefore understand the difference between negotiating and selling. A combination of sales ability and determination, without negotiating skills, can be a positive disadvantage. The too-eager salesmen, using closing techniques to clinch the sale, can be a disaster when negotiation is needed.

Negotiating is quite different from selling. Negotiating begins when each party realizes that the other has something that they want. Negotiation is about the art of manoeuvre in order to secure the best possible deal. The salesman therefore needs to be able to exert influence over his side of the deal.

He needs knowledge of costs and margins, measures of the profitability of his major customers, awareness of the impact of profit on minor variations in volume, price, costs and sales mix, and he has continually to improve his planning and handling of customer negotiations if he is to be truly effective.

IDENTIFYING THE BUYER

The industrial salesman is faced with the problem of convincing a number of people or groups within an organization over an extended period. He is also faced with the problem of finding who actually has the power to make or influence the purchase decision. It is very easy for him to waste his time attempting to achieve the impossible – selling to someone who cannot give a decision or who has no real influence on the decision process.

There can be two reasons for this failure; poor preparation and fear. Once he has done his preparatory homework the industrial salesman can, or should, approach his task with confidence. Even so, many salesmen prefer to meet in the organization people with whom they are familiar and whom they count as their friends, rather than risk meeting a buyer who holds an important position – such as a financial director, works director or managing director – even though they know the more senior executives have greater buying power.

These fears are groundless. Most senior managers are very reasonable people to deal with and few try to dominate the interview with questions to catch him out. In reality it is the assistant – the junior buyer, the secretary or local manager – who makes life difficult for the salesman. A buyer may be protected by a host of such people. It must be the salesman's objective to bypass these guards and to see the person who can really make or influence the decision.

We have stressed the importance of preparation. This means that a great deal of research may be needed into the whole organization and product – design strategy of potential customer companies.

BASIC RESEARCH

The industrial salesman must first find out as much as he can about his potential customers. He must also keep this information up to date:

► What sort of company is it and what is its business?
► What new businesses is it entering?
► What new products is it developing?
► How big is it?
► Is it part of a group?
► How is the buying done?
► Who within the organization has the real authority to choose the supplier, and who influences him?
► What past relationships have there been between the vendor and purchaser companies?
► Is the company profitable? How is it doing at present?
► Is it in an expanding, declining or static industry?
► How strong is competition in the area (has a competitor an office close to the buyer's works)?
► Who supplies the company at present?
► Are the directors traditional or modern-minded businessmen? Have there been any changes at the top recently?
► Have representatives from the company ever visited the salesman's company exhibitions or showrooms?

Such information can be culled from many sources. For example:

- ▶ past records of dealings with the company;
- ▶ other salesmen;
- ▶ other customers;
- ▶ the company itself – telephone inquiries and unofficial sources of information such as receptionists and gatekeepers;
- ▶ chambers of trade;
- ▶ productivity organizations;
- ▶ national and local newspapers;
- ▶ trade press;
- ▶ classified telephone directories;
- ▶ trade directories;
- ▶ exhibition catalogues;
- ▶ association membership lists;
- ▶ *Kompass*;
- ▶ *Kelly*;
- ▶ *Extel* cards;
- ▶ the prospect's own literature.

A great deal of work is involved in this sort of basic research, but the salesman should consider the time this research can save if it ensures that he is able to see the right person and know all about his organization and its products before he meets the buyer.

IDENTIFYING WHO HAS INFLUENCE

We have seen that a large number of people are involved in each buy phase and that many of them will be able to influence the decision process. The salesman will have to spend a lot of time selling to these people. Sound preparation will identify the influential; poor preparation may result in time being wasted on intermediaries who do not have influence.

Although the organization of each manufacturer differs in some way from every other, a number of basic operations have to be performed irrespective of the size of the organization or the nature of the end product. At one end of the spectrum there is the one-man firm, in which the proprietor may perform all the operations himself. At the other, each of the basic operations will be the concern of a separate, highly specialized department. In very large organizations the necessary operations may be further subdivided in an effort to increase efficiency by yet greater specialization.

The industrial salesman must understand the elements of the typical manufacturing company, how these interact and how they depend upon each other to influence the final purchase decision. Armed with this knowledge a salesman will be able to decide when and where to concentrate his efforts for maximum effect. Typical activities of the various departments of a company are summarized below.

Marketing An important task of the marketing department is to identify market needs and opportunities. A long and complex procedure is followed before full-scale design and production work can begin. This may involve a market survey, a design feasibility study, an evaluation of available manufacturing resources and a financial study. Assuming these studies are successful, the new project then becomes the responsibility of a design department. The industrial salesman can influence a prospective customer's marketing department by showing how. his products can open up new market opportunities.

The design department This department has many titles and many sections, for example dealing with development, research, design, engineering and drawing. The main task of the department is to design a product which will meet a specified market requirement. The starting point may be a sales specification and the theoretical finishing point may be the production of a prototype model, design drawings and a performance specification. During the design phase, designers will call upon other departments and also may have to seek specialist assistance from existing or potential component or material suppliers. The industrial salesman has a vital part to play at this stage.

Production engineering department In broad terms, the function of the production engineering department is to specify how the product should be made and to provide the manufacturing departments with the equipment needed to make it. The department's responsibilities are very broad-ranging. They include resolving such matters as whether to purchase from outside or manufacture in-house, and whether to utilize existing plant as opposed to new acquisitions. It decides the source for the purchase of materials and provides estimates of manufacturing costs. The industrial salesman may well find some very powerful allies in this department.

Production control department This department is responsible for the logistics of the manufacturing operation. The prime function is to ensure that men, materials and machines are all brought together at the right time to meet planned production programmes. Supplies of the majority of raw materials and components are usually secured well in advance and the department tries to maintain stock levels that provide the optimum balance between insufficient stock, which can create long delivery times, and excessive stocks which are expensive to maintain. Industrial salesmen will invariably work closely with this department.

Purchasing department This department buys little on its own behalf, but seeks and vets suppliers, negotiates contracts and monitors performance. On the face of it, one might think that purchasing departments play an important part in the selection of suppliers. However, in many cases, the selection of the supplier is more strongly influenced by other departments and the purchasing department's eventual selection is almost a formality. This is particularly the case when design or production engineering departments have received technical help or advice from a potential supplier at an early stage of development. If the supplier has been able to guide the design or manufacturing process towards the use of his product, then his chances of achieving a subsequent order are usually higher than that of competitors who have not been so involved. The purchasing department is not therefore necessarily the right place for the industrial salesman to direct his main effort. The salesman may negotiate and obtain the actual order from this department, but usually his real selling effort will have been directed elsewhere, long before reaching this final stage.

TERRITORY PLANNING AND OBTAINING THE INTERVIEW

Let us now turn our attention briefly to the sales process itself, starting with territory planning and obtaining the interview.

The industrial salesman must plan his life to ensure that maximum time is spent selling and minimum time is spent on travelling, administration, planning and other activities. A systematic approach to territory planning is needed to ensure that all customers receive regular visits.

Although some calls will be made 'on spec', the majority will be by appointment. Appointments between buyers and industrial salesmen are usually arranged on the telephone. Thorough preparation is needed before the call, to enable the salesman to decide who is to be spoken to, what is the objective for the call and what is the lever which is to be used to arouse the prospect's interest. It is not always easy to get through to the prospect or, once connected, to persuade him to agree to the interview. There is a range of techniques the salesman can use to persuade the telephone operator and the prospect's secretary to connect him with the prospect, and for persuading the prospect to agree to an interview. This process of persuasion is a form of selling, which is discussed later in this chapter.

The salesman should always try to suggest the times for his appointments. This will enable him to fit four or five appointments a day into a schedule which is economical in terms of travel and efficient in the use of time.

OPENING TECHNIQUES

The salesman will only succeed if he handles his sales interviews effectively. He must establish clear objectives for each call and have a plan of how he intends to achieve these objectives.

A useful sequence to follow in any call is the 'ABC' sequence in order to achieve the required objectives. The salesman should arrest the prospect's attention (A), sell benefits (B) and move to a close (C). The sales offer has to be preplanned and the necessary facts, information and supporting sales-kit of literature, samples, data and other aids needed to achieve the interview objectives must be assembled.

It is essential to arrive in plenty of time for an interview. The salesman must be neat and tidy and he must pre-plan his opening remarks in order to create a good impression from the outset and to secure the client's immediate interest. Pleasantries and social chat should be kept to the minimum. The salesman may open by asking a question, giving new information, quoting a reference, using a sales aid, demonstrating something or linking his visit with some previous business. The aim must be to arrest the prospect's interest from the very outset.

BENEFIT SELLING

Throughout this book we have referred to the fact that customers do not buy products or services, but rather they seek to acquire benefits. Every product or service has its features, but the potential customer is only interested in the benefits which will accrue from these features. Since people buy products and services for what they will do for them – that is, the **benefits** of having those products or services – the salesman must sell these benefits rather than the features.

For the salesman, a simple formula to ensure this customer-orientated approach is adopted is always to use the phrase 'which means that' to link a feature to the benefit it brings.

The salesman must undertake a detailed analysis to underline the full range of benefits he has to offer his customers. He should seek to identify standard benefits (those benefits which arise directly from the features of what he offers), company benefits (benefits which are offered by the salesman's company) and differential benefits (those benefits which differentiate between the salesman's product or service and those of his competitors). A 'benefit analysis form' should be used to ensure a methodical analysis is conducted and proof should be given to substantiate every claim.

DEALING WITH OBJECTIONS

The buyer will almost invariably raise objections during the sales interview. An objection is a statement or question which puts an obstacle in the path leading towards closure of the sale. A buyer may raise a fundamental objection when he cannot see a need for the product or service on offer. He may raise standard objections when he recognizes his need but either wishes to delay a decision or needs further convincing before concluding a deal.

The salesman should always seek to forestall objections before they are raised. This can be done by identifying possible objections and 'answering them' in his offer. When faced with a fundamental objection, the salesman has to sell the need for the product in question rather than the benefits entailed. There is a range of techniques for dealing with standard objections but, if the buyer continues to raise objections without actually concluding the interview, there may be a hidden objection. It is often possible to discover what this is by asking an incomplete question, such as, 'and your other reason for not deciding is . . .?'

The salesman should not fear a price objection. This can usually be overcome by talking in terms of value rather than cost. Furthermore, the salesman is sometimes able to negotiate over price in order to secure an order.

CLOSING TECHNIQUES

The sale is closed when the buyer makes a firm commitment to place an order. The salesman should constantly look for opportunities to close the sale.

The buyer will often show interest, make committing statements and ask questions; these are buying signals which the salesman should follow up by asking a question in order to confirm that he has correctly interpreted the buying signals.

Trial closes should be used throughout the sales offer to test the buyer's reactions, uncover objections, determine buyer interest and speed the sale. Trial closes also help the salesman retain the initiative and accumulate small commitments from the buyer. The salesman should use direct and indirect questions to obtain buyer commitment. It is sometimes possible to offer alternatives which lead the buyer into stating a preference which, once expressed, can pave the way to an immediate close. Other opportunities to close can be created by the summary technique, giving a quotation or by offering a concession.

The salesman will only achieve a final close if he **asks for an order.**

The successful close is the culmination of a great deal of preparation, planning and hard work. It is the moment which makes it all worthwhile. But the close is not the end of the matter, it is just a step in a continuous process. The salesman must always remember that his objective is not only to close the sale, but also to open up a lasting relationship with the customer. In the final analysis, this is what makes a successful salesman.

ADVANTAGES OF PERSONAL SELLING

- ▶ It is a two-way form of communication, giving the prospective purchaser the opportunity to ask questions of the salesman about the product or service.
- ▶ The sales message itself can be made more flexible and therefore can be more closely tailored to the needs of individual customers.
- ▶ The salesmen and women can use in-depth product knowledge to relate their messages to the perceived needs of the buyers and to deal with objections as they arise.

▶ Most important of all, the sales representatives can ask for an order and perhaps negotiate on price, delivery or special requirements.

Once an order has been obtained from a customer, and there is a high probability of a re-buy occurring, the sales representative's task changes from persuasion to reinforcement. All communications at this stage should contribute to underlining the wisdom of the purchase.

Clearly, in different markets different weighting is given to the various forms of communication available. In the grocery business, for example, advertising and sales promotion are extremely important elements in the communications process. However, the food manufacturer must maintain an active sales force which keeps in close contact with the retail buyers. This retail contact ensures vigorous promotional activity within the chain. In the wholesale hardware business frequent and regular face-to-face contact with retail outlets through a sales force is the key determinant of success. In industries where there are few customers (such as capital goods and specialized process materials), and in-depth understanding of the customers' production processes has to be built up, personal contact is of paramount importance. In contrast, many fast-moving industrial goods are sold into fragmented markets for diverse uses. In this area, forms of communication other than personal selling take on added importance. One such form of communication is sales promotion.

SALES PROMOTION

The term **advertising** (often referred to as 'above-the-line expenditure') can be defined as all non-personal communication through media. This includes television, cinema, radio, print and outdoor media.

Sales promotion, for which the term 'below-the-line

expenditure' is often used as a synonym, is not so easily defined. For example, the Americans use the term to describe all forms of communication, including advertising and personal selling. In the United Kingdom some use the term to describe any non-face-to-face activity concerned with the promotion of sales. Some people use it to describe any non-media expenditure, whilst others use it specifically to mean in-store merchandising. The fact that none of these definitions is an accurate reflection of how sales promotion works in practice is an indication of why there is so much confusion about many aspects of this important area of marketing activity.

In practice, sales promotion is a specific activity, which can be defined as the making of a featured offer to defined customers within a specific time limit. In other words, for an activity to qualify as a sales promotion, someone must be offered something which is 'featured' rather than just being an aspect of trade. Furthermore, the offer must include benefits not inherent in the product or service, as opposed to the intangible benefits offered in advertising (such as adding value through appeals to imagery). Seen this way, every other element of the marketing mix, including advertising, personal selling, point-of-sale material, pricing and after sales service can be used as part of a structured activity in order to achieve specified objectives.

How can we use Sales Promotion? Essentially, this is a problem-solving activity designed to encourage customers to behave more in line with the economic interests of the company. Typical tasks for sales promotion are: encouraging stock movement; counteracting competitive activity; encouraging repeat purchase; securing marginal buyers; getting bills paid on time and inducing trial purchases. From this, it will be seen that sales promotion is not necessarily concerned with volume increases. For example, it is often used to assist production and distribution scheduling by persuading customers to bring forward their peak buying from one period to another.

To summarize, sales promotion seeks to influence:

- Salesmen   ▷ to sell
- Customers ▷ to buy
- Customers ▷ to sell   MORE, FASTER, EARLIER
- Users   ▷ to buy
- Users   ▷ to use

Although in recent years sales promotion activity has increased to such an extent that it now accounts for as much expenditure as above-the-line advertising, it is important to realize that, on its own, sales promotion will not replace selling, change long-term trends or build you long-term customer loyalty. Nevertheless, whilst sales promotion is essentially a tactical device, it has also an important strategic role to play.

What different kinds of promotion are there? Many and varied types of sales promotions are listed in Figure 15.1 overleaf. Each of these different types are appropriate for different circumstances and each has advantages and disadvantages. For example, points schemes are flexible, have wide appeal, do not involve the company in holding stocks of gifts, prevent customers from easily valuing gifts and are easy to administer.

PREPARING THE SALES PROMOTION PLAN

There is widespread acknowledgement that sales promotion is one of the most mismanaged of all marketing functions. This is mainly because of the confusion about what sales promotion is, which often results in expenditures not being properly recorded. Some companies include it in advertising; others as part of sales force expenditure; some as a general marketing expense and others as a manufacturing expense (as in the case of extra product, special labels or packaging); whilst the loss of revenue from special price reductions is often not recorded at all.

Such failures can be extremely damaging because sales promotion is such an important part of marketing strategy. Also, with increasing competition from Common Market countries, troubled economic conditions and growing pressures from the

TARGET MARKET	TYPE OF PROMOTION					
	MONEY		GOODS		SERVICES	
	Direct	Indirect	Direct	Indirect	Direct	Indirect
Consumer	Price reduction	Coupons Vouchers Money equivalent Competitions	Free goods Premium offers (e.g. 13 for 12) Free gifts Trade-in offers	Stamps Coupons Vouchers Money equivalent Competitions	Guarantees Group participation Special exhibitions and displays	Cooperative advertising Stamps, coupons Vouchers for services Competitions
Trade	Dealer loaders Loyalty schemes Incentives Full range buying	Extended credit Delayed invoicing Sale or return Coupons Vouchers Money equivalent	Free gifts Trial offers Trade-in offers	Coupons Vouchers Money equivalent Competitions	Guarantees Group participation events Free services Risk reduction schemes Training	Stamps, coupons Vouchers for services Competitions

TARGET MARKET	TYPE OF PROMOTION					
	MONEY		GOODS		SERVICES	
	Direct	Indirect	Direct	Indirect	Direct	Indirect
Trade continued					Special exhibitions, displays Demonstrations Reciprocal trading schemes	
Sales force	Bonus Commission	Coupons Vouchers Points systems Money equivalent Competitions	Free gifts	Coupons Vouchers Points systems Money equivalent	Free services Group participation events	Coupons Vouchers Points systems for services Competitions

Figure 15.1   Sales Promotions

trade, sales promotion is becoming more widespread and more acceptable. This means that companies can no longer afford not to set objectives, nor to evaluate results after the event, nor to fail to have some company guidelines. For example, a £1 case allowance on a product with a contribution rate of £3 per case has to increase sales by 50 per cent just to maintain the level of contribution. Failure to realize this, or to set alternative objectives for the promotion, can easily result in loss of control and a consequent reduction of profits.

In order to manage a company's sales promotion expenditure effectively there is one essential step that must be taken. An objective for sales promotion must be established in the same way that an objective is developed for advertising, pricing or distribution and the objectives for each promotion should be clearly stated – such as trial, repeat purchase, distribution, display, a shift in buying peaks or combating competition.

Thereafter, the following process should apply:

▶ Select the appropriate technique;
▶ pre-test;
▶ mount the promotion;
▶ evaluate in depth.

Spending must be analysed and categorized by type of activity (for example, special packaging, special point of sale material and loss of revenue through price reductions).

One company manufacturing self-assembly kitchens embarked on a heavy programme of sales promotion after a dramatic reduction in consumer demand. Whilst they managed to maintain turnover, they were worried that their sales promotional activities had been carried out in such a haphazard and piecemeal fashion that they were unable to evaluate the cost effectiveness of what they had done. They were also very concerned about its effect on company image and their long-term consumer franchise. So the company made a concentrated study of this area of expenditure, which now represented over half of their communication budget. Next time round they had clear objectives, a clear promotional plan properly integrated into the marketing plan, and an established means of assessment.

As for the sales promotional plan itself, the objectives, strategy and brief details of timing and costs should be included. It is important that too much detail should **not** appear in the sales promotional plan. Detailed promotional instructions will follow as the marketing plan is revealed. For example, the following checklist outlines the kind of detail that should eventually be circulated. However, only an outline of this should appear in the marketing plan itself.

Checklist for Promotional Instruction

1	**Introduction**	Briefly summarize content – What? Where? When?
2	**Objectives**	Marketing and promotional objectives for new product launch.
3	**Background**	Market data. Justification for technique. Other relevant matters.
4	**Promotional Offer**	Detail the offer: special pricing structure; description of premium, etc. Be brief, precise and unambiguous.
5	**Eligibility**	Who? Where?
6	**Timing**	When is the offer available? Call, delivery or invoice dates?
7	**Date Plan**	Assign dates and responsibilities for all aspects of plan prior to start date.
8	**Support**	Special advertising. POS. Presenters. Leaflets. PR. Samples, etc.
9	**Administration**	Invoicing activity. Free goods invoice lines. Depot stocks. Premium (re)ordering procedure. Cash drawing procedures.
10	**Sales Plan**	Targets. Incentives. Effect on routing. Briefing meetings. Telephone sales.

11	Sales Presentation	Points to be covered in call.
12	Sales Reporting	Procedure for collection of required data not otherwise available.
13	Assessment	How will the promotion be evaluated?

SUMMARY

Sales and marketing are clearly linked yet require separate attention. The marketing process is only completed when a sale is made. It is essential that a sales strategy be developed which is closely integrated with the overall marketing strategy. Similarly it must be recognized that selling is ultimately part of the communications and promotional element of the marketing mix, and thus a high level of co-ordination between direct selling and the other mix elements is essential.

Not every business needs a sales force, but every business has to sell. The issue is what approach to communications and promotion is most likely to achieve a sale.

CHAPTER 16

Managing the Sales Force

IN THIS chapter we turn our attention to methods of determining the size of the sales force, establishing sales territories, setting sales objectives and managing the sales force effort.

HOW MANY SALESMEN AND WOMEN DO WE NEED?

The organization should begin its consideration of how many sales representatives it needs by finding out exactly how work is allocated at the present time. Start by listing all the things the current sales force actually does. These might include opening new accounts, servicing existing accounts, demonstrating new products, taking repeat orders and debt collecting. This analysis should be utilized to investigate alternative ways of carrying out these responsibilities.

For example, telephone selling has been shown to be a perfectly acceptable alternative to personal visits, particularly in respect of repeat business. The sales force can thus be freed for pioneering work, which is not so susceptible to the telephone approach. Can debts be collected by mail or by telephone? Can products be demonstrated in showrooms or at exhibitions? It is only by asking these kinds of questions that we can be certain that we have not fallen into the common trap of committing the company to a decision and then seeking data and reasons to justify the decision. At this stage, the manager should concentrate on collecting relevant, quantified data and then use judgement and experience to help him come to a decision.

WORKLOAD

Basically, all sales force activities can be categorized under three headings: making calls, travelling, and performing administrative functions. These tasks comprise the **workload**. If we first decide what constitutes a reasonable workload for a salesman, in hours per month, we can measure how long the current activities take and then work out the exact extent of the workload. There are, of course, several ways of measuring workload; one major consumer goods company used its Work Study department to measure sales force effectiveness. The results of this study are summarized in the following table.

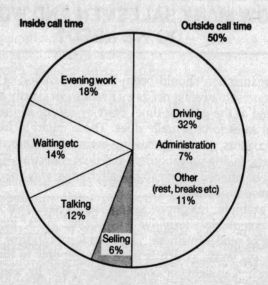

Figure 16.1   Breakdown of a Salesman's Total Daily Activity

This table showed the company how a salesman's time was spent and approximately how much of his time was actually available for selling. One immediate action taken by the company was to initiate a training programme which enabled more time to be spent on selling as a result of better planning. Another was to improve the quality of the sales performance whilst face-to-face with the customers.

There are, of course, other methods of measuring current sales force performance. One such method involves getting salesmen to carry out their own measurement. Research shows that salesmen carry out this measurement task diligently over the prescribed measurement period. The method involves getting them to record their daily starting time and the miles on the car clock, and to repeat this throughout the working day for all calls. The only additional information required is the account category called on, and the time in and time out.

From this, it is possible to calculate over a two month period, for example, the *average* time it takes to make a particular type of call (such as to a wholesaler, a chemist, a doctor, a hospital or a consultant). It is also possible to measure, given the type of territory (for example, town or country), how long it takes in travel to cover a given territory size. Finally, since administration is likely to be a fixed period of time for everyone, the company now has in its possession the vital information to measure, *territory by territory*, the precise workload of every salesman. Territories can now be equitably allocated to all salesmen.

There are, of course, many methods of calculating workload, but there is one further factor which is worthy of consideration here. This is a subject which we have researched over a number of years and which has proved extremely valuable in helping companies to allocate their salesmen more effectively.

During the 1970s, it was fashionable to predict the death of the salesman as a key component in commercial success. Enthusiasts predicted that marketing methods would become so sophisticated and precisely targeted that the need for personal selling would vanish. But the salesman is still around: indeed, even now, many companies spend considerably more on personal selling than on advertising and sales promotion put together.

The reason is not hard to find. Despite his very high cost, no one has yet discovered a more effective agency than the human being for communicating the full benefit of product offerings and for smoothing out customers' concerns. Moreover, research shows that, even in industries which doubt the usefulness of the personal selling process, customers take a different line. For example – and one that confounds popular belief – according to a recent survey medical representatives are actually welcomed by doctors and are considered to be a most valuable source of information about developments in the pharmaceutical industry.

As the pendulum has swung back towards personal selling, companies have invested heavily to improve the productivity of one of their scarcest resources: the group of individuals who have a direct interface with the customers. And indeed, today's salesmen are significantly better than those of a decade ago. But it is not the quality of the 'reps' themselves that has changed, so much as the quality of their direction and management. Creative, highly-motivated and productive salesmen could certainly be found in 1975; but, where excellence existed, it often stemmed from an individual's personal imagination and desire to excel rather than from the wherewithal provided by the company's training and management development processes. Some salesmen were excellent performers despite the firm's management, not because of it.

Clearly, this is a broad generalization. Some companies were as excellent at selling a decade ago as the best performers today. But even now, despite the improvements, there are all too few companies which, on close reflection and with honest self-appraisal, can truly claim a level of salesmanship that exceeds the mediocre.

Increasing the productivity of a sales force is a major challenge for the most enlightened and results-oriented sales manager, well aware that an increased call rate, higher revenue targets, a larger client base and similar objectives are not the only yardsticks. It is becoming fully recognized that productivity calls for a combination of both quantitative and qualitative performance measures.

Some of the methods and ideas that have been used to improve the productivity of sales forces during the last decade have proved very useful. Among those which have become fairly standard in competently managed organizations are (1) the development of imaginative and thorough training modules covering areas like communication techniques, body language, human behaviour and motivation, observation skills, transactional analysis and effective planning; (2) the introduction of performance measurement, supported by evaluation procedures; (3) the design of creative and productive sales aids; (4) the establishment of systems for tapping and cross-fertilizing creative ideas generated by the firm's sales force; and (5) the development of effective incentive systems.

DIRECTING THE SALES EFFORT

Every company places a slightly different emphasis on each one of these items, making many interesting and creative variations. But direct observation of a large number of seemingly effective and productive sales forces over the last few years has revealed a serious weakness in the way the majority of them are directed in one important area: salesmen are rarely guided on how their communication effort should be changed when addressing loyal customers at one end of the spectrum and hostile customers at the other. For instance, one salesman on an in-company training programme proudly told a seminar that he was in the habit of calling on one outlet 135 times a year, on the grounds that the account was worth $500,000 and the client was so loyal that 'one needed to reciprocate'.

The fact is that a firm's clientele normally consists of many types of customer. Some are large and some are small. Some represent a high sales potential; others the opposite. Some clients are loyal to the point of folly; others are sufficiently

cynical to change patronage at the slightest provocation. Yet
others are almost phobic about the supplying company and need
superhuman persuasion to change their attitude towards it.
Sheer common sense demands that customers of different
potential should have different amounts of sales time invested in
them.

The trouble is that, understandably enough, the average salesman enjoys calling on the loyal customer and dislikes the prospect of being constantly rebuffed by the hostile one. The result,
also understandable, is that salesmen tend to concentrate on the
loyal customers who will probably continue to buy from their
company regardless. A simple analysis of a salesman's call record
can highlight the incestuous relationship developing between
reps and the buyer. Both sides are quite happy to fête each other
at frequent intervals, although it is really a 'mutual admiration
society' from which little additional commercial and marketing
value can be derived.

The main difficulty is that if the salesman achieves his sales
budget little notice is normally taken of the fact that a lot of his
time is directed unproductively – towards a customer who is
literally 'in the bag'. Salesmen would no doubt reply that, if they
are neglected, even loyal customers may lose 'affection' for their
pet supplier. This is obviously true. However, it is no less true
that the main thrust of his communication with a very loyal
customer should be quite different from that which takes place in
front of a hostile prospect. In the former case, the main purpose
of the sales call is to maintain contact; to reassure the customer
that his loyalty is a wise one and to cement a happy relationship.
In the latter case, the aim is to try to understand the reasons for
the hostility, to attempt to remove them and then 'sell' the
product. These are totally different tasks; they call for different
approaches and should yield different results.

This notion can be taken a stage further. A firm's clientele can
be divided into three major groupings: those who love the
supplier (the 'Philes'); those who are totally indifferent to the
identity of the supplier as long as the offering is right (the
'Promiscuous' companies); and those who are hostile to the
selling company and reluctant to buy from it at all (the 'Phobes').

The point is that each of the three groups needs to be addressed with different selling and communication techniques. In fact, there is a strong case for developing individual sales aids for each case.

The situation is further complicated by the need to distinguish between the level of sales effort that is directed towards the large, medium and small potential customer. Since each of the three Phile, Promiscuous and Phobe groupings can represent a large, medium or small prospect, there are a possible nine types of customer. Obviously, some of the cells of the matrix represent better opportunities than others. A small Phobe is probably not worth bothering about, since the results of even a successful combating of the phobia will not justify the effort involved. A small Phile, on the other hand, will probably buy from the supplier anyway. Since it only represents a small potential, however, the right approach is for the supplier to call infrequently and then concentrate on assuring the customer that the affection is reciprocated. Spending any more time than the absolute minimum on such a client is unproductive.

Large Philes are both loyal and important. They should be handled with a maintenance policy, under which a representative should do only what is necessary to maintain the business. In practice, this might consist of a personal telephone call once a week only. The frequency of personal visits is a matter of management judgement, since there is always an element of vulnerability to strong competitive moves. The medium Philes can be handled along the same principles, although obviously the call frequency will have to be less.

The most promising pay-off for the time invested by the representative clearly comes from the company which is both large and 'promiscuous'. The appropriate treatment here is an investment policy which might mean a much higher call frequency with additional support from the company in whatever ways are thought necessary. The objective, if possible, is to move it up to the status of Phile. Medium and small Promiscuous customers can be handled likewise, but with a decreasing call frequency.

Large Phobes are an interesting challenge. The first thing to establish here is the precise reason for the antipathy to the selling firm. If that can't be discovered, it may not be worth spending too much time on them.

Figure 16.2   'Philes, Promiscuous and Phobes'

To go into the suggested selling postures more deeply we will take the customer types one by one. First, Phile/Large (Box 1) – an important customer which has proved to be very loyal. The main selling task thus consists of: (1) maintaining contact – no more calls than are absolutely necessary; (2) communicating details of all new developments; (3) responding to complaints (if any); and (4) collecting information about general developments pertaining to the use of the product and/or competitive practices. It is important that the client receives a copy of the company's annual report – and that salesmen are authorized to spend £x twice a year on entertaining appropriate members of the client's organization.

Promiscuous/Large (Box 4), on the other hand, is a fairly difficult customer, apt to change allegiance at the slightest opportunity and very sensitive to price. However, it is a large potential user and the business is worth having. So the main selling task consists of: (1) identifying the motivational stimuli of the members of the decision-making unit in such companies: (What makes them tick?); (2) planning sales presentations capable of demonstrating the cost/benefit and 'value-in-use' of the product; (3) maintaining a careful record of competitive pressures likely to affect sales; (4) demonstrating the selling company's ability and willingness to respond to problems and queries at all times; and (5) endeavouring to change the attitude of the prospect from Promiscuous to Phile. Success in doing so will form part of the salesman's performance appraisal system. Salesmen can be authorized to spend £x on entertaining members of the client's decision-making unit provided they have identified the most appropriate person and they can see a probability of a pay-off.

The Phobe/Large (Box 7) is a much more difficult customer to acquire and/or maintain. For some reason, known or unknown, it dislikes the supplying company to the point of phobia. It has large sales potential, but the amount of effort needed to convert the potential into results is probably prohibitive. This being so, the sales force should limit the time and effort it spends on such customers to: (1) maintaining a low-profile contact, if possible; (2) endeavouring to diagnose the real reasons for the current hostility and trying alternative solutions to any problems identified; (3) monitoring changes in the company's ownership or personnel which might affect future relationships; and (4) keeping vigilant for serious let-downs or stock-out problems with other suppliers. In general, salesmen must refrain from spending too much time or money on such unproductive clients until a change in attitude can be discerned.

The Phile/Medium (Box 2) is a loyal customer with a fairly good potential sales turnover. It is likely to buy without excessive sales effort. In this case, the main selling task should consist of: (1) maintaining contact – no more than a few visits a year unless there are specific problems (strong telephone contact is preferred); (2) communicating details of all new developments – mostly by means of letters and/or personalized mail-shots. Lavish entertainment should be discouraged, but customers in this category should be invited to fairs, exhibitions and other public promotional events. They should also be given preference for gifts planned for anniversary celebrations and Christmas.

The Promiscuous/Medium (Box 5) is an awkward, fickle customer, but one whose business is not insignificant. Beware of wasting too much time on penetrating such accounts. The main objective must be to 'flirt' with them in a fairly low-key attempt to persuade them to mend their ways. More specifically, the selling task is to: (1) identify the motivations of the decision-making unit to find what incentive is likely to convert its members from 'promiscuity' to loyalty; (2) communicate at frequent intervals (although not through personal visits) the great benefits of using the company's products. Emphasis here is to be through mail-shots, telephone calls and literature. Correspondingly, entertainment expenses must be kept to an absolute minimum and should only be used in exceptional circumstances.

The Phobe/Medium (Box 8), on the other hand, is a hostile customer with only medium purchasing potential. There is little justification for wasting too much selling effort on it. The selling task is limited to: (1) trying to determine the reason for the company's hostility; (2) tracking and recording changes in the organization which might alleviate the phobia; (3) if the hostility stems from past mistakes, ensuring that any corrective measures are brought to the notice of the client; and (4) maintaining an up-to-date client dossier.

Now take the Phile/Small (Box 3). Although its loyalty is appreciated, the seller can't reciprocate by giving it too much non-productive selling time. The selling emphasis should rather be placed on: (1) organizing an annual meeting to inform all the small Philes of developments in both the industry and the selling company (the meeting is a good opportunity for the small Philes and their friends in the sales force to demonstrate their mutual admiration); (2) maintaining frequent (and less costly) telephone contact; (3) ensuring that the restricted contact does not make the small and loyal customers feel unwanted. Happy communication can often be maintained through members of the sales administration team, which should be trained accordingly.

Promiscuous/Small companies (Box 6) should mostly be ignored. They are small customers who feel that their limited purchasing power is sufficiently attractive to make selling organizations fight hard for their business. The only exceptions to this rule are when: (1) there are indications that the firm is likely to become big in the near future; (2) the customer is part of a larger organization which the selling company would like to penetrate. In all other cases, very little time should be allocated to them. When they decide to become more loyal, they will receive more attention and affection. Finally, Phobe/Small (Box 9): forget it! This customer is more trouble than he is worth. Allow him to indulge his phobias in happy isolation.

WHAT DO WE WANT OUR SALESMEN AND WOMEN TO DO?

Whatever the method used to organize the salesman's day, there is always comparatively little time available for selling. In these circumstances, it is vital that a company should know as precisely as possible what it wants its sales force to do. Sales force objectives can be either **quantitative** or **qualitative**.

Quantitative Objectives Principal quantitative objectives are concerned with the following measures:

- How much to sell (the value of unit sales volume);
- what to sell (the mix of unit sales volume);
- where to sell (the markets and the individual customers that will take the company towards its marketing objectives);
- the desired profit contribution (where relevant and where the company is organized to compute this);
- selling costs (in compensation, expenses and supervision).

The first three types of objectives are derived directly from the marketing objectives, which were discussed in an earlier question, and constitute the principal components of the sales plan. There are many other kinds of quantitative objectives which can be set for the sales force; these are summarized below.

Some Quantitative Objectives for a Sales Force

▶ number of point-of-sale displays organized
▶ number of letters written to prospects
▶ number of telephone calls to prospects
▶ number of reports turned or not turned in
▶ number of trade meetings held
▶ use of sales aids in presentations
▶ number of service calls made
▶ number of customer complaints
▶ safety record
▶ collections made
▶ training meetings conducted
▶ competitive activity reports
▶ general market condition reports

Qualitative Objectives These can be a potential source of problems if sales managers try to assess the performance of the sales force along dimensions which include abstract terms such as 'loyalty', 'enthusiasm' and 'cooperation', since such terms are difficult to measure objectively. In seeking qualitative measurements of performance, managers often resort to highly subjective interpretations which cause resentment and frustration amongst those being assessed.

However, managers can set and measure qualitative objectives which actually relate to the performance of the sales force on the job. It is possible, for example, to assess the skill with which a person applies their product knowledge on the job, the skill with which the work is planned or the skill with which objectives are overcome by the representative during a sales interview. While still qualitative in nature, these measures relate to standards of performance understood and accepted by the sales force.

Given such standards, it is not too difficult for a competent field sales manager to identify deficiencies; to get agreement on them; to coach in skills and techniques; to build attitudes of professionalism; to show how to self-train; to determine which training requirements cannot be tackled in the field and to evaluate improvements in performance and the effect of any past training.

One consumer goods company with thirty field sales managers discovered that most of them were spending much of the day in their offices engaged in administrative work, most of it self-made. The company proceeded to take the offices away and insisted that the sales managers spend most of their time in the field training their sales representatives. To assist them in this task they trained them how to appraise and improve salesmen's performance in the field. As a result, there was a dramatic increase in sales and consequently in the sales managers' own earnings. This quite rapidly overcame their resentment at losing their offices.

HOW SHOULD WE MANAGE OUR SALES FORCE?

Sales force motivation has received a great deal of attention in recent times, largely as a result of the work undertaken by psychologists in other fields of management. It is now widely accepted that it is not enough to give someone a title and an office and expect to achieve good sales results. Effective leadership is as much 'follower-determined' as it is determined by management, and so we shall mention briefly some important factors that contribute to effective sales force management.

If a sales manager's job is to improve the performance of his or her sales force, and if performance is a function of incentives minus 'disincentives', then the more he can increase incentives and reduce disincentives the better will be performance. Research has shown that an important element of sales force motivation is a sense of doing a worthwhile job. In other words, desire for praise and recognition, the avoidance of boredom and monotony, the enhancement of self-image, freedom from fear and worry and the desire to belong to something believed to be worthwhile all contribute to enhanced performance.

However, remuneration will always be a most important determinant of motivation. This does not necessarily mean paying the most money, although clearly unless there are significant financial motivations within a company it is unlikely that people will stay. In drawing up a remuneration plan, which would normally include a basic salary plus some element for special effort such as bonus or commission, the objectives summarized in the following list should be considered.

Remuneration Objectives

▶ To attract and keep effective salesmen;
▶ to remain competitive;
▶ to reward salesmen in accordance with their individual performance;
▶ to provide a guaranteed income plus an orderly individual growth rate;
▶ to generate individual sales initiative;
▶ to encourage teamwork;
▶ to encourage the performance of essential non-selling tasks;
▶ to ensure that management can fairly administer and adjust compensation levels as a means of achieving sales objectives.

A central concept of sales force motivation is that the individual salesman or woman will exert more effort if he is led to concentrate on:

▶ EXPECTATIONS of accomplishing the sales objectives and
▶ PERSONAL BENEFITS derived from accomplishing those objectives.

The theory of sales force motivation is known as the **path-goal** approach because it is based on the particular path the sales representative follows to a particular sales objective – and the particular goals associated with successfully travelling down that path. Representatives estimate the probability of success of travelling down various paths or sales approaches and estimate the probability that their superiors will recognize their goal accomplishments and will reward them accordingly. Stated less formally, the motivational functions of the sales manager consist of increasing personal pay-offs to sales representatives for work-goal attainment, making the path to these pay-offs easier to travel by clarifying it, reducing road-blocks and pitfalls and increasing the opportunities for personal satisfaction *en route*.

PREPARING THE SALES PLAN

No two sales plans will contain precisely the same headings. However, some general guidelines can be given. The following is an example of setting objectives for an individual sales representative. Clearly, these objectives will be the logical result of the breaking-down of the marketing objectives into actual sales targets.

All companies set themselves overall objectives which in turn imply the development of specific marketing objectives. In this question we have discussed personal selling in the context of the overall marketing activity. This approach leads us to the following hierarchy of objectives: corporate objectives, marketing objectives and sales objectives, as outlined in the diagram overleaf:

Figure 16.3   The Link between Corporate Markets and Sales Objectives

SUMMARY

The benefits to sales force management of following the approach detailed in this chapter can be determined as:

▶ Coordination of corporate and marketing objectives with actual sales effort;
▶ establishment of a circular relationship between corporate objectives and customer wants;

▸ improvement of sales effectiveness through an understanding of the corporate and marketing implications of sales decisions.

The sales force is a vital but very expensive element of the marketing mix and as much care should be devoted to its management as to any other area of marketing management. This is most likely to be achieved if intuitive sense, which is associated with experience, can be combined with the kind of logical framework suggested in this chapter.

Task	Standard	How to Set Standard	How to Measure Performance	Performance Shortfalls
1. To achieve personal sales target.	Sales target per period of time for individual groups and/or products.	Analysis of – territory potential – individual customers' potential. Discussions and agreement between salesman and manager.	Comparison of individual salesman's product sales against targets.	Significant shortfall between target and achievement over a meaningful period.
2. To sell the required range and quantity to individual customers.	The achievement of specified range and quantity of sales to a particular customer or group of customers within an agreed time period.	Analysis of individual customer records of – potential – present sales. Discussion and agreement between manager and salesman.	Scrutiny of – individual customer records – observation of selling in the field.	Failure to achieve agreed objectives. Complacency with range of sales made to individual customers.

3. To plan journeys and call frequencies to achieve minimum practicable selling cost.	To achieve appropriate call frequency on individual customers. Number of live customer calls during a given time period.	Analysis of individual customers' potential. Analysis of order/call ratios. Discussion and agreement between manager and salesman.	Scrutiny of – individual customer records Analysis of order/call ratio. Examination of call reports.	High ratio of calls to an individual customer relative to that customer's yield. Shortfall on agreed total number of calls made over an agreed time period.
4. To acquire new customers.	Number of prospect calls during time period. Selling new products to existing customers.	Identify total number of potential and actual customers who could produce results. Identify opportunity areas for prospecting.	Examination of – call reports – records of new accounts opened – ratio of existing to potential customers.	Shortfall in number of prospect calls from agreed standard. Low ratio of existing to potential customers.
5. To make a sales approach of the required quality.	To exercise the necessary skills and techniques required to achieve the identified objective of each element of the sales approach.	Standard to be agreed in discussion between manager and salesman related to company standards laid down.	Regular observations of field selling using a systematic analysis of performance in each stage of the sales approach.	Failure to identify – objective of each stage of sales approach – specific areas of skill, weakness – use of support material.

Figure 16.4 Setting Objectives for an Individual Sales Representative
Based on original work of Stephen P. Morse when at Urwick Orr and Partners

CHAPTER 17

Marketing Planning

WHAT IS MARKETING PLANNING?

IN THIS chapter we shall consider one of the most difficult aspects of the marketing task – actually making it all work in practice by means of a system within the company. This is something that many people seem to overlook. Yet no investigation of marketing management can be complete without a fairly detailed consideration of how all the structures and frameworks presented in the earlier chapters are to be effectively implemented.

To make marketing work, it is necessary to have available a logical 'common format' for implementation of strategy, i.e. a **marketing plan**. In effect the planner is attempting to manage the future by deciding **what to do about the possible different trading environments.**

Issues to be Considered in Marketing Planning

▶ **When** should it be done; **how often**; by **whom** and **how**?
▶ Is it different in a **large** and a **small** company?
▶ Is it different in a **diversified** and an **undiversified** company?
▶ Is it different in an **international** and a **domestic** company?
▶ What is the role of the **chief executive**?
▶ What is the role of the **planning department**?

- Should marketing planning be 'top down' or 'bottom up'?
- What is the relationship between operational (one year) and strategic (longer-term) planning?

Let us now remind ourselves what marketing planning is about. It is a logical sequence and a series of activities leading to the setting of marketing objectives and the formulation of plans for achieving them. It is a management *process*. Formalized marketing planning by means of a planning system is, *per se*, little more than a structured way of identifying a range of options for the company, making them explicit in writing, formulating marketing objectives which are consistent with the company's overall objectives and scheduling and costing out the specific activities most likely to bring about the achievement of the objectives.

BENEFITS OF FORMALIZED MARKETING PLANNING

In one study, 90 per cent of the industrial goods companies involved did not, by their own admission, produce anything approximating to an integrated, coordinated and internally consistent plan for their marketing activities. This included a substantial number of companies that had highly formalized procedures for marketing planning. Certainly, few of these companies enjoyed the claimed benefits of formalized marketing planning which are outlined below.

Benefits of Formalized Marketing Planning

- Coordination of the activities of many individuals whose actions are interrelated over time.
- Identification of expected developments.
- Preparedness to meet changes when they occur.
- Minimization of non-rational responses to the unexpected.
- Better communication among executives.

▶ Minimization of conflicts among individuals which would result in a subordination of the goals of the company to those of the individual.

WHY IS MARKETING PLANNING ESSENTIAL?

There can be little doubt that marketing planning is essential when we consider the increasingly hostile and complex environment in which companies operate. Hundreds of external and internal factors interact in a bafflingly complex way to affect our ability to achieve profitable sales. Also, let us consider for a moment the four typical objectives which companies set:

▶ The maximization of revenue;
▶ the maximization of profit;
▶ the maximization of return on investment;
▶ the minimization of costs.

Each one of these has its own special appeal to different managers within the company, depending on the nature of their particular function. In reality, the best that can ever be achieved is a kind of optimal compromise, because each of these objectives is often in conflict with another.

Managers of a company have to understand, or at least have a view of, how all these variables interact; and managers try to be rational about their business decisions no matter how important intuition, feel and experience are as contributory factors in the process of rationality. Most managers accept that some kind of formalized procedure for marketing planning is desirable because it may help to reduce the complexity of business operations and add a dimension of realism to the company's hopes for the future. Without some procedures for dealing with these issues there is a danger that the company will exhaust much of its energies in mutually destructive disputes, whilst its marketing is at risk of becoming little more than an uncoordinated mixture of interesting bits and pieces.

Ideally, what is required is some kind of institutionalized process designed to work out and write down in advance the particular competitive stance that the company plans to take. This should be communicated throughout the company so that everyone is conscious of what has to be done to take the company towards its objectives. A useful way of achieving this synergy is through the marketing planning process.

THE MARKETING PLANNING PROCESS

Figure 17.1 illustrates the several stages that have to be worked through in order to arrive at a marketing plan. The dotted lines joining up steps 5, 6 and 7 are meant to indicate the reality of the

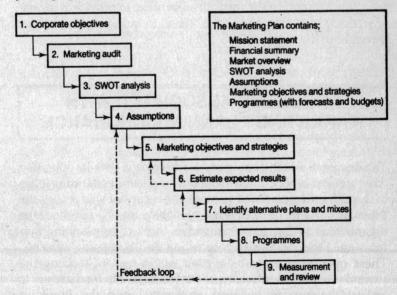

Figure 17.1   The Marketing Planning Process

planning process in that each of these steps is likely to have been worked through more than once before final programmes can be written.

Although it is generally accepted that each of the marketing planning steps is applicable in most cases, the degree to which each of the separate steps in the diagram needs to be formalized depends to a large extent on the size and nature of the company.

For example, an *undiversified* company generally uses less formalized procedures, since top management tends to have greater functional knowledge and expertise than subordinates and because the lack of diversity of operations enables direct control to be exercised over most of the key determinants of success. Thus situation reviews or the setting of marketing objectives, for example, are not always made explicit in writing, although these steps still have to be considered.

In contrast, in a *diversified* company it is usually not possible for top management to have greater functional knowledge and expertise than subordinate management, hence the whole planning process tends to be formalized in order to provide a consistent discipline for those who have to make the decisions throughout the organization.

PROBLEMS ASSOCIATED WITH MARKETING PLANNING IGNORANCE

The degree to which a company is able to cope with its operating environment is very much a function of the understanding it has of the marketing planning process as a means of sharpening the rationality and focus of all levels of management throughout the organization. What most companies think of as planning systems are little more than forecasting and budgeting systems. These give impetus and direction to the task of tackling the current operational problems of the business, but tend merely to project the current business unchanged into the future, a phenomenon often referred to as **tunnel vision**.

The problem with this approach is that, because companies are dynamically-evolving systems within a dynamically-evolving business environment, some means of evaluation of the way in which the two interact has to be found in order that they should be better matched. Otherwise, because of a general unpreparedness, a company will suffer increased pressures in the short term in trying to react to and to cope with environmental pressures.

Many companies, having gone through various forms of rationalization or efficiency-increasing measures, become aware of the opportunities for making profit which have been lost to them because of their unpreparedness but are still confused about how to make better use of their limited resources. This problem increases in importance in relation to the size and diversity of companies.

In other words, there is widespread awareness of lost market opportunities through unpreparedness and real confusion over what to do about it. Also, there is a strong relationship between these two problems and the techniques most widely used in place of formal marketing planning – that is, *sales forecasting* and *budgeting systems*. The following table lists the most frequently observed operating problems resulting from a reliance on traditional sales forecasting and budgeting procedure in the absence of a marketing planning system:

Operating Problems in the Absence of Marketing Planning

- Lost opportunities for profit
- Meaningless numbers in long-range plans
- Unrealistic objectives
- Lack of actionable market information
- Interfunctional strife
- Management frustration
- Proliferation of products and markets
- Wasted promotional expenditure
- Pricing confusion
- Growing vulnerability to environmental change
- Loss of control over the business.

It is not difficult to see the connection between all of these problems. Perhaps what is not apparent is that each of these operational problems is in fact a symptom of a much larger problem which emanates from the way in which a company sets its objectives. The eventual effectiveness of any objective is dependent upon the quality of the informational inputs about the business environment. However, objectives also need to be realistic, and to be realistic they have to be closely related to the company's particular capabilities in the form of its assets, competences and reputation that have evolved over a number of years.

Some kind of appropriate system has to be used to enable meaningful and realistic marketing objectives to be set. A frequent complaint is that there is preoccupation with short-term thinking and an almost total lack of what has been referred to as **strategic** thinking. Another complaint is that plans consist largely of numbers which are difficult to evaluate in any meaningful way, since they do not highlight and quantify opportunities, emphasize the key issues, show the company's position clearly in its markets, nor delineate the means of achieving the sales forecasts. Indeed, very often the actual numbers that are written down bear little relationship to any of these things. Sales targets for the sales force are often inflated in order to motivate them to higher achievement, whilst the actual budgets themselves are deflated in order to provide a safety net against shortfall. Both act as demotivators and both lead to the frequent use of expressions such as 'ritual' and the 'numbers game'. It is easy to see how the problems listed above begin to manifest themselves in this sort of environment. Closely allied to this is the frequent reference to profit as being the only objective necessary to successful business performance.

Characteristics of a Company with an Effective Marketing Planning System

▶ Widely understood objectives
▶ Highly motivated employees
▶ High levels of actionable market information

- Greater interfunctional coordination
- Minimum waste and duplication of resources
- Acceptance of the need for continuous change
- A clear understanding of priorities
- Greater control over the business and less vulnerability from the unexpected

However, even though many British companies have made the making of profit almost the sole objective, many of them have gone into decline.

Why should this be so? It is partly because some senior managers believe that all they have to do is to set profit targets and that middle managers will somehow make everything come right automatically. Financial objectives, whilst being essential measures of the desired performance of a company, are of little practical help since they say nothing about *how* the results are to be achieved. The same applies to sales forecasts and budgets, which are *not* marketing objectives and strategies.

To summarize, a structured approach to the situation is necessary, irrespective of the size or complexity of the organization. Such a system should:

- Ensure that comprehensive consideration is given to the definition of strengths and weaknesses and to problems and opportunities;
- ensure that a logical framework is used for the presentation of the key issues arising from this analysis.

Very few companies in Britain have planning systems which possess these characteristics. Those that do manage to cope with their environment more effectively than those that do not. They find it easier to set meaningful marketing objectives; are more confident about their future; enjoy greater control over their business and react less on a piecemeal basis to ongoing events. In short, they suffer less operational problems and are as a result more effective organizations.

In the case of companies without effective marketing planning systems, whilst it is possible to be profitable over a number of years, especially in high growth markets, such companies will

tend to be less profitable over time and to suffer problems which
are the very opposite of the benefits referred to above. Furthermore, companies without effective marketing planning systems
tend to suffer more serious commercial and organizational consequences when environmental and competitive conditions
become hostile and unstable.

HOW TO PREPARE A MARKETING PLAN

So far we have discussed the total marketing planning process
and in Chapter 5 we considered one of the most important steps
in the planning process – the marketing audit. Before turning
our attention to the other important steps in the marketing
planning process, it will be useful to discuss how marketing
planning relates to the corporate planning process. Figure 17.2
shows five steps in this process.

As we can see, the starting point is usually a statement of
corporate financial objectives for the long-range planning period
of the company; these are often expressed in terms of turnover,
profit before tax and return on investment.

More often than not this long-range planning horizon spans
five years; but the precise period should be determined by the
nature of the markets in which the company operates. For
example, five years would not be a long enough period for a
glass manufacturer, since it takes that period of time to commission a new furnace; whereas in some fashion industries five
years would be too long a period. A useful guideline in determining the planning horizon is that there should be a market for
the company products for long enough at least to depreciate any
capital investment associated with those products.

At this stage it is worth pointing out that one of the main
purposes of the corporate plan is to provide a long-term vision
of what the company is – or is striving to become – taking into
account shareholder expectations, environmental trends,
resource market trends, consumption market trends and the

Step 1	2 Management audit	3 Objective strategy setting	4 Plans	5 Corporate plans
	Marketing audit Marketing	Marketing objec- tives, strategies	Marketing plan	Issue of corporate plan, to include corporate object- ives and strategies,

	Distribution audit
	  Stocks and control; trans-
	  portation; warehousing
		Distribution
		objectives,
		strategies
			Distribution
			plan
				production object-
				ives and strategies
				etc.; long range

Corporate
financial
objectives
	Production audit
	  Value analysis; engineering
	  development; work study;
	  quality control; labour;
	  materials, plant and space
	  utilisation; production
	  planning; factories
		Production
		objectives,
		strategies
			Production
			plan
				P & L accounts and
				balance sheets

	Financial audit
	  Credit, debt, cash flow
	  and budgetary control;
	  resource allocation;
	  CAPEX; long term finance
		Financial
		objectives,
		strategies
			Financial
			plan	

	Personnel audit
	  Management, technical and
	  administrative ability etc.
		Personnel
		objectives,
		strategies		

Measurement, review and amendment (if necessary) of operating plans (continuous)

Figure 17.2   Steps in the Corporate Planning Process

distinctive competence of the company as revealed by the management audit. What this means in practice is that the corporate plan will contain the following elements:

- desired level of profitability
- business boundaries ▷ what kinds of products will be sold to what kinds of market (markets)
  - ▷ what kinds of facilities will be developed (production and logistics)
  - ▷ the size and character of the labour force (personnel)
  - ▷ funding (finance)
- other corporate objectives such as social responsibility, corporate image, stock market image, employee image.

Such a corporate plan, containing projected profit-and-loss

accounts and balance sheets – being the result of the process described above – is more likely to provide long-term stability for a company than plans based on a more intuitive process and containing forecasts which tend to be little more than extrapolations of previous trends.

The headquarters of one major multinational company, with a sophisticated budgeting system, used to receive plans from all over the world and coordinate them in quantitative and cross-functional terms (such as number of employees, units of sale, items of plant and square feet of production area) together with the associated financial implications. The trouble was that this whole complicated edifice was built on the initial sales forecasts, which were themselves little more than a time-consuming numbers game. The really key strategic issues relating to products and markets were lost in all the financial activity, which eventually resulted in grave operational and profitability problems.

THE STEPS IN THE PLANNING PROCESS

Let us briefly remind ourselves of some of the principal points made about the **marketing audit** in Chapter 5.

▶ A checklist of questions must be agreed and issued.
▶ Checklists need to be customized according to level in the organization to make them meaningful/relevant.
▶ It is essentially a data base of all relevant company/market related issues.
▶ It should be continuous/dynamic.
▶ Do not hide behind vague terms e.g. 'poor economic conditions'.
▶ Do incorporate PLCs and portfolio matrices. (See Chapters 8 and 9). Diagrams and corresponding words should match.
▶ It is a valuable 'transfer device' for incoming personnel.

Brief mention was made in Chapter 5 of the SWOT analysis.

COMPILING THE SWOT ANALYSIS

To decide on marketing objectives and future strategy, it is first necessary to summarize the unit's *present* position in its market(s).

The marketing audit must now be summarized in the form of a *SWOT* analysis. The word SWOT derives from the initial letters of the words **strengths, weaknesses, opportunities** and **threats**. In simple terms:

▶ What are the opportunities?
▶ What are the present and future threats to the unit's business in each of the segments which have been identified as being of importance?
▶ What are the unit's *differential* strengths and weaknesses *vis à vis* competitors? In other words, why should potential customers in the target markets prefer to deal with you rather than with any of your competitors?

GUIDELINES FOR COMPLETING THE SWOT ANALYSIS

The marketing audit will have identified what are considered to be the key markets on which the company should focus. For presentation purposes, it is helpful if a brief SWOT for each of these key products can be completed. Each of these SWOTs should be brief and interesting to read.

Section A, which follows, is intended to indicate how the **opportunities** and **threats** section of the SWOT should be completed. Section B concerns **strengths** and **weaknesses**.

A. Summary of Outside Influences and their Implications

This should include a brief statement about how important environmental influences, such as technology, government policies and regulations and the economy have affected this segment. There will obviously be some opportunities and some threats.

B. Some Important Factors for Success in this Business

How does a competitor wishing to provide products in this segment succeed? There are always relatively few factors that determine success. Factors such as product performance, quality of software, breadth of services, speed of service and low costs are often the most important factors for success.

A brief statement should now be made about the company's strengths and weaknesses in relation to these most important factors for success that have been identified. To do this, it will probably be necessary to consider other specialist suppliers to the same segment in order to identify why your company can succeed and what weaknesses must be addressed in the long-range plan.

PLANNING ASSUMPTIONS

Having completed our marketing audit and SWOT analysis, assumptions now have to be made and explicitly written down. There are certain key determinants of success in all companies about which assumptions have to be made before the planning process can proceed. For example, it would be no good receiving plans from two product managers, one of whom believed the economy was going into decline by 2 per cent whilst the other believed the economy was about to grow by 10 per cent.

Examples of assumptions might be:

'With respect to the company's industrial climate, it is assumed that:

1 Industrial overcapacity will increase from 105 per cent to 115 per cent as new industrial plants come into operation;
2 price competition will force price levels down by 10 per cent across the board;
3 a new product will be introduced by our major competitor before the end of the second quarter.'

Assumptions should be few in number, and if a plan can be

robust, that is possible irrespective of any assumption made, then so much the better.

MARKETING OBJECTIVES AND STRATEGIES

The next step in marketing planning is the writing of marketing objectives and strategies, the key step in the whole process.

▶ **Objectives** are what you want to achieve.
▶ **Strategies** are how you plan to achieve your objectives.

Therefore, there can be objectives and strategies at all levels in marketing. For example, there can be advertising objectives and strategies, and pricing objectives and strategies.

However, it is important to remember that marketing objectives are about *products* and *markets* only. Common sense will confirm that it is only by selling something to someone that the company's financial goals can be achieved, and that advertising, pricing and service levels are the means (or strategies) by which we might succeed in doing this. Thus pricing objectives, sales promotion objectives and advertising objectives should not be confused with marketing objectives. In other words, we can say that marketing objectives are about one or more of the following:

▶ Existing products in existing markets;
▶ new products for existing markets;
▶ existing products for new markets;
▶ new products for new markets.

They should be capable of measurement, otherwise they are not objectives. Directional terms such as 'maximize', 'minimize', 'penetrate' and 'increase' are only acceptable if quantitative measurement can be attached to them over the planning period. Measurement should be in terms of sales volume, money value (pounds, francs or dollars, for example), market share and percentage penetration of outlets.

Marketing strategies are the means by which marketing objectives will be achieved and generally are concerned with the four Ps – that is product, pricing, place and promotion decisions.

Having completed this major planning task, it is normal at this stage to employ judgement, experience and field tests to assess the feasibility of the objectives and strategies in terms of market share, sales, costs and profits.

PROGRAMMES

The general marketing strategies are now developed into specific 'sub-objectives', each supported by more detailed strategy and action statements, with timings and responsibilities clearly indicated.

USE OF MARKETING PLANS

A written marketing plan is the background against which operational decisions are taken on an ongoing basis; consequently too much detail should not be included. We should remember that its major function is to determine where the company is *now*, where it wants to *go* and *how* to get there. This is central to the company's revenue-generating activities, and from it flow all other corporate activities, such as the timing of the cash flow and the size and character of the labour force. Finally, the marketing plan should be distributed to those who need to know what is going on, since its purpose is as an aid to effective management.

CAN MARKETING PLANNING FAIL?

As a rule, formalized marketing planning procedures result in greater profitability and stability in the long term and also help to reduce friction and operational difficulties within organizations.

When marketing planning fails, it is generally because companies place too much emphasis on the procedures themselves, and the resulting paperwork, rather than on generating information useful to and consumable by management. Also, when companies relegate marketing planning to a 'planner' it invariably fails, for the simple reason that planning for line management cannot be delegated to a third party. The real role of the planner should be to help those responsible for implementation to plan. Failure to recognize this simple fact can be disastrous. Equally, planning failures often result from companies trying too much too quickly and without training staff in the use of procedures.

One Swedish company selling batteries internationally tried unsuccessfully four times to introduce a marketing planning system, each one failing because management throughout the organization was confused by what was being asked of them. Furthermore not only did they not understand the need for the new systems, but they were also not provided with the necessary resources to make the system work effectively. Training of managers and careful thought about resource requirements would have overcome this particular company's problems to a great extent.

In contrast, a major multinational company, having suffered grave profitability and operational difficulties through not having an effective marketing planning system, introduced one over a three-year period. It included a training programme in the use of new procedures and the provision of adequate resources to make them work effectively. This company is now firmly in control of its diverse activities and has recovered its confidence and profitability.

SUMMARY

There are a number of points to be watched for, which may signal the beginning of a marketing plan failure. Recognition of these will reinforce the purpose of a marketing plan, which is to aid effective management. It cannot be a substitute. These points are summarized below:

Marketing Planning Systems Design and Implementation Problems

- ▶ Weak support from chief executive and top management
- ▶ Lack of a plan for planning
- ▶ Lack of line management support
  - ▷ hostility
  - ▷ lack of skills
  - ▷ lack of information
  - ▷ lack of resources
  - ▷ inadequate organization structure
- ▶ Confusion over planning terms
- ▶ Numbers in lieu of written objectives and strategies
- ▶ Too much detail, too far ahead
- ▶ Once-a-year ritual
- ▶ Separation of operational planning from strategic planning
- ▶ Failure to integrate marketing planning into a total corporate planning system
- ▶ Delegation of planning to a planner.

What Goes into a Marketing Plan?

S.W.O.T.

- ▶ Only the SWOT (not the audit) goes in a marketing plan.
- ▶ A summary emanating from the marketing audit.
- ▶ A brief, interesting, concise commentary.
- ▶ Focus on *key* factors only.
- ▶ List *differential* strengths and weaknesses *vis à vis* competitors.
- ▶ List *key* external opportunities and threats.
- ▶ Identify and pin down the *real issues*. Not a list of unrelated points.
- ▶ The reader should be able to grasp instantly the main thrust of the business; he should even be able to write your marketing objectives.
- ▶ Follow the implied question, 'which means that . . .?' to get to the real implications.
- ▶ Do not over-abbreviate.
- ▶ Spend time on the SWOT. It is worth it.

Assumptions

▶ Must be few in number.
▶ If a plan can happen irrespective of the assumption, the assumption is unnecessary.

Marketing Objectives and Strategies

Marketing Objectives
▶ Products/services and markets only.
▶ They articulate what we are committing ourselves to, and the corresponding resource implications.
▶ They flow from the SWOT and must be compatible.
▶ They should be quantifiable and measureable. Avoid directional terms like 'increase', 'improve', etc.
▶ There will be a hierarchy of objectives throughout the organization.
▶ Set priorities for the chosen marketing objectives.
▶ Do not mix up objectives and strategies.
   (Objectives – what we want to achieve
      Strategies – how)

Marketing Strategies
▶ Product, Pricing, Place and Promotion Policies.
▶ Marketing strategies must eventually be transformed into detailed marketing actions.

Programmes

▶ Forecasts come last (not simple extrapolations), they are not objectives.
▶ Specific sub-objectives for products and segments, with detailed strategy and action statements (What, Where, When, Costs, etc.).
▶ Include budgets and forecasts and a consolidated budget.
▶ Budgets and forecasts *must* reflect marketing objectives. Objectives, Strategies and Programmes *must* reflect agreed budgets and sales forecasts.

CHAPTER 18

Organization and Control of Marketing

ORGANIZATION for effective marketing is a subject which is fraught with difficulty, largely because all companies and all markets are different. The complexities arising from the possible combinations of product, market, geography, function and size make it impossible to be prescriptive about the way a company should organize for marketing. Nonetheless, there are some general principles which are abiding.

At a 'macro' level, there are basically two kinds of organization which can be described as decentralized or centralized. In decentralized organizations, the company frequently has a strategic level of management at headquarters, supported by a number of managers making up central services such as product development, finance, personnel and production. At the divisional or subsidiary level there is often a similar kind of organization, with each divisional chief in charge of his own area of responsibility, being largely independent as long as profits are satisfactory.

The point about this kind of decentralized organizational structure is that it inevitably leads to duplication of effort and differentiation of strategies, with all the consequent problems, unless a major effort is made to get some synergy out of the several systems by means of a company-wide planning system. One company in the telecommunications industry had a range of 1500 products; one of those products had 1300 different variations; all of which was the result of a totally decentralized marketing-orientated approach in the subsidiary companies. It was not surprising that any sensible economies of scale in production were virtually impossible, with the result that the company made a substantial loss. The same problems apply to marketing research, advertising, pricing, distribution and other business areas. When someone takes the trouble to find out, it is often very salutary to see the reaction of senior managers at headquarters when they are told, for example, that the very same market problem is being researched in many different countries around the world, all at enormous expense.

It is this kind of organization structure which, above all others, requires strong central coordination by means of some kind of planning system; otherwise everyone wastes enormous amounts of corporate resources striving to maximize their own small part of the business. If, however, some system can be found of gaining synergy from all the energy expended, then the rewards are great indeed.

In a *centrally* controlled company there is often no strategic level of management in the subsidiary units, particularly in respect of new product introductions. This kind of organizational form tends to lead to standardized strategies, particularly in respect of product management. For example, when a new product is introduced it tends to be designed at the outset with as many markets as possible in mind, while the benefits from market research in one area are passed on to other areas, and so on. The problem here, of course, is that unless great care is exercised the company can easily become less sensitive to the needs of individual markets, and hence lose flexibility in reacting to competitive moves. The point is that marketing in this kind of system means something different from marketing in the kind of system described above.

There is a difference between financial manipulation and business management in respect of the headquarters role. There is a difference between a corporation and its individual components, and often there is confusion about what kind of planning should be done by managers at varying levels in the organization, such confusion arising because the chief executive has not made it clear what kind of business he is managing.

We have looked briefly at two principal organizational forms, both of which consist essentially of a central office and various decentralized divisions, each with its own unique products, processes and markets which complement the others in the group. In enterprises of this type, planning within the divisions applies to the exploration of markets and improved efficiency within the boundaries laid down by headquarters,. The problems and opportunities that this method throws up tend to make the role of headquarters one of classifying the boundaries for the enterprise as a whole in relation to new products and markets that do not appear to fall within the scope of one of the divisions.

In this type of organization, the managers of affiliated companies are normally required to produce the level of profit set by headquarters management within the constraints imposed on them. Such companies need to institutionalize this process by providing a formal structure of ideas and systems so that operating management know what they are expected to do and whether they are doing the essential things. The point about these kinds of organization seems to be that some method has to be found of planning and controlling the growth of the business in order to utilize effectively the evolving skills and growing reputation of the firm, and so avoid an uncontrolled dissipation of energy. It is probably easier to do this in a centrally-organized firm, but, as we have pointed out, both forms of organization have their disadvantages.

Finally, the financial trust type of organization needs to be mentioned briefly. The primary concern of its central management is the investment of shareholders' capital in various businesses. The buying and selling of interests in various firms is done for appreciation of capital rather than for building an enterprise with any logic of its own. Planning in this type of operation requires different knowledge and skills, and addresses itself to different kinds of problems from those of the two organizational forms described above.

There are two further points worth making briefly about organizing for marketing. The first is that where marketing and sales are separated at board level, marketing planning is going to be a very different kind of activity from a situation in which both functions are coordinated at board level. Figure 18.1 illustrates these two different situations:

Figure 18.1 Alternative Marketing/Sales Organizations

In the first of these organizational forms, marketing is very much a staff activity, with the real power vested in the sales organization. While a strong chief executive can ensure that the two activities are sensibly coordinated, unfortunately this rarely happens because he is often too busy with production, distribution, personnel and financial issues to devote enough of his time to sales and marketing. The point here is that a sales force is quite correctly concerned with today's products, problems and customers, while the marketing manager needs to be thinking about the future. The sales force is also quite correctly concerned mainly with individual products, problems and customers, while a marketing manager needs to be thinking about groups of products and customers (portfolio management and market segmentation). The two jobs are closely connected, but fundamentally different, and great care is necessary to ensure that what the marketing department is planning is the same as what the sales force is actually doing in the field. All too often it is not.

The second kind of organizational form tends to make it easier to ensure a sensible coordination between planning and doing.

Whatever the marketing organizational form, there are a number of issues that all firms have to address. These are:

► Functions (such as advertising, market research, pricing)
► Products
► Markets
► Geographical locations
► Channels

Of these, most firms would readily agree that in most cases the two main issues are products and markets, which is why many companies have what are called 'product managers' and/or 'market managers'. There can be no right or wrong answer to the question of which of these is the better, and commonsense will dictate that it is market circumstances alone that will determine which is most appropriate for any one company.

Each has its strengths and weaknesses. A product manager orientated system will ensure good strong product orientation, but can also easily lead to superficial market knowledge. Many a company has been caught out by subtle changes in their several markets causing a product to become practically redundant. In consumer goods, for example, many companies are beginning to admit that their rigid product/brand management system has allowed their major customers, for example retail chains, to take the initiative; and many are now changing belatedly to a system in which the focus of marketing activity revolves around major customer/market groups rather than individual products.

On the other hand, a market manager orientated system can easily result in unnecessary product differentiation and poor overall product development.

Ideally, therefore, whatever organizational form is adopted, the two central issues of products and markets constantly need to be addressed. This conundrum can be summarized in the following brief case study.

Wessol Ltd manufactures two basic types of machinery, mechanical and electrical, that are supplied to a number of markets, principally oil, gas, water, automotive and farming.

Wessol have both a product management and market management structure (see Figure 18.2). The basic role of the product

Figure 18.2   Wessol's Product/Market Management Structure

manager is to ensure that the product is properly managed, while the role of the market manager is to pay particular attention to the needs of the market. Close liaison between the two is obviously necessary, and a basic principle of this kind of organization is that ultimate authority for the final decision must be vested in either one or the other. Even when this is done, however, communications can still be difficult, and great care is necessary to ensure that vested interests are not allowed to dominate the real product/market issues.

This is the basis of the classic matrix organization which in the case of Wessol can be represented as in Figure 18.3 overleaf.

To summarize, no one particular form of organization can be recommended, commonsense and market needs being the final arbiters. However, the following factors always need to be considered:

Figure 18.3   A Matrix Organization

- ▶ Marketing 'centres of gravity' (i.e. key product/market segments);
- ▶ interface areas (for example present/future; salesmen/drawing office);
- ▶ authority and responsibility;
- ▶ ease of communication;
- ▶ coordination;
- ▶ flexibility;
- ▶ human factors.

What is certain is that one of the major determinants of the effectiveness of any marketing plan which is attempted within a company will be the way that it organizes for marketing. The purpose of this section has been to point out some of the more obvious issues and pitfalls before attempting to outline a number of approaches to control, to which we will now turn.

CONTROL

Just as there is a hierarchy of objectives, so there has to be a hierarchy of information and control data. For example, at the *macro* level in a company information will have to be generated to show overall sales volume; whilst at the *micro* level varying degrees of individual account detail will have to be generated according to the needs of the company.

At the next level down, each department will need to generate its own specific control data, so that, for example, if an advertising objective is to achieve an attitude change over a given period, then it will require an attitude survey in order to ascertain whether this particular objective has been achieved. Or, if the objective was to convey a particular piece of information to a specific target market, then again research will be necessary to establish whether this objective was achieved. The same principle would also apply to the sales department, which ideally will have a series of control data generated and distributed according to need, as well as establishing its own specialized control procedures when circumstances demand information which cannot be generated by the general company information and control system.

Any information system should be closely related to the company's organization and objectives so that relevant information for decision-making can be presented to each level of management. Thus, the objective of a company's sales information and control system may include some or all of the following objectives:

▶ To provide a weekly guide to sales performance indicating any likely budget shortfalls;

▶ to review, each period, product performance in total and within each category of trade, providing comparison against last year and against sales forecast;

▶ to examine the contribution of each product to both sales and gross profit and to assess the effect of 'mix' on the overall profit percentage of each market;

▶ to provide for marketing management information allowing them to identify strengths and weaknesses by product, by market and by geographical region;

▶ to provide sales-operating statements for senior management;

▶ to provide information by geographical unit for the use of sales and distribution management in restructuring territories and redefining distribution boundaries;

▶ to enable sales management to review the trading situation of any customer in terms of profit;

▶ to encourage development of profitable accounts not only through greater sales but also increased delivery drop size and more relevant discounts;

▶ to enable sales management to monitor trading agreements;

▶ to enable salesmen to schedule their work according to a predetermined calling cycle;

▶ to ensure that, in the call, the salesman is equipped with accurate and up-to-date information on the customer's order pattern, overall sales performance, and mix of sales;

▶ to analyse for sales management the productivity of salesmen in terms of calling rate and product placement;

▶ to identify by type of outlet and product the penetration achieved and the potential in existing accounts.

These and many more are the kind of objectives which result in the detailed output which a system will produce, such as brand performance.

The important fact which emerges from any review of information and control procedures is that its purpose should be to provide management with the necessary information to enable it to monitor its progress towards its predetermined objectives, thus providing the necessary loop in the planning cycle.

Nonetheless, the basic tool for controlling the marketing effort is the budget, which itself derives from the marketing plan.

SETTING THE MARKETING BUDGET

Perhaps the most central and frequent question asked in respect of a marketing programme is, 'how much should we spend?' Certainly, this is one of the most difficult problems facing any marketing manager. It may explain also why relatively little attention is given to this problem, compared to other aspects of marketing. However, before we decide how much we should spend, it is worth trying to isolate those costs which are justifiable marketing costs.

IDENTIFYING MARKETING COSTS

Many people contend that the marketing budget is an unambiguous concept – it is quite simply a statement of marketing costs. However, in practice the marketing budget should be much more than this. Strictly, a comprehensive marketing budget will include all direct and indirect costs of the marketing organization, such as those outlined below.

Direct and Indirect Costs of a Marketing Organization

- **Staff Costs**
- **Office and Equipment Expenses**
- **Marketing Mix Costs** ▷ *Product Policy*
  (packaging, new product launches, modification launches, etc.)
  ▷ *Pricing*
  (discounts given, price lists, commissions, etc.)

> *Communications*
>   (advertising media and production
>   costs, sales promotions, public
>   relations, sales force office and field
>   costs, etc.)
> *Distribution*
>   (transport of finished goods,
>   storage, warehousing, special deals
>   with distributors, etc.)

However, this is not normal practice and there are a number of reasons for this. First, there is often some reluctance to identify marketing as a cost centre. It is easier, given the problems of cause and effect analysis, to consider marketing as little more than an overhead, or a charge against profits, rather than a revenue creator and profit maker.

The figure above falls into the trap of combining **controllable** and **uncontrollable** costs; this inevitably invalidates the use of the budget as a planning and a control mechanism. For example, in one European company the largest component of the marketing budget was **distributor commission**; that is the difference between sales value at list prices and revenues received from distributors. In fact, since commission rates were set by the finance department and senior management, this was to a great extent an 'uncontrollable factor' for the marketing department and sales managers.

Another related problem is the danger of confusing **overheads** with direct or **incremental** costs. A product manager may plan sales promotions and construct a budget for them, but he is unlikely to be involved in determining the costs of administering the sales office and order processing system.

Even more difficult – yet essential if one is to improve the productivity of the sales effort – is to attempt to allocate costs right down to individual customer accounts in order to determine the true costs associated with dealing with specific outlets.

Such an approach is based on the principle that the individual customer is the ultimate profit centre and that costs incurred after production are primarily related to the customer and the unique factors associated with serving him, such as order size, sales discounts, returned goods, promotional items and delivery costs. A customer profitability model is given below. This is followed by a worked example.

	£	£
Gross sales value		80,000
Less discounts	8,000	
Net sales value		72,000
Less production costs	44,000	
Gross profit		28,000
Less sales and distribution costs:		
(1) Selling cost	9,000	
(2) Order processing	6,500	
(3) Warehousing and order assembly	6,400	
(4) Cost of holding stock	800	
(5) Inbound freight	1,600	
(6) Outbound freight	2,700	
(7) Returns	250	
(8) Merchandizing	4,500	
(9) Cost of credit	1,100	
TOTAL	32,850	
Net contribution		(4,850)

Figure 18.4 Customer Profitability Model

(1) Selling
includes costs of sales force (including sales management) and sales administration, allocated according to visit frequency and call duration.

(2) Order processing
includes costs relating to credit rating, stock checking, processing the order, raising invoices, and the accounts and credit control departments, allocated according to turnover.

(3) Warehousing and order assembly
includes warehousing, fixed costs, order picking, assembly and loading, allocated on the basis of work study measurements.

(4) Cost of holding stock
includes credit, insurance, shrinkage, pilferage, staff.

(5) Inbound Freight
costs of transport from factory to warehouse, allocated according to order size.

(6) Freight out
costs of transport from warehouse to customer. A standard unit of cost.

(7) Returns
includes cost of returned goods, plus returns of packaging materials.

(8) Merchandising
cost of merchandising, i.e. price marking, shelf stacking, displays etc.

(9) Cost of Credit
cost of credit over the average period of outstanding debts.

The **comprehensive budget** implies a particular form of marketing organization and a particular type and degree of marketing management responsibility. Empirical studies have shown that it is all too easy to exaggerate the real responsibilities of the marketing manager. At its simplest, for instance, if the marketing department has no responsibility for physical distribution, then it has no real place in the budget. This then highlights the whole question of what is, and what is not, a marketing cost.

Let us take the example of an Anglo-Arab joint publishing venture operating in the Middle East. This was a comparatively infant enterprise employing expatriate staff whose general manager reported to the parent company in England as well as to the local Arab directors. The marketing function of the company embraced a sales force of six, headed by a marketing manager. The production function of the company was subcontracted to the British parent company, and the editorial policy and financial functions, whilst run from the Middle East base, were controlled also by the parent company. In practice, the two line managers, the company accountant and the marketing manager reported to the general manager and were concerned only with the marketing income and expenditure of the company. This covered not only the costs of the sales team, marketing channels, advertising and promotion, but also the costs of inventory storage and shipment, together with all the fixed overheads of the Middle East operation. Equally, the company's sources of income were derived solely through publication and advertising-space sales achieved by the marketing department. In effect the planning and control of the marketing budget was the company's profit and loss account.

In other words, it is necessary to accept that the components of the marketing budget vary very greatly between companies. It is not the place in a book of this nature to give step-by-step guidelines for all the principal permutations. Rather, we consider as many elements and models for approaching the marketing budget process as possible, so that you can apply the most appropriate to your own particular circumstances.

Such is the ambiguity on the subject that one management accountant was recorded recently as saying:

'Unfortunately, it may well be that many controllers have resigned themselves to assuming that marketing cost is an impossible area to analyse and control.'

Fortunately, however, all is not gloom and disarray! An

American survey has demonstrated that three-quarters of a
sample of large industrial companies in the United States of
America budgeted around the following concepts – and successfully:

▶ *order-filling activities* – mainly concentrated on physical distribution costs like transport, warehousing, order handling,
  credit and stocking.
▶ *order-getting activities* – mainly centred upon advertising, sales
  promotion and merchandizing.

In many companies the marketing budget is in effect the budget
for advertising and promotion. The substantive control of an
important budget may, in organizational terms, be both a source
of power and a sign of that power to others. It has been noted, for
instance, that in companies with a large TV advertising spend,
real control has passed from the marketing department to general
managers and company directors.

BUDGETS AS MANAGERIAL TOOLS

All budgets, no matter how they are constructed, still serve the
original purpose. That is, they enable managers to pull together
their commitments, their plans and projects, and all the costs
involved into one comprehensive document – in this case a marketing budget. Above all it is a managerial tool, not just a financial
device. One of the best ways to approach a marketing budget is to
ask the simple question: 'What are the expected results?'

Budgets are expressed in monetary terms, but we should
regard monetary terms as a kind of shorthand for the actual
efforts needed. They should be based on real values. In other
words, the marketing budget should be a tool by which we can
think through the relationship between desired results and available means. Whatever we do, we should avoid the worst pitfall of
all, that is a tendency to regard last year's expenditure as being
'about right' and to project this into the new budget.

BUDGET ALTERNATIVES

It is important that each manager responsible for the marketing function should identify the costs and revenue for which he or she is accountable. As we mentioned earlier, care must be taken to assess the relevance of including the following in a marketing budget:

▶ Fixed costs;
▶ variable costs;
▶ controllable costs;
▶ uncontrollable costs.

It will be all too easy for the marketing department to find itself responsible for certain capital investment costs, depreciation of equipment costs, research and development expenditure and public relations activity, when, in reality, the demarcation as to which item belongs to which department is a grey area because it has never been correctly allocated. Until this is clear, marketing objectives and strategies cannot be quantified in terms of expected results.

Zero-based budgeting is growing in popularity, since, rather than starting with last year's expenditure, new targets and objectives are the primary concern. Questions are asked such as: 'Are we operating in the right area? Is the area a priority?'

The marketing director is asked to justify his marketing expenditure each year from a zero base against the tasks he wishes to perform, and for which he can forecast revenue expectations, rather than starting with last year's budget and adding a percentage.

This should not be too difficult if the procedures outlined in Chapter 17 are adhered to; a hierarchy of objectives will be built up in such a way that every item of budget expenditure can be related back directly to its own specific objective and ultimately to the corporate financial objectives. Thus, having identified sales promotion as a major promotional strategy for achieving an objective in a particular market – when sales promotional items appear in the programme – each one has a specific purpose which can be related back to a major objective.

Doing it this way not only ensures that every item of expenditure is fully accounted for as part of a rational objective and task approach, but also that when changes have to be made during the period to which the plan relates they can be made in a way that causes least damage to the company's long-term objectives.

Zero-based budgeting can, and should, be used by every organization as a tool for the periodic systematic review of all products, markets and related activities, so helping the systematic abandonment of the obsolescent, the unproductive, and above all the unnecessary.

Life-cycle budgeting is based on the principle that the budget should start out with the appropriate time cycle. What portion of the expenditure needed over this time cycle belongs in this current budgeting period? This will be particularly relevant to marketing operations where product life cycles have to be viewed in relation to the phasing-in of new products and the phasing-out of those which have reached maturity or decline. This will also allow for other expenditure such as pilot testing of new products, marketing research and the projected cash-generation life of cash cows and stars.

One of the best known examples of life-cycle budgeting is that which Robert McNamara introduced into the American defence budget while Secretary of Defence under President Kennedy's administration in the early 1960s. Under the budgeting process of the US government, as it had been practised earlier, the Armed Services submitted their requests for money for the development of a new weapon, such as a new fighter plane, on an annual basis. In other words, they asked for enough money to get a project started without disclosing how much money it would take to get the project finished. Then, when the first few hundred million dollars had been spent, they always argued that to abandon a product because its costs were rising sharply (as the new plan moved from drawing board into production) would lead to a waste of money already spent. When the first prototype of the plane rolled off the production line and when it became apparent that there would be need for an expensive and extensive training programme (and also for very large sums of money to buy replacement parts for the plane) they could argue that not to provide these sums in the future budget would mean a waste of very large sums already spent.

Under life-cycle costing the Armed Services are supposed to present total cost estimates over the life of the proposed weapon, including the training expenses and the expense for maintaining, repairing, and replacing equipment. This, in theory at least, enables the Secretary of Defence, the President and the Congress to know in advance the size of the commitment and its impact on future budgets.

Life-cycle costing, or some variant of it, is increasingly standard practice in many companies. In fact, it is now regarded as poor budgeting practice to assume that a new product – whether involving capital investment or an activity such as an advertising campaign – will cost less in the future. In other words, marketing managers should always think through the implications of how much more money will be required to run with success.

Operating budget and opportunities budget. Many companies nowadays separate their budgets into two parts. One is the **operating budget** which deals with all the things that are already being done. The other is sometimes called the **opportunities budget** which deals with new products, development, research and testing.

In terms of the operating budget the marketing manager should ask questions such as :

▶ What is the minimum that needs to be done in this area to prevent damage?
▶ How much effort and resources do we need to keep this activity operational?
▶ What are the minimum requirements needed to prevent unacceptable performance?

In respect of the opportunities budget, the first question should be:

▶ Is this the right opportunity?

If the answer is yes, then the next questions must be:

▶ What is the optimum, in terms of resources and money, that this opportunity can absorb at the present level?
▶ Can we hope to speed up the development process of a badly needed new product by putting more people to work on it?
▶ Will this create confusion?

Human Resources budgeting.   Most budgets provide only for money and specify where it should be spent. They do not contain the necessary provisions to make reasonably sure that the expected results can be obtained. They do not provide for the only resource that can produce results: accomplished people. This is particularly relevant to marketing managers, where skilled sales representatives, market researchers, advertising personnel and public relations executives are crucial to the survival of the company. Recruitment and training must be accounted for both in terms of time and money resources.

Sales Budget.   Whilst the overall marketing commitment is the responsibility of any marketing manager, it may be that in smaller companies considerations such as product research and development, testing and extensive marketing research are not relevant in terms of a young or comparatively small operation. It may be that the sales budget will be central to the marketing manager's objectives.

SUMMARY

Whilst this chapter has not attempted to address specific financial questions, it has demonstrated the issues and problems associated with marketing budgeting before any 'numbers are crunched'. The numbers can be worked out with comparative ease once the criteria for expected results have been explored fully and marketing management have a clear brief as to what they are accountable for and what marketing objectives must be satisfied.

The essential feature of marketing organization and control is that it 'closes the loop' and connects marketing plans to marketing actions. Ultimately, therefore, the way we manage marketing is the major determinant of commercial success or failure.

Further Reading

Oliver, G., *Marketing Today*, (Prentice-Hall International 1986)

Baker, M., *Marketing Strategy and Management*, (Macmillan 1985)

O'Shaughnessy, J., *Competitive Marketing: a Strategic Approach*, (Unwin Hyman 1989)

Day, G. S., *Analysis for Strategic Market Decisions*, (West Publishing Co. 1986)

McDonald, M. H. B., *Marketing Plans: How to Prepare Them, How to Use Them*, (Heinemann 1988)

Porter, M. E., *Competitive Strategy*, (Free Press 1980)

Ohmae, K., *The Mind of the Strategist*, (Penguin 1985)

Davidson, H., *Offensive Marketing*, (Penguin 1987)

Christopher, M., et al, *Strategy: A Guide to Marketing for Senior Executives*, (Gower Press 1989)

Peters, T. J., & Waterman, R. H., *In Search of Excellence*, (Harper & Row 1982)

Levitt, T., *The Marketing Imagination*, (Free Press 1983)

Index

communications *continued*
plan 243–9
competitive advantage 1, 11,
20, 26–7, 55–61
competitive benchmarking
67–70
conjoint analysis 219–24
consumer behaviour 87–110,
114–18, 240–1;
and personal influencing
factors, 92–100;
and external influencing
factors 100–107
consumer marketing 12, 25,
121–2
consumer panel 50
corporate communications
audit 238–9
corporate planning process
304–6
corporate values 11
cost advantage 56–8, 60–1
cost/benefit appraisal 50–1
cultural trends 37–9, 53, 100–1
cumulative volume 57
customer account profitability
analysis 207
customer benefits 128–9,
212–14, 266–7
customer needs 4–5
customer orientation 11
customer profitability model
325
customer service 27–8, 197–
210;
pre-transaction/transaction/
post-transaction elements
200;

and market research 203–4;
package 205–7;
culture 208–10

data bank 66
decentralized organizations
314–15, 316
decisionmaking unit (DMU)
109
demand curve 102, 214–15,
223
design department 263
desk research 48–9
differential advantage 7–9, 17,
21, 58–9, 205, 213
directional policy matrix
151–2, 155
direct mail 236–7
discounted cash flow 9
distribution:
network 3, 20–1, 27;
strategy 171–2;
channels 182–96;
audit 305
Domino's Pizzas 28

EEC 49
exchange control 40
exhibitions 234
experience:
effect 3;
curve 57–8, 60, 226–8
experimentation 47–8

family life cycle 103–4
fast-moving consumer goods
(FMCG) 12
'fast-track' marketing 31–3

Dr Peter Hanson
Stress for Success £6.99

Stress is the key to excellence – when you know how to manage it!

Badly managed stress can squeeze the breath out of a healthy body . . . and the life out of business performance. But, properly managed, that same stress can be used to create advantage in the workplace – and to become a powerful secret ally.

In *The Joy of Stress* Dr Peter Hanson showed how to harness stress as a rewarding way to better health and personal success. In this book he shows how stress can be used effectively to gain long-term advantage, to create new solutions and to increase adaptability in any business enterprise.

The Hanson prescription contained in *Stress for Success* provides the clearly charted way to the achievement of excellence – concisely analysing the parameters of the Working World, targeting the key areas of Situational Stress, and providing the tools to improve your Stress Fitness in the most effective way.

For, in the rapidly changing world of business, stress is the one constant factor. It is by adapting to stress – and by being prepared to use it in the most effective way – that you can navigate successfully through the storm waters of work stress that will capsize the unaware.

All Pan books are available at your local bookshop or newsagent, or can be ordered direct from the publisher. Indicate the number of copies required and fill in the form below.

Send to: Pan C. S. Dept
              Macmillan Distribution Ltd
              Houndmills Busingstoke RG21 2XS
or phone: 0256 29242, quoting title, author and Credit Card number.

Please enclose a remittance* to the value of the cover price plus: £1.00 for the first book plus 50p per copy for each additional book ordered.

*Payment may be made in sterling by UK personal cheque, postal order, sterling draft or international money order, made payable to Pan Books Ltd.

Alternatively by Barclaycard/Access/Amex/Diners

Card No.

Expiry Date

Signature:

Applicable only in the UK and BFPO addresses

While every effort is made to keep prices low, it is sometimes necessary to increase prices at short notice. Pan Books reserve the right to show on covers and charge new retail prices which may differ from those advertised in the text or elsewhere.

NAME AND ADDRESS IN BLOCK LETTERS PLEASE:

....

Name _____

Address _____

_____

_____

_____

6/92